MW00903198

# STUDY GUIDE
## Steven Cox *Queens University of Charlotte*
## Alyssa Cox

# MANAGEMENT
## *Ninth Edition*

# Stephen P. Robbins
# Mary Coulter

PEARSON
Prentice
Hall

Upper Saddle River, New Jersey 07458

**VP/Editorial Director:** Jeff Shelstad
**Acquisitions Editor:** Michael Ablassmeir
**Assistant Editor:** Denise Vaughn
**Associate Director, Manufacturing:** Vincent Scelta
**Production Editor & Buyer:** Carol O'Rourke
**Printer/Binder:** Offset Paperback Manufacturing

---

Pearson Prentice Hall™ is a trademark of Pearson Education, Inc.

10  9  8  7  6  5  4  3
ISBN 0-13-225746-7

# Table of Contents

# Chapter 1  Introduction to Management and Organizations

## Learning Outline

**Who Are Managers?**
- Explain how managers differ from nonmanagerial employees.
- Describe how to classify managers in organizations.

**What Is Management?**
- Define management.
- Explain why efficiency and effectiveness are important to management.

**What Do Managers Do?**
- Describe the four functions of management.
- Explain Mintzberg's managerial roles.
- Describe Katz's three managerial skills and how the importance of these skills changes depending on managerial level.
- Discuss the changes that are impacting managers' jobs.
- Explain why customer service and innovation are important to the manager's job.

**What Is an Organization?**
- Describe the characteristics of an organization.
- Explain how the concept of an organization is changing.

**Why Study Management?**
- Explain the *universality of management* concept.
- Discuss why an understanding of management is important.
- Describe the rewards and challenges of being a manager.

---

**A Manager's Dilemma**

As you read about Jovita Carranza, vice president of air operations at United Parcel Service (UPS), consider the following questions. Compare your thoughts to **Managers Respond** at the end of the chapter.

1. What is Ms. Carranza's management philosophy?
2. How has her attitude toward working with teams helped her to be successful?
3. What managerial skills should she encourage her first-line supervisors to develop in order to reach her goals for the organization?

---

## Lecture Outline

I. Introduction
   A. Effective management plays a large role in a company's employee productivity and financial performance.
   B. The rapid pace of change in the world today requires managers to blend traditional and innovative approaches in the way they manage their organizations.

II. Who Are Managers?
   C. Distinguish between managers and nonmanagerial employees in a traditionally structured organization.
   D. Classification of managers by managerial levels. (Refer to Exhibit 1-1)
   E. Even in nontraditional organizational settings, where responsibilities may shift as work demands change, someone must fulfill the role of the manager on each project.
   F. Learning Review.
   - Explain how managers differ from nonmanagerial employees.
   - Describe how to classify managers in organizations.
   G. Key Terms.
       1. Manager – Someone who coordinates and oversees the work of other people so that organizational goals can be accomplished.
       2. First-line managers – The lowest level of management who manage the work of nonmanagerial employees, who typically are directly or indirectly involved with producing the organization's products or servicing the organization's customers.
       3. Middle managers – Managers between the first level and the top level of the organization who manage the work of first-line managers.
       4. Top managers – Managers at or near the upper levels of the organization structure who are responsible for making organization-wide decisions and establishing the plans and goals that affect the entire organization.

III. What Is Management?
   H. Coordination distinguishes the work of managers and nonmanagers.
   I. Distinguish between efficiency and effectiveness (Refer to Exhibit 1-2).
   J. Learning Review.
   - Define management.
   - Explain why efficiency and effectiveness are important to management.
   K. Key Terms.
       1. Management – Coordinating and overseeing the work activities of others so that their activities are completed efficiently and effectively.
       2. Efficiency – Doing things right, or getting the most output from the least amount of inputs.
       3. Effectiveness – Doing the right things, or completing activities so that organizational goals are attained.

---

**Thinking Critically About Ethics**

You are the catering manager at a local country club. The club manager has asked you to lie about your group's efficiency.
1. Is lying always wrong?
2. If an employee's job is at stake, is it acceptable to lie to protect the employee?
3. Is distorting information the same as lying?
4. Is giving incomplete information the same as lying?

IV. What Do Managers Do?

L. Management Functions – accepted as the most useful way of describing the manager's job. (Refer to Exhibit 1-3)
1. Planning.
2. Organizing.
3. Leading.
4. Controlling.

M. Mintzberg's Management Roles – managers at all levels and in all types of organizations perform similar roles. (Refer to Exhibit 1-4)
1. Interpersonal roles.
   a. Figurehead.
   b. Leader.
   c. Liaison.
2. Informational roles.
   a. Monitor.
   b. Disseminator.
   c. Spokesperson.
3. Decisional roles.
   a. Entrepreneur.
   b. Disturbance handler.
   c. Resource allocator.
   d. Negotiator.

N. Management Skills – needed to perform the duties and activities associated with being a manager; identified by Robert Katz. (Refer to Exhibits 1-5, 1-6, and 1-7)
1. Technical skills – most important at lower levels of management.
2. Human skills – important at all levels of management.
3. Conceptual skills – most important at top management levels.

O. How the Manager's Job Is Changing. (Refer to Exhibit 1-8)
1. Importance of customers to the manager's job: employee attitudes and behaviors play a crucial role in customer satisfaction.
2. Importance of innovation to the manager's job: "Nothing is more risky than not innovating."

P. Learning Review.
- Describe the four functions of management.
- Explain Mintzberg's managerial roles.
- Describe Katz's three essential managerial skills and how the importance of these skills changes depending on the managerial level.
- Discuss the changes that are impacting managers' jobs.
- Explain why customer service and innovation are important to the manager's job.

Q. Key Terms
1. Planning – Management function that involves defining goals, establishing strategies for achieving those goals, and developing plans to integrate and coordinate activities.
2. Organizing – Management function that involves arranging and structuring work to accomplish the organization's goals.

3. Leading – Management function that involves working with and through people to accomplish organizational goals.
4. Controlling – Management function that involves monitoring, comparing, and correcting work performance.
5. Management roles – Specific categories of managerial behavior.
6. Interpersonal roles – Managerial roles that involve people and other duties that are ceremonial and symbolic in nature.
7. Informational roles – Managerial roles that involve collecting, receiving, and disseminating information.
8. Decisional roles – Managerial roles that revolve around making choices.
9. Technical skills – Job-specific knowledge and techniques needed to proficiently perform specific tasks.
10. Human skills – The ability to work well with other people individually and in a group.
11. Conceptual skills – The ability to think and to conceptualize about abstract and complex situations.

V. What Is an Organization?
   R. Characteristics of an Organization.  (Refer to Exhibit 1-9)
      1. Distinct Purpose.
      2. People.
      3. Deliberate Structure
   S. Contrast the Traditional Organization with the New Organization (Refer to Exhibit 1-10)
   T. Learning Review.
      • Describe the characteristics of an organization.
      • Explain how the concept of an organization is changing.
   U. Key Terms.
      1. Organization – A deliberate arrangement of people to accomplish some specific purpose.

VI. Why Study Management?
   V. The Universality of Management.  (Refer to Exhibit 1-11)
   W. Well-managed organizations develop a loyal customer base, grow, and prosper.
   X. The Reality of Work – You don't have to aspire to be a manager to gain something valuable from an understanding of management.
   Y. Rewards and Challenges of Being a Manager. (Refer to Exhibit 1-12)
   Z. Learning Review.
      • Explain the *universality of management* concept.
      • Discuss why an understanding of management is important.
      • Describe the rewards and challenges of being a manager.
   AA.   Key Terms.
      1. Universality of management – The reality that management is needed in all types and sizes of organizations, at all organizational levels, in all organizational areas, and in organizations in all countries around the globe.

| Focus on Leadership: Do Organizations Need Managers or Leaders or Both? |
|---|
| Organizations need both strong leadership and strong management for optimal effectiveness. |
| 1. What functions do managers serve? |
| 2. What function do leaders serve? |
| 3. How can leadership training improve management skills? |

**Multiple-Choice Questions**

1. A manager is a(n) _____.
   a) uncompensated employee
   b) coordinator of work activities to accomplish organizational goals
   c) head of the organization
   d) first-line worker
   (p. 5)

2. Regional managers, project leaders, and division managers are all considered to be _____.
   a) first-line managers
   b) nonmanagerial workers
   c) middle managers
   d) top managers
   (pp. 6-7)

3. Mary reports to the VP of marketing and has both supervisors and some hourly employees who report directly to her. Mary is a(n) _____.
   a) first-line manager
   b) middle manager
   c) top manager
   d) operative
   (pp. 6-7)

4. Those responsible for making organization-wide decisions and establishing plans and goals for the entire organization are termed _____.
   a) top managers
   b) middle managers
   c) first-line managers
   d) nonmanagerial employees
   (p. 7)

5.  One thing that distinguishes a managerial position from a nonmanagerial one is _____.
    a)  the amount of money paid to an employee
    b)  coordinating the work of others
    c)  initiating new projects
    d)  having technical skills
    (p. 7)

6.  If Bianca focuses on reducing waste, she is working at being a more _____ manager.
    a)  efficient
    b)  effective
    c)  goal oriented
    d)  technically skilled
    (p. 8)

7.  Effectiveness is often described as _____.
    a)  work activities that will help the organization reach its goals
    b)  delegating as much responsibility as possible
    c)  managing processes by yourself
    d)  defining the project in terms of dollars
    (p. 8)

8.  Whereas _____ is concerned with the *means* of getting things done, _____ is concerned with the *ends*, or attainment of organizational goals.
    a)  effectiveness; economy
    b)  effectiveness; efficiency
    c)  efficiency; effectiveness
    d)  economy; efficiency
    (p. 8)

9.  Planning involves _____.
    a)  directing and motivating others
    b)  monitoring activities to ensure they are accomplished
    c)  determining what needs to be done by whom
    d)  defining goals and establishing strategy
    (p. 9, Exhibit 1-3)

10. When a manager is determining what needs to be done and how it will be accomplished, he or she is _____.
    a)  planning
    b)  organizing
    c)  leading
    d)  controlling
    (p. 9, Exhibit 1-3)

11. Comparing actual performance with previously set goals is a part of _____.
    a) planning
    b) organizing
    c) leading
    d) controlling
    (p. 9, Exhibit 1-3)

12. Jennifer's supervisor has asked her to explain the difference between the amounts spent by her division and the amounts that were budgeted. The supervisor is performing the management function of _____.
    a) planning
    b) organizing
    c) leading
    d) controlling
    (p. 9)

13. Selecting the most effective communication channel for use among organization members is part of which management function?
    a) Planning
    b) Organizing
    c) Leading
    d) Controlling
    (p. 9)

14. Which of the following is an example of a manager's decisional role?
    a) Initiating and overseeing new projects
    b) Monitoring the sharing of information
    c) Hiring and training of new employees
    d) Working as a liaison between work groups
    (p. 11, Exhibit 1-4)

15. Collecting, receiving, and disseminating information is part of the manager's _____.
    a) decisional role
    b) organizational role
    c) interpersonal role
    d) informational role
    (p. 10)

16. According to Mintzberg, a manager's interpersonal role includes functioning as a _____.
    a) leader
    b) monitor
    c) spokesperson
    d) resource allocator
    (p. 11, Exhibit 1-4)

17. Technical skills are most important to _____.
    a) the middle manager
    b) an executive
    c) a first-line manager
    d) a top manager
    (p. 12)

18. _____ involve the ability to work well with other people, both individually and in a group.
    a) Human skills
    b) Decisional skills
    c) Conceptual skills
    d) Technical skills
    (p. 12)

19. _____ are especially crucial if managers are to fulfill their interpersonal roles.
    a) Human skills
    b) Decisional skills
    c) Conceptual skills
    d) Technical skills
    (p. 12)

20. _____ skills are most important at the top management levels.
    a) Technical
    b) Human
    c) Financial
    d) Conceptual
    (p. 12)

21. All of the following are examples of communication skills listed by your text EXCEPT _____.
    a) credibility among colleagues, peers, and subordinates
    b) listening and asking questions
    c) selecting critical information from masses of data
    d) presentation skills
    (p. 13, Exhibit 1-6)

22. An organization is best described as _____.
    a) a business conglomerate
    b) a deliberate arrangement of people to accomplish some specific purpose
    c) a business with an emphasis on resource allocation
    d) corporation listed on a national exchange
    (p. 17)

23. Which of the following is true about organizations?
    a) They seldom risk their own finances in their ventures.
    b) They are oriented towards the achievement of short-term goals.
    c) They have a distinct purpose, include people or members, and have some type of deliberate structure.
    d) They have a difficult time accepting mistakes and failure.
    (p. 18)

24. Which of the following is a characteristic of the contemporary organization, but not the traditional organization?
    a) Team oriented
    b) Hierarchical relationships
    c) Permanent jobs
    d) Command-oriented
    (p. 18, Exhibit 1-10)

25. The universality of management means that _____.
    a) all managers use the same style
    b) there is one best management style
    c) management is needed in all organizations
    d) management is unimportant
    (p. 19)

## True/False Questions

1. T  F  The changing nature of organizations and work has, in many organizations, blurred the clear lines of distinction between managers and nonmanagerial employees.
   (p. 4)

2. T  F  A chief operating officer or division manager is most likely a first-line manager.
   (p. 6)

3. T  F  Middle managers are responsible for establishing the plans and goals that affect the entire organization.
   (p. 6)

4. T  F  Coordinating the work of others is what distinguishes a managerial position from a nonmanagerial one.
   (p. 7)

5. T  F  Effectiveness refers to "doing things right."
   (p. 8)

6.  T  F  Efficiency is important to managers because they are dealing with scarce inputs.
(p. 8)

7.  T  F  The ability to do the right things is the basic definition of efficiency.
(p. 8)

8.  T  F  Controlling is a process used to make sure an organization's actions are consistent with the organization's plans.
(p. 9)

9.  T  F  Arranging work to accomplish the goals of the organization is called organizing.
(p. 9)

10. T  F  A manager is currently hiring new workers. This is an example of her interpersonal role.
(p. 11, Exhibit 1-4)

11. T  F  Monitoring the environment, giving information to outsiders, and serving as an expert are all examples of a manager's decisional role.
(p. 11, Exhibit 1-4)

12. T  F  Mintzberg's managerial roles include interpersonal roles, informational roles, and leadership roles.
(p. 11, Exhibit 1-4)

13. T  F  Follow-up studies generally support Mintzberg's idea that managers – regardless of the type of organization or level in the organization – perform similar roles.
(p. 12)

14. T  F  Mintzberg's interpersonal role includes the roles of figurehead, leader, and spokesperson.
(p. 11, Exhibit 1-4)

15. T  F  Many of Mintzberg's roles align well with one or more of the functions. For instance, resource allocation is part of organizing.
(p. 12)

16. T  F  Conceptual skills are most important to people in middle management.
(p. 12)

17. T  F  Focusing on customers is mostly the responsibility of employees in marketing.
(p. 16)

18. T   F   Innovative ideas may not involve changing technology.
          (p. 17)

19. T   F   Innovation is so risky that companies who innovate are generally less
          successful than those who don't.
          (p. 17)

20. T   F   All organizations share three characteristics: distinct purpose, strict financial
          management, and technology.
          (p. 18)

21. T   F   One result of changing technology is more flexible work arrangements.
          (p. 15, Exhibit 1-8)

22. T   F   Traditional organizations typically include lateral and networked
          relationships.
          (p. 18, Exhibit 1-10)

23. T   F   Management is typically not as important in not-for-profit organizations.
          (p. 20, Exhibit 1-11)

24. T   F   Organizations that are poorly managed tend to develop a loyal customer base,
          grow, and prosper.
          (p. 20)

25. T   F   Most people in the work force either manage or are managed.
          (p. 20)

## Match Terms with Definitions

a. Planning     d. Controlling    g. Interpersonal roles    j. Technical skills
b. Organizing    e. Efficiency    h. Informational roles    k. Human skills
c. Leading    f. Effectiveness    i. Decisional roles    l. Conceptual skills

_____ 1. Skills that include knowledge of and proficiency in a specialized field.

_____ 2. Roles that include monitoring, disseminating, and spokesperson activities.

_____ 3. Includes motivating subordinates, directing others, selecting the most efficient communication channels, and resolving conflicts.

_____ 4. Determining what tasks are to be done, who is to do them, how the tasks are to be grouped, who reports to whom, and where decisions are to be made.

_____ 5. Roles that include figurehead, leader, and liaison activities.

_____ 6. The ability to think about abstract situations, to see the organization as a whole, and to visualize how the organization fits into its broader environment.

_____ 7. The ability to work well with other people, both individually and in a group.

_____ 8. Roles that include those of entrepreneur, disturbance handler, and resource allocator.

_____ 9. Goal attainment.

_____ 10. The relationship between inputs and outputs, seeks to minimize resource costs.

_____ 11. Includes defining goals, establishing strategy, and developing plans to coordinate activities.

_____ 12. Monitoring activities to ensure that they are being accomplished as planned and correcting any significant deviations.

## Essay Questions

1. Explain efficiency and effectiveness and their importance for managers.
   (p. 8)

2. List and briefly define the four functions of management.
   (p. 9, Exhibit 1-3)

3. Henry Mintzberg described three groups of management roles. Identify the three types of roles and give an example of each.
   (p. 11, Exhibit 1-4)

4. Katz identified three essential skills needed by managers at different levels in the organization. What are the three types of skills and at which level of management is each needed?
   (pp. 12-13, Exhibit 1-5, Exhibit 1-6)

5. Describe two ways in which managers' jobs are impacted by change. What is the impact of these changes?
   (pp. 15-17, Exhibit 1-8)

# Chapter 2  Management Yesterday and Today

## Learning Outline

### Historical Background of Management
- Explain why studying management history is important.
- Describe some early evidences of management practice.

### Scientific Management
- Describe the important contributions made by Frederick W. Taylor and Frank and Lillian Gilbreth.
- Explain how today's managers use scientific management.

### General Administrative Theory
- Discuss Fayol's contributions to management theory.
- Describe Max Weber's contributions to management theory.
- Explain how today's managers use general administrative theories of management.

### Quantitative Approach
- Explain what the quantitative approach has contributed to the field of management.
- Discuss how today's managers use the quantitative approach.

### Toward Understanding Organizational Behavior
- Describe the contributions of the early advocates of OB.
- Explain the contributions of the Hawthorne Studies to the field of management.
- Discuss how today's managers use the behavioral approach.

### The Systems Approach
- Describe an organization using the systems approach.
- Discuss how the systems approach helps us understand management.

### The Contingency Approach
- Explain how the contingency approach differs from the early theories of management.
- Discuss how the contingency approach helps us understand management.

### Current Trends and Issues
- Explain why we need to look at the current trends and issues facing managers.
- Describe the current trends and issues facing managers.

---

**A Manager's Dilemma**

John R. Hoke III wants to foster more innovation within Nike outside the design team. As you read the Manager's Dilemma, think about the following questions, and then compare your thoughts to **Managers Respond** at the end of the chapter.

1. How does Mr. Hoke define "sustainable design"?
2. How does Mr. Hoke encourage his design team to think creatively about footwear design?
3. In what ways can Hoke's strategy be used to promote creating thinking elsewhere within Nike.

---

# Lecture Outline

I. Historical Background of Management.
   A. Egyptian pyramids.
   B. China's Great Wall.
   C. Fifteenth century Venetian business practices.
   D. Since the 1770s. (Refer to Exhibit 2-1)
      1. Adam Smith – *The Wealth of Nations*: economic advantage of division of labor.
      2. Industrial Revolution – Mechanization of work
   E. Learning Review.
     • Explain why studying management history is important.
     • Describe some early evidences of management practice.
   F. Key Terms.
      1. Division of labor (job specialization) – The breakdown of jobs into narrow and repetitive tasks.
      2. Industrial Revolution – The substitution of machine power for human power, which made it more economical to manufacture goods in factories rather than in the home.

II. Scientific Management.
   A. Important Contributions.
      1. Frederick W. Taylor – *Principles of Scientific Management*, 1911.
        a. Midvale and Bethlehem Steel Companies.
        b. Applications of Scientific Method.
        c. Improvement of Production Efficiency.
        d. Four Principles of Management. (Refer to Exhibit 2-2)
      2. Frank and Lillian Gilbreth.
        a. Worked to Eliminate Wasteful Movements.
        b. Therbligs – Basic Hand Movements.
   B. How Do Today's Managers Use Scientific Management?
   C. Learning Review.
      1. Describe the important contributions made by Frederick W. Taylor and Frank and Lillian Gilbreth.
      2. Explain how today's managers use scientific management.
   D. Key Terms.
     • Scientific management – Using the scientific method to determine the "one best way" for a job to be done.
     • Therbligs – A classification scheme for labeling 17 basic hand motions.

III. General Administrative Theory.
   A. Important contributions.
      1. Henri Fayol.
        a. Contemporary of Taylor.
        b. Management Functions.
        c. Principles of Management. (Refer to Exhibit 2-3)

        2. Max Weber.
            a.  German Sociologist.
            b.  Bureaucracy as "Ideal" Organization. (Refer to Exhibit 2-4)
    B.  How Do Today's Managers Use General Administration Theories?
        1.  Functional View – Fayol.
        2.  Bureaucracy – Weber.
    C.  Learning Review.
        • Discuss Fayol's contribution to management theory.
        • Describe Max Weber's contribution to management theory.
        • Explain how today's managers use general administrative theories of
          management.
    D.  Key Terms.
        1.  General administration theory – A theory of management that focused on
            describing what managers do and what constitutes good management practice.
        2.  Principles of management – Fundamental rules of management that could be
            taught in schools and applied in all organizational situations.
        3.  Bureaucracy – A form of organization characterized by division of labor, a
            clearly defined hierarchy, detailed rules and regulations, and impersonal
            relationships.

IV. Quantitative Approach.
    A.  Important Contributions.
        1.  Quantitative approach evolved from World War II military solutions.
        2.  Whiz Kids – Robert McNamara and Charles "Tex" Thornton.
        3.  Applications of Quantitative Approaches.
    B.  How Do Today's Managers Use the Quantitative Approach?
        1.  Budgeting.
        2.  Scheduling.
        3.  Quality Control.
        4.  Approach implemented using specialized software.
    C.  Learning Review.
        • Explain what the quantitative approach has contributed to the field of
          management.
        • Discuss how today's managers use the quantitative approach.
    D.  Key Terms.
        1.  Quantitative approach – The use of quantitative techniques to improve
            decision making.

V.  Toward Understanding Organizational Behavior.
    A.  OB is concerned with the behaviors of people at work.
    B.  Early Advocates. (Refer to Exhibit 2-5)
        1.  Shared common belief that people were an organization's most important
            asset.
        2.  Robert Owen.
        3.  Hugo Munsterberg.
        4.  Mary Parker Follett.

  5. Chester Barnard.
 C. The Hawthorne Studies.
  1. Conducted at the Western Electric Company Works in Cicero, Illinois, as scientific management experiment.
  2. Originally studied effects of illumination levels on worker productivity.
  3. Mayo reached several conclusions.
   a. Behavior and attitudes are closely related.
   b. Group factors significantly affect individual behavior.
   c. Group standards establish individual worker output.
   d. Money is less a factor in determining output than are group standards, group attitudes, and security.
  4. Led to a new emphasis on the human behavior factor in the management of organizations.
 D. How Do Today's Managers Use the Behavioral Approach?
  1. Behavioral approach has largely shaped today's organizations.
  2. Hawthorne Studies provided foundation for current theories.
 E. Learning Review.
  • Describe the contributions of the early advocates of OB.
  • Explain the contributions of the Hawthorne Studies to the field of management.
  • Discuss how today's managers use the behavioral approach.
 F. Key Terms.
  1. Organizational behavior – The field of study concerned with the actions (behavior) of people at work.
  2. Hawthorne Studies – A series of studies during the 1920s and 1930s that provided new insights into individual and group behavior.

VI. The Systems Approach.
 A. In 1960s researchers began using systems approach.
  1. Closed systems.
  2. Open systems. (Refer to Fig. 2-6)
 B. The Systems Approach and Managers.
  1. Emphasizes interdependence.
  2. Actions in one area influence other areas.
  3. Organizations are not self-contained.
 C. Learning Review.
  • Describe an organization using the systems approach.
  • Discuss how the systems approach helps us understand management.
 D. Key Terms.
  1. System – A set of interrelated and interdependent parts arranged in a manner that produces a unified whole.
  2. Closed Systems – Systems that are not influenced by or do not interact with their environment.
  3. Open Systems – Systems that interact with their environment.

VII. The Contingency Approach.
   A. Different and changing situations require use of different approaches and techniques.
   B. The Contingency Approach and Managers.
      1. Contingency approach stresses that there are no simplistic or universal rules for managers.
      2. Four popular contingency variables. (Refer to Exhibit 2-7)
         a. Organization Size.
         b. Routineness of Task Technology.
         c. Environmental Uncertainty.
         d. Individual Differences.
   C. Learning Review.
      • Explain how the contingency approach differs from the early theories of management.
      • Discuss how the contingency approach is appropriate for studying management.
   D. Key Terms.
      1. Contingency approach – A management approach that says that organizations are different, face different situations (contingencies), and require different ways of managing.

VIII. Current Trends and Issues.
   A. Globalization.
      1. Working with People from Different Cultures.
      2. Coping with Anticapitalism Backlash.
      3. Movement of Jobs to Countries with Low-Cost Labor.
   B. Ethics.
      1. Ethical issues are difficult.
      2. Process for Addressing Ethical Dilemmas. (Refer to Exhibit 2-8)
   C. Workforce Diversity.
      1. Workforce 2020.
      2. Fastest growth will be Asian and Hispanic workers.
      3. Aging population will offer challenges.
      4. Workforce diversity is a managerial issue in all developed countries.
      5. "Melting Pot" approach replaced by recognition and celebration of differences.
   D. Entrepreneurship.
      1. Three important themes.
         a. Pursuit of opportunities.
         b. Innovation.
         c. Growth.

E. Managing in an E-Business World. (Refer to Exhibit 2-9)
    1. E-Business Enhanced Organization.
    2. E-Business Enabled Organization.
    3. Total E-Business Organization.
F. Knowledge Management and Learning Organizations.
    1. Learning Organization vs. Traditional Organization. (Refer to Exhibit 2-10)
    2. Managers create learning capabilities.
    3. Managers must deliberately manage the organization's base of knowledge.

G. Quality Management.
    1. TQM (Total Quality Management).
    2. What Is Quality Management? (Refer to Exhibit 2-11)
H. Learning Review.
    • Explain why we need to look at the current trends and issues facing managers.
    • Describe the current trends and issues facing managers.
I. Key Terms.
    1. Workforce diversity – A workforce that's heterogeneous in terms of gender, race, ethnicity, age, and other characteristics that reflect differences.
    2. Entrepreneurship – The process whereby an individual or group of individuals uses organized efforts to pursue opportunities to create value and grow by fulfilling wants and needs through innovation and uniqueness, no matter what resources the entrepreneur currently has.
    3. E-business (electronic business) – A comprehensive term describing the way an organization does its work by using electronic (Internet-based) linkages with its key constituencies in order to efficiently and effectively achieve its goals.
    4. E-Commerce (electronic commerce) – The sales and marketing component of e-business.
    5. Intranet – A Web-based internal communication system accessible only by organizational employees.

6. Learning organization – An organization that has developed the capacity to continuously learn, adapt, and change.
7. Knowledge management – Cultivating a learning culture where organizational members systematically gather knowledge and share it with others in the organization so as to achieve better performance.
8. Quality management – A philosophy of management that is driven by continual improvement and responding to customer needs and expectations.

## Multiple-Choice Questions

1. Division of labor can best be described as _____.
   a) the breakdown of jobs into narrow and repetitive tasks
   b) dividing the workforce into teams
   c) delegation of authority
   d) analytical study of the total workforce
   (p. 28)

2. _____ published *The Wealth of Nations*, in which he argued for the economic advantages that organizations and society would gain from the division of labor.
   a) Frederick Taylor
   b) Max Weber
   c) Adam Smith
   d) Henri Fayol
   (p. 28)

3. Which of the following occurred during the Industrial Revolution?
   a) Machine power was substituted for human power.
   b) The manufacture of goods moved from the home to the factory.
   c) The demand for managers increased.
   d) All of the above
   (p. 29)

4. The use of scientific methods to define the "one best way" for a job to be done was developed by _____.
   a) Frederick Taylor
   b) Max Weber
   c) Adam Smith
   d) Henri Fayol
   (p. 30)

5. Frank and Lillian Gilbreth devised a classification scheme to label 17 basic hand motions which they called _____.
   a) widgets
   b) handlets
   c) therbligs
   d) lillians
   (p. 31)

6. Who developed 14 principles of management that he/she felt were universal truths that applied to all management systems?
   a) Mary Parker Follett
   b) Max Weber
   c) Adam Smith
   d) Henri Fayol
   (p. 32)

7. _____ is a form of organization characterized by division of labor, a clearly defined hierarchy, detailed rules and regulations, and impersonal relationships which was developed by Max Weber.
   a) Bureaucracy
   b) Learning system
   c) Matrix
   d) E-business
   (p. 32)

8. The _____ evolved from the development of mathematical and statistical solutions to military problems during World War II.
   a) quantitative approach
   b) learning organization
   c) e-business
   d) bureaucracy
   (p. 34)

9. Who proposed more people-oriented ideas than scientific management followers and thought organizations should be based on group ethic?
   a) Hugo Munsterberg
   b) Chester Barnard
   c) Mary Parker Follett
   d) Robert Owen
   (p. 36, Exhibit 2-5)

10. The Hawthorne Studies examined the _____.
    a) safety needs of workers
    b) physiological needs of displaced homemakers
    c) effect of various illumination levels on worker productivity
    d) esteem needs of top corporate management personnel
    (p. 37)

11. The Hawthorne Studies had a dramatic impact on management beliefs about the
    _____.
    a) importance of top management commitment
    b) role of human behavior in organizations
    c) importance of scientific principles for management
    d) many ways an organization can apply bureaucratic principles
    (p. 37)

12. Today when we describe organizations as systems, we mean _____.
    a) open systems
    b) closed systems
    c) TQM systems
    d) global systems
    (p. 38)

13. Steve is examining the human resources, capital, and technology used by his
    company to make its products. In terms of an open system, Steve is examining the
    system's _____.
    a) inputs
    b) outputs
    c) transformation process
    d) organizational interdependence
    (p. 38, Exhibit 2-6)

14. Which of the following is another name for the contingency approach?
    a) Situational approach
    b) Variable approach
    c) Conceptual study approach
    d) Evaluative perspective study
    (p. 39)

15. Jim's company employs fifteen people and takes a collaborative team approach to develop company goals and objectives. Julia's company employs 150 people and company goals and objectives are developed by a top management group and then explained to the rest of the employees. This difference in company goal development between Jim's company and Julia's company is largely the result of which of the following contingency variables?
    a) Organization size
    b) Routineness of task technology
    c) Environmental uncertainty
    d) Individual differences
    (p. 40, Exhibit 2-7)

16. Which of the following is NOT among the four popular contingency variables listed in your text?
    a) Organization size
    b) Degree of globalization
    c) Environmental uncertainty
    d) Individual differences
    (p. 40, Exhibit 2-7)

17. In the first part of the twenty-first century, _____ will make up over half of the new entrants in the U.S. workforce.
    a) Asians
    b) minorities
    c) women
    d) teenagers
    (p. 43)

18. Intelligent managers recognize that diversity can be an asset because it _____.
    a) brings a broad range of viewpoints and problem-solving skills to a company
    b) demonstrates concern for people, concern for task, and the ability to integrate the two
    c) is the process where a group of individuals pursue opportunities
    d) displays autocratic, democratic, laissez-faire, and initiating structure
    (p. 44)

19. The melting pot assumption has been replaced by _____.
    a) an understanding that assimilation has no effect on the workforce
    b) management's realization that diversity is decreasing
    c) recognition and celebration of differences
    d) increased reliance on laws prohibiting discrimination
    (p. 44)

20. Three important themes in the definition of entrepreneurship are pursuit of opportunities, innovation, and _____.
    a) education
    b) emphasis on family businesses
    c) risk
    d) growth
    (pp. 44-45)

21. _____ is a comprehensive term describing the way an organization does its work by using electronic linkages with its key constituencies.
    a) Entrepreneurship
    b) E-business
    c) Business-to-business
    d) Computer network
    (p. 45)

22. A _____ is one that has developed the capacity to continuously learn, adapt, and change.
    a) diverse workforce
    b) traditional organization
    c) learning organization
    d) chief knowledge officer
    (pp. 46-47)

23. Knowledge management involves cultivating a(n) _____ culture where knowledge is shared.
    a) learning
    b) international
    c) traditional
    d) ethical
    (p. 47)

24. Deming and Juran inspired the development of _____.
    a) impoverished management.
    b) management by objectives.
    c) total quality management.
    d) reengineering.
    (p. 48)

25. _____ is a philosophy of management involving continual improvement and responding to customer needs and expectations
    a) The contingency approach
    b) The systems approach
    c) Knowledge management
    d) Quality management
    (p. 48)

## True/False Questions

1. T  F  The concept of division of labor was first introduced by Adam Smith in *The Wealth of Nations*.
(p. 28)

2. T  F  The Industrial Revolution saw many cases of human power replaced by machine power.
(p. 29)

3. T  F  The first major step towards developing a formal theory to guide managers in running large organizations was developed by the Egyptians.
(p. 29)

4. T  F  Frederick W. Taylor is known as the "father" of scientific management.
(p. 30)

5. T  F  Frank and Lillian Gilbreth were major contributors to the contingency approach to management.
(p. 31)

6. T  F  Fayol's principles of management included division of work, authority, discipline, unity of command, and equity.
(p. 33, Exhibit 2-3)

7. T  F  Mary Parker Follett developed a theory of authority structures and relations and described the "ideal bureaucracy."
(pp. 33-34)

8. T  F  The Hawthorne Studies consisted of several different experiments, lasted over a period of years, and were the most important contribution to the developing organizational behavior field.
(p. 37)

9. T  F  The conclusions of the Hawthorne Studies led to a new emphasis on the human behavior factor in the management of organizations and the attainment of goals.
(p. 37)

10. T  F  A system is a set of independent parts arranged in a manner that produces a unified whole.
(p. 38)

11. T  F  A systems perspective helps managers look at an organization as individual units and thereby isolate each area where there may be a problem.
(p. 38)

12. T   F   Management activities, employee work, and the use of technology all take place during the transformation stage of an open system.
(p. 38, Exhibit 2-6)

13. T   F   The contingency approach to management is deciding what principles work in a given situation and using them appropriately
(p. 39)

14. T   F   Ethical issues are typically simple and clear-cut.
(p. 42)

15. T   F   *Workforce 2020* stated that the U.S. labor force would continue its ethnic diversification, although at a slower pace.
(p. 43)

16. T   F   Managers today generally use a "melting pot" assumption and encourage assimilation as the goal for diverse workers.
(p. 43)

17. T   F   Entrepreneurship involves the discovery of opportunities and the resources to exploit them.
(pp. 44-45)

18. T   F   Entrepreneurs are generally content for their organizations to stay small.
(p. 45)

19. T   F   The sales and marketing component of e-business is termed e-commerce.
(p. 45)

20. T   F   An intranet is accessible only to organizational employees.
(p. 46)

21. T   F   In the learning organization, the manager's job is to enable others to innovate and work more effectively and efficiently.
(p. 47, Exhibit 2-10)

22. T   F   Part of a manager's responsibility is to create learning capabilities throughout the organization.
(p. 47)

23. T   F   Knowledge management refers to those functions performed by a Technology Services Department of a large firm.
(p. 47)

24. T  F  Total quality management was developed by an American who first taught it to the Japanese in the 1950s.
(p. 48)

25. T  F  Quality management is based on the belief that low costs are the only road to increased productivity.
(pp. 48-49)

## Match Terms With Definitions

a. Workforce diversity
b. Total quality management
c. General administration theory
d. Industrial Revolution
e. Learning organization

f. Organizational behavior
g. Knowledge management
h. Scientific management
i. Hawthorne Studies
j. Contingency approach

k. Bureaucracy
l. Intranet
m. Therbligs
n. E-business
o. Division of labor

_____ 1.  Different and changing situations require managers to use different approaches and techniques.

_____ 2.  The use of the scientific method to define the "one best way" for a job to be done.

_____ 3.  Mayo's conclusions about this led to a new emphasis on the human behavior factor in management.

_____ 4.  A theory of management that focused on describing what managers do and what constitutes good management practice.

_____ 5.  A form of organization advocated by Max Weber and marked by division of labor, hierarchy, rules and regulations, and impersonal relationships.

_____ 6.  A learning culture where information is gathered and shared to achieve better performance.

_____ 7.  The advent of machine power, mass production, and efficient transportation.

_____ 8.  Employees in organizations are heterogeneous in terms of race, gender, religion, disabilities, or ethnicity.

_____ 9.  An internal communication system that uses Internet technology.

_____ 10.  Organization that has developed the capacity to continuously learn, adapt, and change.

_____ 11.  The field of study concerned with the actions of people at work.

_____ 12.  An organization that does its work using Internet-based linkages.

_____ 13.  The breakdown of jobs into narrow, repetitive tasks.

_____ 14.  A philosophy of management that is driven by customer needs and expectations.

_____ 15.  A classification scheme for labeling 17 basic hand motions.

## Essay Questions

1. Give three examples where management was evident prior to 1700.
   (p. 28)

2. Pick two of the following organizational behavior theorists and compare and contrast their work: Robert Owen, Hugo Munsterberg, Mary Parker Follett, and Chester Barnard.
   (p. 36, Exhibit 2-5)

3. List and explain three popular contingency variables.
   (p. 40, Exhibit 2-7)

4. Explain the process suggested in your text for addressing ethical dilemmas.
   (p. 42, Exhibit 2-8)

5. List and briefly explain at least three of the most important current trends in management.
   (pp. 40-49)

# Chapter 3  Organizational Culture and the Environment:  The Constraints

## Learning Outline

**The Manager:  Omnipotent or Symbolic?**
- Contrast the actions of managers according to the omnipotent and symbolic views.
- Explain the parameters of managerial discretion.

**The Organization's Culture**
- Describe the seven dimensions of organizational culture.
- Discuss the impact of a strong culture on organizations and managers.
- Explain the source of an organization's culture.
- Describe how culture is transmitted to employees.
- Describe how culture affects managers.

**Current Organizational Culture Issues Facing Managers**
- Describe the characteristics of an ethical culture, an innovative culture, and a customer-responsive culture.
- Explain why workplace spirituality seems to be an important concern.
- Describe the characteristics of a spiritual organization.

**The Environment**
- Describe the components of the specific and general environments.
- Discuss the two dimensions of environmental uncertainty.
- Identify the most common organizational stakeholders.
- Explain the four steps in managing external stakeholder relationships.

---

**A Manager's Dilemma**

Yves Guillemot, CEO of Ubisoft, a leading maker of videogames, operates gaming studios in some 20 countries worldwide.  As you read the Manager's Dilemma, think about the following questions, and then compare your thoughts to the **Managers Respond** at the end of the chapter.

1.  What kind of organizational environment does Mr. Guillemot try to foster at Ubisoft?
2.  How has that environment helped the company develop award-winning video games?
3.  How can Mr. Guillemot ensure that Ubisoft's culture is transmitted to new employees as Ubisoft continues to expand worldwide?

---

## Lecture Outline

I.  The Manager:  Omnipotent or Symbolic?
   A. The Omnipotent View.
      1.  Reflects a dominant assumption in management theory.
      2.  Differences in an organization's performance are due to the decisions and actions of its managers.
      3.  Isn't limited to business organizations.

4. Manager is held directly responsible for organizational success or failure.
   B. The Symbolic View.
      1. Organization's results are influenced by factors outside the control of managers such as the economy, customers, governmental policies, etc.
      2. Managers symbolize control and influence.
         a. They create meaning out of randomness, confusion, and ambiguity.
         b. They try to innovate and adapt.
      3. Managers' part in organizational success or failure is minimal.
   C. Reality Suggests a Synthesis.
      1. Managers are neither helpless nor all powerful.
      2. Internal and external constraints restrict a manager's options. (Refer to Exhibit 3-1)
   D. Learning Review.
      • Contrast the actions of managers according to the omnipotent and symbolic views.
      • Explain the parameters of managerial discretion.
   E. Key Terms.
      1. Omnipotent view of management – The view that managers are directly responsible for an organization's success or failure.
      2. Symbolic view of management – The view that much of an organization's success or failure is due to external forces outside manager's control.

II. The Organization's Culture.
   A. An organization's personality is called its *culture*.
   B. What Is Organizational Culture?
      1. Shared values and practices that determine organizational behavior.
      2. Three implications of definition of culture.
      3. Seven dimensions of organizational culture. (Refer to Exhibit 3-2)
      4. Contrasting Organizational Cultures. (Refer to Exhibit 3-3)
   C. Strong Versus Weak Cultures. (Refer to Exhibit 3-4)
      1. Strong cultures have greater influence on employees than weak cultures.
      2. Factors influencing strength/weakness of organization's culture.
      3. Most organizations have moderate to strong cultures.
      4. Strong cultures are associated with high organizational performance.
   D. The Source of Culture.
      1. Reflects vision of founder.
      2. Impact of founder not unique to U.S. organizations.
   E. How an Organization's Culture Continues. (Refer to Exhibit 3-5)
      1. Organizational practices.
      2. Selection of employees.
      3. Actions of top executives.
      4. Employees learn organizational culture through socialization.
   F. How Employees Learn Culture.
      1. Stories.
      2. Rituals.
      3. Material Symbols.

4. Language.
G. How Culture Affects Managers.
   1. Cultural constraints are rarely explicit.
   2. Link between values and managerial behavior.
   3. Managerial decisions are affected by culture.  (Refer to Exhibit 3-6)

---

**Managing Workforce Diversity:  Creating an Inclusive Workplace Culture**
A key challenge for managers is creating a workplace culture that advocates and encourages diversity.  Consider the following questions as you think about workforce diversity.
1.  Identify an advantage to workplace diversity.
2.  How did Marriott and Prudential assist managers to handle diversity in better ways?
3.  Identify ways organizations can reinforce employee behaviors that exemplify inclusiveness in the workforce.

---

H. Learning Review.
- Describe the seven dimensions of organizational culture.
- Discuss the impact of a strong culture on organizations and managers.
- Explain the source of an organization's culture and how that culture continues.
- Describe how culture is transmitted to employees.
- Describe how culture affects managers.
I. Key Terms.
   1. Organizational culture – The shared values, principles, traditions, and ways of doing things that influence the way organizational members act.
   2. Strong cultures – Organizational cultures in which the key values are intensely held and widely shared.
   3. Socialization – The process that adapts employees to the organization's culture.

III. Current Organizational Culture Issues Facing Managers.
  A. Creating an Ethical Culture.  (Refer to Exhibit 3-6)
    1. Culture influences ethical climate and ethical behavior in an organization.
    2. Description of culture that is most likely to shape high ethical standards.

---

**Thinking Critically About Ethics**
Think about the relationship between a manager's values and organizational culture.  Do you think a manager with high ethical standards can live by values of a corporation that tolerates unethical practices?

---

  B. Creating an Innovative Culture.
    1. Successful organizations in all types of industries need cultures that support innovation.
    2. Eight characteristics of an innovative culture.
  C. Creating a Customer-Responsive Culture.
    1. Six characteristics of a customer-responsive culture.
    2. Managers can create a more customer-responsive culture. (See Exhibit 3-8)

D. Spirituality and Organizational Culture.
  1. Workplace spirituality is embraced by a growing number of organizations.
  2. Importance of workplace spirituality.
  3. Five characteristics of spiritual organizations.
     a. Strong Sense of Purpose.
     b. Focus on Individual Development.
     c. Trust and Openness.
     d. Employee Empowerment.
     e. Toleration of Employee Expression.
  4. Criticisms of emphasis on workplace spirituality.
E. Learning Review.
  • Describe the characteristics of an ethical culture, an innovative culture, and a customer-responsive culture.
  • Explain why workplace spirituality seems to be an important concern.
  • Describe the characteristics of a spiritual organization.
F. Key Terms.
  1. Workplace spirituality – A culture where organizational values promote a sense of purpose through meaningful work that takes place in the context of community.

IV. The Environment.
  A. Defining the External Environment.  (Refer to Exhibit 3-9)
     1. Specific Environment.
        a. Customers.
        b. Suppliers.
        c. Competitors.
        d. Pressure Groups.
     2. The General Environment.
        a. Economic Conditions.
        b. Political/Legal Conditions.  (Refer to Exhibit 3-10)
        c. Sociocultural Conditions.
        d. Demographic Conditions.
        e. Technological Conditions.
        f. Global Conditions.
  B. How the Environment Affects Managers.
     1. Assessing Environmental Uncertainty.  (Refer to Exhibit 3-11)
        a. Degree of change ranges from a dynamic environment to a stable environment.
        b. Degree of environmental complexity is measured in terms of the knowledge an organization needs to have about its environment.
        c. Uncertainty is a threat to an organization's effectiveness.
  C. Managing Stakeholder Relationships.
     1. Who are stakeholders?  (Refer to Exhibit 3-11)
     2. Importance of managing stakeholder relationships.
        a. Can influence outcomes.
        b. It's the "right" thing to do.

      c.  Four steps in managing stakeholder relationships.
         i.  Identify organization's stakeholders.
         ii.  Determine particular interests or concerns of stakeholders.
         iii. Decide which stakeholders are critical.
    iv.     iv. Determine how to manage the external stakeholder relationships.
D.  Learning Review.
- Describe the components of the specific and general environments.
- Discuss the two dimensions of environmental uncertainty.
- Identify the most common organizational stakeholders.
- Explain the four steps in managing external stakeholder relationships.

E.  Key Terms.
1. External environment – Those factors and forces outside the organization that affect an organization's performance.
2. Specific environment – Those external forces that have a direct impact on managers' decisions and actions and are directly relevant to the achievement of the organization's goals.
3. General environment – Broad external conditions that may affect the organization.
4. Environmental uncertainty – The degree of change and complexity in an organization's environment.
5. Environmental complexity – The number of components in an organization's environment and the extent of the organization's knowledge about those components.
6. Stakeholders – Any constituencies in the organization's environment that are affected by the organization's decisions and actions.

## Multiple-Choice Questions

1. If a firm holds to an omnipotent view of a manager, then the organization sees managers as _____.
   a) only having a limited effect on organizational outcomes
   b) directly responsible for the success or failure of an organization
   c) heavily constrained by external environmental factors
   d) creating value for the benefit of shareholders, customers, and the public, at the expense of the employees
   (p. 58)

2. Bill is a take-charge business executive who believes that he can overcome any obstacle in carrying out the organization's goals. Bill adheres to the _____ view of management.
   a) objective
   b) symbolic
   c) subjective
   d) omnipotent
   (p. 58)

3. The symbolic view of management suggests that a manager's ability to affect outcomes is influenced by _____.
   a) attention to detail
   b) external factors
   c) aggressiveness
   d) innovation and risk taking
   (pp. 58-59)

4. The definition of organizational cultures implies all of the following EXCEPT that _____.
   a) culture is a perception
   b) there is a shared aspect of culture
   c) culture is prescribed by managers
   d) culture is a descriptive term
   (pp. 59-61)

5. Strong corporate cultures are marked by _____.
   a) key values that are held intensely and widely shared
   b) a high degree of diversity in priorities and values
   c) an omnipotent view of management
   d) a symbolic view of management
   (pp. 61-62)

6. A company with a strong corporate culture would usually _____.
   a) focus intently on details
   b) focus on results such as customer service
   c) be associated with a strong entrepreneurial spirit
   d) be associated with high organizational performance
   (p. 62)

7. An organization can help employees adapt to its culture through the process of _____.
   a) outplacement
   b) organizational development
   c) strategic planning
   d) socialization
   (p. 64)

8. Corporate _____ are a narrative of significant events or people.
   a) stories
   b) symbols
   c) rituals
   d) personalities
   (p. 64)

9. When employees learn a firm's culture through repetitive sequences of activities, they are learning culture through _____.
   a) stories
   b) material symbols
   c) language
   d) rituals
   (pp. 65-66)

10. Which of the following best describes the effect of an organization's culture on management?
    a) It creates implicit constraints on management practice.
    b) Its constraints are explicit and apparent to managers.
    c) It has little if any restraining force on management practice.
    d) It is more influenced by management than influencing on management.
    (pp. 67-68)

11. In organizations where the culture conveys a basic distrust of employees, managers are more likely to _____.
    a) use a democratic leadership style
    b) employ an authoritarian style of leadership
    c) require a major organizational restructuring program
    d) embrace and welcome a diverse workforce
    (p. 68)

12. An organizational culture most likely to shape high ethical standards is one that is _____.
    a) high in aggressiveness and high in risk tolerance
    b) low to moderate in aggressiveness and focuses on outcomes
    c) low in risk tolerance and high in aggressiveness
    d) high in risk tolerance and low to moderate in aggressiveness
    (p. 69)

13. A(n) _____ culture would be characterized by challenge and involvement, freedom, trust and openness, idea time, playfulness, conflict resolution, debates, and risk taking.
    a) ethical
    b) customer-responsive
    c) innovative
    d) spiritual
    (pp. 69-70)

14. A(n) _____ culture would be characterized by employees who are outgoing and friendly, few rigid rules and regulations, empowered employees, good listening kills, role clarity, and conscientious employees.
    a) ethical
    b) customer-responsive
    c) innovative
    d) spiritual
    (p. 71)

15. The recognition that people have an inner life that nourishes and is nourished by meaningful work is referred to as _____.
    a) faith
    b) workplace spirituality
    c) applied socialism
    d) working smarter
    (p. 71)

16. The specific environment includes _____.
    a) suppliers
    b) economic conditions
    c) technology
    d) global pressures and competition
    (p. 74, Exhibit 3-9)

17. The aspect or element of the environment that is directly relevant to achievement of an organization's goals is _____.
    a) environmental complexity
    b) the general environment
    c) the specific environment
    d) environmental uncertainty
    (p. 75)

18. Special-interest groups that attempt to influence the actions of organizations are _____.
    a) pressure groups
    b) technology awareness groups
    c) financial resources groups
    d) environmental rights groups
    (p. 75)

19. Sociocultural conditions of the general environment include _____.
    a) changes in disposable income
    b) specific attitudes of legislators toward business
    c) consumer values and tastes
    d) the use of technology
    (pp. 76-77)

20. The general environment includes _____ conditions which encompass trends in the physical characteristics of a population such as gender, age, level of education, geographic location, and so forth.
    a) economic
    b) sociocultural
    c) technological
    d) demographic
    (p. 77)

21. A firm working in an environment that has few components, has a minimal need for sophisticated knowledge of the components, and is unpredictable is working in an environment that is _____.
    a) simple but dynamic
    b) simple and stable
    c) complex and dynamic
    d) complex but stable
    (p. 79, Exhibit 3-11)

22. If the components in an organization's environment change frequently, we call it a(n) _____ environment. If change is minimal, we call it a(n) _____ environment.
    a) autocratic; pluralistic
    b) general; specific
    c) dynamic; stable
    d) omnipotent; symbolic
    (p. 79)

23. The dimension of environmental uncertainty that deals with the number of components in the environment and the extent of the knowledge the organization has about those components is environmental _____.
    a) stability/instability
    b) complexity
    c) relativity
    d) competitive intelligence
    (p. 80)

24. Constituencies in an organization's external environment that are affected by the organization's decisions and actions are _____.
    a) unions
    b) shareholders
    c) competitors
    d) All of the above
    (p. 81, Exhibit 3-12)

25. When an external stakeholder is critical and environmental uncertainty is high _____.
   a) managers should use stakeholder partnerships
   b) managers should buy corporate stock
   c) managers should use boundary spanning
   d) managers should use an autocratic leadership style
   (p. 82)

## True/False Questions

1. T  F  The symbolic view of the manager is that an organization's outcomes are influenced by a number of factors outside the control of management.
   (p. 58)

2. T  F  The best perspective on management is somewhere between the omnipotent and symbolic views.
   (p. 59)

3. T  F  An organization's culture constrains management behavior but has little influence on organizational performance.
   (pp. 60-61)

4. T  F  An organization's personality is called its *culture*.
   (p. 59)

5. T  F  The strength or weakness of a culture depends on an organization's size, history, amount of turnover experienced, and intensity with which the culture was originated.
   (p. 62)

6. T  F  The primary source of an organization's culture is its founder.
   (p. 63)

7. T  F  The impact of a founder on an organization's culture is unique to the United States.
   (p. 63)

8. T  F  Employees learn a firm's mission through the stories that are told, its rituals, material symbols, and language.
   (pp. 64-66)

9. T  F  The link between organizational values and managerial behavior is fairly straightforward.
   (p. 67)

10. T   F   The content and strength of an organization's culture influences its ethical climate and ethical behavior of its members.
(p. 69)

11. T   F   Among the characteristics of an innovative culture would be risk taking, freedom, and playfulness/humor.
(pp. 69-70)

12. T   F   Widespread employee empowerment and role clarity are characteristics routinely seen in customer-responsive cultures.
(p. 70)

13. T   F   Organizations that promote a spiritual culture recognize that people have a mind and a spirit, seek to find meaning and purpose in their work, and desire to connect with other human beings and be part of a community.
(p. 71)

14. T   F   The external environment is made up of the organizational environment and the country environment.
(p. 73)

15. T   F   Customers, suppliers, competitors, and pressure groups make up the general environment.
(pp. 74-75)

16. T   F   Although suppliers and customers are part of a firm's specific environment, competitors and the government are not.
(pp. 74-75)

17. T   F   Interest rates, inflation, and stock market fluctuations are examples of economic conditions within the general environment.
(p. 76)

18. T   F   Technological and demographic conditions are elements of the general environment.
(pp. 77-78)

19. T   F   Environmental uncertainty refers to the number of components in an organization's environment.
(p. 79)

20. T   F   If the components in an organization's environment change frequently, it is said to be a dynamic environment.
(p. 79)

21. T  F  Environmental complexity can be measured in terms of the knowledge an organization needs to have about its environment.
(p. 80)

22. T  F  Because uncertainty is not a threat to an organization's effectiveness, managers try to maximize it.
(p. 80)

23. T  F  Stakeholders can include internal and external groups.
(p. 81)

24. T  F  Managers of high-performing companies tend to consider the interests of all major stakeholder groups as they make decisions.
(p. 81)

25. T  F  The more critical the stakeholder and the more certain the environment, the more managers need to rely on establishing explicit stakeholder partnerships.
(p. 82)

## Match Terms with Definitions

a. Organizational culture
b. Symbolic view of management
c. Environmental uncertainty
d. Omnipotent view of management
e. Environmental complexity
f. Organizational personality
g. Specific environment
h. General environment

i. Stories
j. Material symbols
k. Environmental change
l. Workplace spirituality
m. Stakeholders
n. Rituals
o. Socialization

_____ 1. The process that adapts employees to the organization's culture.
_____ 2. The view that managers are directly responsible for an organization's success or failure.
_____ 3. The result of different organizational culture themes; how an organization approaches its business.
_____ 4. Repetitive sequences of activities that express and reinforce the values of the organization.
_____ 5. Any constituencies in the organization's external environment that are affected by the organization's decisions and actions.
_____ 6. The recognition that people have an inner life that nourishes and is nourished by meaningful work that takes place in the context of community.
_____ 7. The degree of change and complexity in an organization's environment.
_____ 8. Explanation of significant events or people that explain the values of the organization and how it does business.
_____ 9. The number of components in an organization's environment and the extent of an organization's knowledge about its environmental components.
_____ 10. Everything outside the organization.
_____ 11. The part of the environment that is directly relevant to the achievement of an organization's goals.
_____ 12. The layout of a facility, dress, and the types of automobiles provided to executives are all elements of this aspect of organizational culture.
_____ 13. The view that management has only a limited effect on substantive organizational outcomes because of the limited number of factors outside of management's control.
_____ 14. A system of shared meaning within an organization that determines, in large degree, how employees act.
_____ 15. That element of environmental uncertainty that deals with the amount and frequency of change.

## Essay Questions

1. Compare and contrast the omnipotent view of managers with the symbolic view. (pp. 58-59)

2. Explain the seven dimensions of organizational culture. (p. 61, Exhibit 3-2)

3. How do employees learn culture? (pp. 64-66)

4. How can organizations create an ethical culture? How can they create an innovative culture? (pp. 69-70)

5. Discuss the two components of the external environment. (pp. 73-78)

# Chapter 4  Managing in a Global Environment

## Learning Outline

**What's Your Global Perspective?**
- Define parochialism.
- Contrast ethnocentric, polycentric, and geocentric attitudes toward global business.
- Explain why it's important for managers to be sensitive to global differences.

**Understanding the Global Environment**
- Describe the current status of the European Union.
- Discuss the North American Free Trade Agreement and other regional trade alliances in Latin American.
- Tell about the Association of Southeast Asian Nations.
- Explain the interdependence that globalization involves.
- Discuss the role of the WTO.

**Doing Business Globally**
- Contrast multinational, multidomestic, global, transnational, and born global organizations.
- Describe the different ways organizations can go international.
- Define global sourcing, exporting, importing, licensing, and franchising.
- Describe global strategic alliances, joint ventures, and foreign subsidiaries.

**Managing in a Global Environment**
- Explain how the global legal-political and economic environments affect managers.
- Discuss Hofstede's five dimensions for assessing country cultures.
- Explain the nine GLOBE dimensions for assessing country cultures.
- Discuss the challenges of doing business globally in today's world.

## Lecture Outline

> **A Manager's Dilemma**
> Zara, the European clothing retailer, is positioned for continued global success. That success is based on a simple principle – in fashion, nothing is more important as time to market. Compare your answers to the following questions with those at the end of the chapter in **Managers Respond.**
> 1. How does Zara get clothes to stores twelve times faster than other manufacturers?
> 2. What cross-cultural problems will Zara face as it continues to open new stores worldwide?

I.   Who Owns What?
    A.  Global company quiz.

II. What's Your Global Perspective?
   A. Parochialism.
   B. Three possible global attitudes.  (Refer to Exhibit 4-1)
      1. Ethnocentric Attitude.
      2. Polycentric Attitude.
      3. Geocentric Attitude.
   C. Successful global management requires enhanced sensitivity.
      1. Examples of Cross-Cultural Blunders. (Refer to Exhibit 4-2)
   D. Learning Review.
      • Define parochialism.
      • Contrast ethnocentric, polycentric, and geocentric attitudes toward global business.
      • Explain why it's important for managers to be sensitive to global differences.
   E. Key Terms.
      1. Parochialism – Viewing the world solely through your own perspective leading to an inability to recognize differences between people.
      2. Ethnocentric attitude – The parochialistic belief that the best work approaches and practices are those of the home country.
      3. Polycentric attitude – The view that the managers in the host country know the best work approaches and practices for running their business.
      4. Geocentric attitude – A world-oriented view that focuses on using the best approaches and people from around the globe.

III. Understanding the Global Environment.
   A. Importance of global trade.
   B. Global trade is shaped by regional trading alliances and agreements negotiated through the World Trade Organization.
   C. Regional Trading Alliances.
      1. The European Union (EU).  (Refer to Exhibit 4-3)
         1. Maastricht Treaty, 1992.
         2. Motivation for creation of the EU.
         3. The euro is a single European currency.
      2. North American Free Trade Agreement (NAFTA), 1992.
         1. An agreement among Canada, U.S., and Mexico.
         2. Eliminates barriers to free trade.
      3. Association of Southeast Asian Nations (ASEAN).  (Refer to Exhibit 4-4)
         1. Trading block of ten Southeast Asia nations.
         2. One of fastest growing economic regions in the world.
      4. Other Trade Alliances.
         1. African Union, 2002.
         2. South Asian Association for Regional Cooperation, 2006.
   D. The World Trade Organization.
      1. Countries are interdependent.
      2. World Trade Organization (WTO) is a multilateral trading system.
      3. The only global organization dealing with the rules of trade among nations.

E. Learning Review.
- Describe the current status of the European Union.
- Discuss the North American Free Trade Agreement and other regional trade alliances in Latin America.
- Tell about the Association of Southeast Asian Nations.
- Explain the interdependence that globalization involves.
- Discuss the role of the WTO.

F. Key Terms.
1. European Union (EU) – A union of 25 European nations created as a unified economic and trade entity.
2. Euro – A single common European currency.
3. North American Free Trade Agreement (NAFTA) – An agreement among the Mexican, Canadian, and U.S. governments in which barriers to free trade have been eliminated.
4. Association of Southeast Asian Nations (ASEAN) – A trading alliance of ten Southeast Asian nations.
5. World Trade Organization (WTO) – A global organization of 149 countries that deals with the rules of trade among nations.

IV. Doing Business Globally.
A. Different Types of Global Organizations.
1. Multinational Corporation (MNC).
   1. Term broadly used to refer to any and all types of international companies that maintain operations in multiple countries.
2. Multidomestic Corporation.
   1. An MNC that decentralizes management and other decisions to the local country.
   2. Local employees typically hired to manage the business and marketing strategies that are tailored to the country's unique characteristics.
   3. Reflects polycentric attitude.
3. Global Company.
   1. Centralizes management and other decisions in the home countries.
   2. Treats the world market as an integrated whole and focuses on the need for global efficiency.
   3. Reflects ethnocentric attitude.
4. Transnational (Borderless) Organization.
   1. Eliminates structural divisions that impose artificial geographic barriers.
   2. Managers choose this form of international organization to increase efficiency and effectiveness in a competitive global market.
   3. Reflects geocentric attitude.
5. Born Global.
   1. Chooses to go global from inception.
   2. Commits resources up front to doing business in more than one country.
   3. Likely to play an increasingly important role in international business.

B. How Organizations Go Global.
   1. Global sourcing.
   2. Exporting and Importing.
   3. Licensing and Franchising.
   4. Strategic alliances.
   5. Joint venture.
   6. Foreign subsidiary.

---

**Managing IT: IT in a Global World**

Managers around the globe are tapping into the power of information technology.
Consider the following questions as you think about managing information
technology.
1. How has technological innovation made employee collaboration more efficient?
2. What are the implications for global managers of differing rates of Internet usage
   in different countries?

---

C. Learning Review.
   - Contrast multinational, multidomestic, global, transnational, and born global
     organizations.
   - Describe the different ways organizations can go international.
   - Define global sourcing, exporting, importing, licensing, and franchising.
   - Describe global strategic alliances, joint ventures, and foreign subsidiaries.
D. Key Terms.
   1. Multinational corporations (MNCs) – A broad term that refers to any and all
      types of international companies that maintain operations in multiple
      countries.
   2. Multidomestic corporation – An international company that decentralizes
      management and other decisions to the local country.
   3. Global company – An international company that centralizes management and
      other decisions in the home country.
   4. Transnational (borderless) organization – A type of international company in
      which artificial geographical barriers have been eliminated.
   5. Born globals – An international company that chooses to go global from
      inception.
   6. Global sourcing – Purchasing materials or labor from around the world
      wherever it is cheapest.
   7. Exporting – Making products domestically and selling them abroad.
   8. Importing – Acquiring products made abroad and selling them domestically.
   9. Licensing – An organization gives another organization the right to make or
      sell its products using its technology or product specifications.
   10. Franchising – An organization gives another organization the right to use its
       name and operating methods.
   11. Strategic alliances – Partnerships between an organization and a foreign
       partner(s) in which both share resources and knowledge in developing new
       products or building production facilities.

12. Joint venture – A specific type of strategic alliance in which the partners agree to form a separate, independent organization for some business purpose.
13. Foreign subsidiary – Directly investing in a foreign country by setting up a separate and independent production facility or office.

V. Managing in a Global Environment.
   A. The Legal-Political Environment.
      1. U.S. managers are accustomed to a stable legal environment.
      2. Some countries have a history of unstable government.
      3. Lower levels of stability result in greater levels of uncertainty.
      4. Legal-political environment doesn't have to be unstable or revolutionary to be of concern to managers.

---

**Thinking Critically About Ethics**
Foreign countries often have lax product-labeling laws. You are responsible for the profitability of a new drug whose side effects can be serious, although not fatal.
1. Is it ethical to allow profit margins to influence decisions?
2. What factors will influence your decision?

---

   B. The Economic Environment.
      1. Types of economic systems.
         1. Market Economy.
         2. Command Economy.
      2. Other economic issues.
         1. Currency exchange rates.
         2. Inflation.
         3. Diverse tax policies.
   C. The Cultural Environment.
      1. National culture has greater effect than organization's culture.
      2. What are Americans like? (Refer to Exhibit 4-6)

---

**Focus on Leadership: Leading Here Is Not Like Leading There**
Consider the following questions as you think about the role of national culture in effective leadership.
1. Is leadership culturally bound?
2. What leadership behaviors are universally deemed to be desirable?
3. What leadership behaviors are universally deemed to be undesirable?

---

      3. Hofstede's Framework for Assessing Cultures.
         1. Individualism vs. Collectivism.
         2. Power Distance.
         3. Uncertainty Avoidance.
         4. Quantity versus Quality of Life.
         5. Long-term and Short-term Orientation.
         6. Examples of Hofstede's Cultural Dimensions. (Refer to Exhibit 4-7)
   D. The GLOBE Framework for Assessing Cultures.

1. Began in 1993 and continues to investigate cross-cultural leadership behaviors of over 18,000 middle managers in 62 countries.
2. Identified nine dimensions on which national cultures differ. (Refer to Exhibit 4-8)
   1. Assertiveness.
   2. Future orientation.
   3. Gender differentiation.
   4. Uncertainty avoidance.
   5. Power distance.
   6. Individualism/collectivism.
   7. In-group collectivism.
   8. Performance orientation.
   9. Humane orientation.
3. Extension of Hofstede's work.

E. Global Management in Today's World.
   1. Managers face challenges arising from the openness associated with globalization.
   2. More serious challenges come from cultural differences.
   3. Successful managing in the global environment will require sensitivity and understanding.

F. Learning Review.
   - Explain how the global legal-political and economic environments affect managers.
   - Discuss Hofstede's five dimensions for assessing country cultures.
   - Explain the nine GLOBE dimensions for assessing country cultures.
   - Discuss the challenges of doing business globally in today's world.

G. Key Terms.
   1. Market economy – An economic system in which resources are primarily owned and controlled by the private sector.
   2. Command economy – An economic system in which all economic decisions are planned by a central government.
   3. National culture – The values and attitudes shared by individuals from a specific country that shape their behavior and beliefs about what is important.
   4. GLOBE – The Global Leadership Organizational Behavior Effectiveness research program which continues to study cross-cultural leadership.

## Multiple-Choice Questions

1. If Evan approaches managing his international workforce from an American perspective because he believes U.S. management methods are the best way to run a business, Evan is demonstrating _____.
   a) parochialism
   b) a polycentric attitude
   c) a geocentric attitude
   d) panethnicity
   (p. 91)

2. When Riya argues that her firm should trust the market knowledge of her host-country managers and that the firm should seek host-country government support, she is demonstrating _____.
   a) parochialism
   b) an ethnocentric attitude
   c) a polycentric attitude
   d) a geocentric attitude
   (p. 92)

3. When Global Marketing, Inc., a U.S.-based marketing firm, promoted one of their German national managers to president of the firm and made it a point to hire and promote managers regardless of nationality, Global was demonstrating _____.
   a) parochialism
   b) an ethnocentric attitude
   c) a polycentric attitude
   d) a geocentric attitude
   (p. 92)

4. Managers with a(n) _____ attitude view every foreign operation as different and hard to understand and are likely to leave the running of their foreign facilities to host country managers.
   a) parochial
   b) ethnocentric
   c) polycentric
   d) geocentric
   (p. 93)

5. The European Union was formed _____.
   a) in 1992 with 12 members
   b) in 1996 with 15 members
   c) in 1920 from the origins of NATO
   d) in 1995 and includes three Eastern European Bloc countries
   (p. 94)

6. The single European currency is the _____.
   a) ecu
   b) euro
   c) lire
   d) kroner
   (p. 95)

7. NAFTA went into effect in 1994 among the United States, Canada, and _____.
   a) Australia
   b) Brazil
   c) Mexico
   d) Venezuela
   (p. 95)

8. Costa Rica, El Salvador, Guatemala, Honduras, and Nicaragua are part of _____, which is intended to liberalize trade between these countries and the United States.
   a) WTO (World Trade Organization)
   b) SCCM (Southern Cone Common Market)
   c) SAFTA (South American Free Trade Agreement)
   d) CAFTA (U.S-Central America Free Trade Agreement.
   (p. 95)

9. ASEAN is _____.
   a) a trading alliance of ten Southeast Asian countries
   b) based in Latin America and has three current members and four more joining
   c) an international regulatory body that overseas trade regulations among countries not in free trade groups
   d) an arm of the World Trade Organization
   (pp. 95-96)

10. An organization of 149 countries that deals with the rules of trade among nations is _____.
    a) ASEAN
    b) the North American Free Trade Association
    c) the Free Trade Area of the Americas
    d) the World Trade Organization
    (p. 96)

11. What organization was formed in 1995 and evolved from the General Agreement on Tariffs and Trade?
    a) ASEAN
    b) WTO
    c) United Nations
    d) WHO
    (p. 96)

12. When a company maintains operations in several countries and decentralizes decision making, it is a _____.
    a) global company
    b) transnational corporation
    c) multidomestic corporation
    d) borderless corporation
    (p. 97)

13. The management of the multidomestic corporation reflects a(n) _____ attitude.
    a) parochialist
    b) geocentric
    c) ethnocentric
    d) polycentric
    (p. 97)

14. One of the first steps when a company wants to go global is to _____.
    a) hire foreign representation
    b) find a joint venture with a host-country business
    c) export to a foreign country
    d) license or franchise their product into the foreign country
    (p. 98, Exhibit 4-5)

15. When companies purchase materials or labor from around the world wherever it is cheapest, this is called _____.
    a) global sourcing
    b) licensing
    c) franchising
    d) exporting
    (p. 98)

16. The _____ is an approach to going global that is a specific type of strategic alliance in which the partners agree to form a separate, independent organization for some business purpose.
    a) licensing agreement
    b) franchise
    c) foreign subsidiary
    d) joint venture
    (p. 99)

17. When a firm studies the stability of a country's government and its policies toward foreign businesses, the firm is examining the country's _____ environment.
    a) economic
    b) cultural
    c) legal-political
    d) technological
    (p. 101)

18. A _____ economy is an economic system in which all economic decisions are planned by a central government.
    a) command
    b) market
    c) laissez-faire
    d) social
    (p. 102)

19. Exchange rates, tax policies, rates of inflation, etc., are all part of a country's _____ environment.
    a) economic
    b) cultural
    c) legal-political
    d) technological
    (p. 102)

20. The cultural element in Hofstede's framework that expresses the value that people expect others to look out after them is _____.
    a) quality of life
    b) collectivism
    c) power distance
    d) uncertainty avoidance
    (p. 105)

21. The extent to which a society accepts the unequal distribution of power in an organization is expressed in Hofstede's framework as the cultural dimension of _____.
    a) quality of life
    b) individualism
    c) power distance
    d) uncertainty avoidance
    (p. 105)

22. A country that is highly rule bound, has little tolerance for unusual ideas, and has a relatively low job mobility could be described as a country with high _____.
    a) quality of life
    b) individualism
    c) power distance
    d) uncertainty avoidance
    (p. 105)

23. The GLOBE (Global Leadership and Organizational Behavior Effectiveness) research program identified all of the following dimensions on which national cultures differ EXCEPT _____.
    a) Individualism/Collectivism
    b) Religiosity
    c) Gender Differentiation
    d) Performance Orientation
    (p. 106)

24. The GLOBE research project identified the dimension of _____ as being the degree to which a society encourages and rewards individuals for being fair, altruistic, generous, caring, and kind to others.
    a) gender differentiation
    b) humane orientation
    c) power distance
    d) in-group collectivism
    (p. 106)

25. Which of the following countries ranked high on performance orientation?
    a) Taiwan
    b) Russia
    c) Greece
    d) Argentina
    (p. 107, Exhibit 4-8)

## True/False Questions

1. T   F   People with a parochial attitude recognize that people in other countries have different ways of living and working.
   (p. 91)

2. T   F   Monolingualism is one of the signs that a nation suffers from parochialism.
   (p. 91)

3. T   F   The polycentric attitude is the view that managers in the host country know the best approaches and practices for running their businesses.
   (p. 92)

4. T   F   The polycentric attitude is a world-oriented view that focuses on using the best approaches and people from around the globe.
   (p. 93)

5. T   F   When trade is allowed to flow freely, countries benefit from economic growth and productivity gains because they specialize in producing the goods they're best at and importing goods that are more efficiently produced elsewhere.
   (p. 94)

6. T   F   The signing of the Maastricht Treaty created the European Union.
   (p. 94)

7. T   F   As a single market, there are no barriers to travel, employment, investment, and trade within the EU.
   (p. 95)

8.　T　F　NAFTA includes the United States, Mexico, and Canada, with the recent addition of Chile.
(p. 95)

9.　T　F　CAFTA is a concept for joining ASEAN, EU, and NAFTA nations into one large free trade area.
(p. 95)

10. T　F　Today, the WTO is the only *global* organization dealing with the rules of trade among nations.
(p. 96)

11. T　F　A global company maintains significant operations in multiple countries but manages them from a base in the home country.
(p. 96)

12. T　F　The borderless organization approaches global business with a geocentric attitude.
(p. 96)

13. T　F　Joint ventures and strategic alliances are considered to be relatively slow and expensive ways for companies to compete globally.
(p. 99)

14. T　F　Licensing and franchising are similar approaches to going global, since both involve an organization's giving another organization the right to use its brand name, technology, or product specifications in return for a lump-sum payment or fee.
(p. 99)

15. T　F　Franchising is an approach to going global that involves partnerships between an organization and a foreign company in which both share resources and knowledge in developing new products or building production facilities.
(p. 99)

16. T　F　A foreign subsidiary is a separate and independent production facility or office.
(p. 100)

17. T　F　The legal-political environment is only of concern to managers when it is unstable or revolutionary.
(p. 101)

18. T　F　In a market economy, resources are primarily owned and controlled by the private sector.
(p. 87; Exhibit 4-21)

19. T　F　In global situations, national culture has more influence on employee behavior than organizational culture.
(p. 102)

20. T　F　A framework to help managers better understand differences between national cultures was developed by Geert Hofstede.
(p. 104)

21. T　F　Power distance, according to Hofstede's model, is a measure of the degree to which people tolerate risk and unconventional behavior.
(p. 105)

22. T　F　Certainty avoidance, according to Hofstede's model, is the degree to which values such as assertiveness, the acquisition of money and material goods, and competition prevail.
(p. 105)

23. T　F　The GLOBE project extended, but did not replace, Hofstede's work in assessing the dimensions of national culture.
(p. 105)

24. T　F　The dimension of national culture identified by the GLOBE project termed *Gender Differentiation* is the extent to which a society maximizes gender-role differences as measured by how much status and decision-making responsibilities women have.
(p. 106)

25. T　F　Both Hofstede's model and the GLOBE model identified *Power Distance* as the degree to which members of a society expect to be unequally treated.
(pp. 105-106)

## Match Terms with Definitions

a. Multinational corporation
b. Market economy
c. Transnational corporation
d. European Union
e. National culture
f. Global company
g. Franchising
h. World Trade Organization

i. NAFTA
j. Foreign subsidiary
k. Ethnocentric attitude
l. Multidomestic corporation
m. Global sourcing
n. Polycentric attitude
o. Geocentric attitude

_____ 1. An international company that centralizes management and other decisions in the home country.

_____ 2. A broad term that refers to any and all types of international companies that maintain operations in multiple countries.

_____ 3. A global organization of 149 countries that deals with the rules of trade among nations.

_____ 4. Directly investing in a foreign country by setting up a separate and independent production facility or office.

_____ 5. A union of 25 European nations created as a unified economic and trade entity.

_____ 6. An agreement among the Mexican, Canadian, and U.S. governments in which barriers to free trade have been eliminated.

_____ 7. The parochialistic belief that the best work approaches and practices are those of the home country.

_____ 8. The view that the managers in the host country know the best work approaches and practices for running their businesses.

_____ 9. A world-oriented view that focuses on using the best approaches and people from around the globe.

_____ 10. An international company that decentralizes management and other decisions to the local country.

_____ 11. An organization gives another organization the right to use its name and operating methods.

_____ 12. An economic system in which resources are primarily owned and controlled by the private sector.

_____ 13. A type of international company in which artificial geographical barriers are eliminated.

_____ 14. Purchasing materials or labor from around the world wherever it is cheapest.

_____ 15. The attitudes and perspectives shared by individuals from a specific country that shape their behaviors and the way they see the world.

**Essay Questions**

1. Compare and contrast the three different global perspectives a manager can have regarding his/her management practices.
   (p. 92, Exhibit 4-1)

2. Discuss the importance of the European Union and NAFTA. Identify their members and how each association benefits its members.
   (pp. 94-95)

3. Discuss three ways that organizations can enter the international market relatively quickly and inexpensively.
   (pp. 98-100)

4. How do the legal-political, economic, and cultural environments impact the business decisions managers must make when going global?
   (pp. 101-104)

5. Discuss Hofstede's framework for understanding the dimensions of national culture. Include each of the five dimensions and briefly explain them.
   (pp. 104-105)

# Chapter 5  Social Responsibility and Managerial Ethics

## Learning Outline

### What Is Social Responsibility?
- Contrast the classical and socioeconomic views of social responsibility.
- Discuss the role that stakeholders play in the four stages of social responsibility.
- Differentiate among social obligation, social responsiveness, and social responsibility.

### Social Responsibility and Economic Performance
- Explain what research studies have shown about the relationship between an organization's social involvement and its economic performance.
- Define social screening.
- Explain what conclusion can be reached regarding social responsibility and economic performance.

### The Greening of Management
- Describe how organizations can go green.
- Relate the approaches to being green to the concepts of social obligation, social responsiveness, and social responsibility.

### Values-Based Management
- Discuss what purposes shared values serve.
- Describe the relationship of values-based management to ethics.

### Managerial Ethics
- Discuss the factors that affect ethical and unethical behavior.
- Discuss the six determinants of issue intensity.
- Tell what codes of ethics are and how their effectiveness can be improved.
- Describe the important roles managers play in encouraging ethical behavior.

### Social Responsibility and Ethics Issues in Today's World
- Explain why ethical leadership is important.
- Discuss how managers and organizations can protect employees who raise ethical issues or concerns.
- Explain what role social entrepreneurs play.
- Describe social impact management.

---

**A Manager's Dilemma**

Cascade Engineering was founded on the belief that business could be profitable and socially and environmentally responsible.  Consider the following questions and compare your answers to **Managers Respond** at the end of the chapter.

1. What are some of the benefits of social responsibility for companies that practice it?
2. What are some of the potential drawbacks of social responsibility for companies that practice it?
3. From a long-term perspective, would it make more sense for Cascade Engineering to be less socially responsible and more focused on profits.

---

I. What Is Social Responsibility?
   A. Two Views of Social Responsibility.
      1. The Classical View.
         a. Advocated by Milton Friedman, economist and Nobel laureate.
         b. Management's only social responsibility is to maximize profits.
         c. Any time managers decide to spend for "social good," they are adding to the costs of doing business.
      2. The Socioeconomic View.
         a. Management's social responsibility also includes protecting and improving society's welfare.
         b. Corporations have a responsibility to the larger society that allows their formation through various laws and regulations and supports them by purchasing their products and services.
      3. Comparing the Two Views.
         a. Four-stage model of the progression of an organization's social responsibility. (Refer to Exhibit 5-1)
            (i)    Stage 1 – classical view; manager obeys laws and regulations and pursues stockholders' interests.
            (ii)   Stage 2 – managers are also responsible to employees as stakeholders and focus on human resources concerns.
            (iii)  Stage 3 – managers are also responsible to stakeholders in the specific environment, particularly customers and suppliers.
            (iv)   Stage 4 – highest socioeconomic commitment; managers are responsible to society as a whole.
   B. Arguments for and Against Social Responsibility. (Refer to Exhibit 5-2)
   C. From Obligations to Responsiveness to Responsibility. (Refer to Exhibit 5-3)
      1. Social Obligation.
      2. Social Responsiveness.
      3. Social Responsibility – Adds an ethical imperative.
   D. Learning Review.
      • Contrast the classical and socioeconomic views of social responsibility.
      • Discuss the role that stakeholders play in the four stages of social responsibility.
      • Differentiate among social obligation, social responsiveness, and social responsibility.
   E. Key Terms.
      1. Classical view – The view that management's only social responsibility is to maximize profits.
      2. Socioeconomic view – The view that management's social responsibility goes beyond making profits to include protecting and improving society's welfare.
      3. Social obligation – When a firm engages in social actions because of its obligation to meet certain economic and legal responsibilities.
      4. Social responsiveness – When a firm engages in social actions in response to some popular social norms.
      5. Social responsibility – A business's intention, beyond its legal and economic obligation, to do the right thing and act in ways that are good for society.

II. Social Involvement and Economic Performance.
   A. How do socially responsible activities affect a company's economic performance?
      1. Most studies showed a positive relationship between social involvement and economic performance.
         a. Difficulties with measuring "social responsibility" and "economic performance."
         b. Causation can't be assumed.
      2. Evaluation of socially responsible mutual stock funds.
         a. Funds use social screening.
         b. Have outperformed average diversified stock fund. (Refer to Exhibit 5-4)
      3. Little evidence supports that a company's social actions hurt long-term economic performance.
   B. Learning Review.
      • Explain what research studies have shown about the relationship between an organization's social involvement and its economic performance.
      • Define social screening.
      • Explain what conclusion can be reached regarding social responsibility and economic performance.
   C. Key Term.
      1. Social screening – Applying social criteria (screens) to investment decisions.

III. The Greening of Management.
   A. There is a close link between an organization's decisions and activities and its impact on the natural environment.
   B. Global Environmental Problems.
      1. Some serious environmental problems.
         a. Natural resource depletion.
         b. Global warming.
         c. Pollution.
         d. Industrial accidents.
         e. Toxic wastes
      2. Affluent societies are most at fault.
   C. How Organizations Go Green.
      1. Approaches to Being Green. (Refer to Exhibit 5-5)
         a. Legal (light green) approach – social obligation.
         b. Market approach – social responsiveness.
         c. Stakeholder approach – social responsiveness.
         d. Activist (dark green) approach – social responsibility.
   D. Evaluating the Greening of Management.
      1. Global Reporting Initiative (GRI).
      2. ISO 14001 Standards.
      3. 100 Most Sustainable Corporations in the World.
   E. Learning Review.
      • Describe how organizations can go green.
      • Relate the approaches to being green to the concepts of social obligation, social responsiveness, and social responsibility.

F.  Key Term.
    1.  Greening of management – The recognition of the close link between an organization's decisions and activities and its impact on the natural environment.

IV. Values-Based Management.
    A.  Approach in which managers establish and uphold an organization's shared values.
    B.  Purposes of Shared Values.  (Refer to Exhibit 5-6)
        1.  Guideposts for managerial decisions and actions.
        2.  Shape employee behavior and communicate organizational expectations.
        3.  Influence marketing efforts.
        4.  Build team spirit.

---

**Thinking Critically About Ethics**
Many organizations donate money to philanthropic and charitable causes and ask their employees to make donations to these causes.
1.  Do you consider this to be ethical conduct on the part of the organizations?
2.  What ethical guidelines might you suggest for individuals and organizational contributions to philanthropic and charitable causes?

---

    C.  The Bottom Line on Shared Corporate Values.
        1.  Managers are responsible for establishing and upholding desired corporate values.
        2.  American Management Association survey of corporate values.  (Refer to Exhibit 5-7)
    D.  Learning Review.
       •  Discuss what purposes shared values serve.
       •  Describe the relationship of values-based management to ethics.
    E.  Key Term.
        1.  Values-based management – An approach to managing in which managers are guided by the organization's shared values in their management practices.

V.  Managerial Ethics.
    A.  Definition of Ethics.
    B.  Factors That Affect Employee Ethics.
        1.  Actions are the result of interactions between stage of moral development and moderating variables.  (Refer to Exhibit 5-8)
        2.  Stage of Moral Development.  (Refer to Exhibit 5-9)
            a.  Preconventional Level.
            b.  Conventional Level.
            c.  Principled Level.
        3.  Individual Characteristics.
            a.  Personal Values.

    b. Personality Variables.
        (i) Ego Strength.
        (ii) Locus of Control.
            a) Internal locus.
            b) External locus.
    4. Structural Variables.
        a. Structural design.
        b. Performance appraisal systems.
        c. Reward allocation systems.
        d. Behavior of managers.
    5. Organization's Culture.
        a. Content and strength influence ethical behavior.
        b. Strong culture vs. weak culture.
    6. Issue Intensity.
        a. Determinants of Issue Intensity. (Refer to Exhibit 5-10)
            (i)     Greatness of harm.
            (ii)    Consensus of wrong.
            (iii)   Probability of harm.
            (iv)    Immediacy of consequences.
            (v)     Proximity to victim(s).
            (vi)    Concentration of effect.
C. Ethics in an International Context.
    1. Social and cultural differences between countries are important.
    2. Foreign Corrupt Practices Act.
    3. The Global Compact. (Refer to Exhibit 5-11)
    4. Organization for Economic Co-operation and Development (OECD)
D. Improving Ethical Behavior.
    1. Employee Selection.
    2. Codes of Ethics and Decision Rules.
        a. Three categories of content in codes of ethics. (Refer to Exhibit 5-12)
            (i)     Be a dependable organizational citizen.
            (ii)    Don't do anything unlawful or improper that will harm the organization.
            (iii)   Be good to customers.
        b. Effectiveness of codes of ethics. (Refer to Exhibit 5-13)
    3. Top Management's Leadership.
    4. Job Goals and Performance Appraisal.
    5. Ethics Training.
        a. Can ethics be taught?
        b. Benefits of ethics training.
    6. Independent Social Audits.
    7. Formal Protective Mechanisms.
E. Learning Review.
    • Discuss the factors that affect ethical and unethical behavior.
    • Discuss the six determinants of issue intensity.
    • Tell what codes of ethics are and how their effectiveness can be improved.

- Describe the important roles managers play in encouraging ethical behavior.

F. Key Terms.
1. Ethics – Principles, values, and beliefs that define what is right and wrong behavior.
2. Values – Basic convictions about what is right and wrong.
3. Ego strength – A personality measure of the strength of a person's convictions.
4. Locus of control – A personality attribute that reflects the degree to which people believe they control their own fate.
5. Code of ethics – A formal statement of an organization's primary values and the ethical rules it expects its employees to follow.

VI. Social Responsibility and Ethics Issues in Today's World.
   A. Managing ethical lapses and social irresponsibility.
      1. Irresponsible and unethical behaviors are prevalent across our society.
      2. Ethical Leadership.
         a. Managers should be good role models.
         b. Ethical leaders should share their values.
         c. Ethical leaders should stress important shared values.
         d. Managers should use the reward system to reinforce ethics.
      3. Protecting Employees Who Raise Ethical Issues.
         a. Whistleblowers.
         b. Ethics hotlines.
   B. Social Entrepreneurship.
      1. "What business entrepreneurs are to the economy, social entrepreneurs are to social change."
      2. Fair Trade.
      3. Senior Lawyers Project.
      4. Program for Appropriate Technology in Health
   C. Social Impact Management.
      1. Managers can address social responsibilities from the perspective of the impacts they have on society.
      2. Managing responsibly and ethically isn't always easy.
   D. Learning Review.
      - Explain why ethical leadership is important.
      - Discuss how managers and organizations can protect employees who raise ethical issues or concerns.
      - Explain what role social entrepreneurs play.
      - Describe social impact management.
   E. Key Terms.
      1. Whistleblower – Individuals who raise ethical concerns or issues to others inside or outside the organization.
      2. Social entrepreneur – An individual or organization who seeks out opportunities to improve society by using practical, innovative, and sustainable approaches.

3. Social impact management – The field of inquiry at the intersection of business practice and wider societal concerns that reflects and respects the complex interdependency between those two realities.

## Multiple-Choice Questions

1. The belief that the primary interest of managers should be protecting the interests of their stockholders by maximizing profits is an example of _____.
   a) the classical view
   b) the socioeconomic view
   c) social responsibility
   d) issue intensity
   (p. 116)

2. When corporations believe they have a social responsibility to the larger society that creates and sustains them, they are reflecting _____.
   a) the classical view
   b) the socioeconomic view
   c) social obligation
   d) issue intensity
   (pp. 116-117)

3. Managers at Sparky Car Repair have expanded their definition of stakeholder to include employees in an effort to attract, keep, and motivate good employees. Sparky Car Repair managers are at _____ in the four-stage model of organizational social responsibility.
   a) Stage 1
   b) Stage 2
   c) Stage 3
   d) Stage 4
   (p. 117, Exhibit 5-1)

4. A company that improves air pollution standards at their firm to meet the minimum levels required by law is practicing _____.
   a) social responsibility
   b) social obligation
   c) social responsiveness
   d) issue intensity
   (p. 119)

5. Those who argue *against* social responsibility because it violates the essence of the classical view of management are making an argument on the basis of _____.
   a) the violation of profit maximization
   b) cost
   c) business having too much power
   d) a dilution of purpose
   (p. 118, Exhibit 5-2)

6. A company that voluntarily recalls a toy when it is discovered to be unsafe is practicing _____.
   a) social responsibility
   b) social obligation
   c) social responsiveness
   d) issue intensity
   (p. 120)

7. _____ adds an ethical imperative to do those things that make a society better and not to do those that could make it worse.
   a) Social responsibility
   b) Social obligation
   c) Social responsiveness
   d) Issue intensity
   (p. 120)

8. Research shows that _____.
   a) there is a negative correlation between social responsibility and corporate profits
   b) social responsibility has no direct impact on corporate profits
   c) there is a positive correlation between social responsibility and corporate profits
   d) the impact on corporate profits by social responsibility depends on issue intensity
   (pp. 120-121)

9. The recognition of the close link between an organization's decisions and activities and its impact on the natural environment is termed _____.
   a) linking pin theory
   b) the greening of management
   c) ecological awareness
   d) stakeholder empowerment
   (p. 123)

10. The highest degree of environmental sensitivity toward the greening of America is termed the _____.
    a) legal approach
    b) activist approach
    c) market approach
    d) stakeholder approach
    (p. 124, Exhibit 5-5)

11. When management recognizes the need to go "green," most organizations begin with the first stage which is a _____ approach.
    a) legal
    b) market
    c) stakeholder
    d) activist
    (p. 124, Exhibit 5-5)

12. An approach to management in which managers establish, communicate, promote, and practice shared corporate values is called _____.
    a) social responsiveness
    b) values-based management
    c) green management
    d) stakeholder management
    (p. 126)

13. Managers develop shared values for a variety of purposes, including _____.
    a) reducing costs
    b) improving productivity and quality
    c) influencing competitors' productivity
    d) shaping employee behavior
    (p. 126, Exhibit 5-6)

14. A survey by the American Management Association reported that 64 percent of respondents said that their corporate values were linked to _____.
    a) industry standards
    b) professional codes of ethics
    c) performance evaluations and compensation
    d) MBO goals
    (p. 127)

15. The term _____ refers to principles and beliefs that define what is right and wrong behavior.
    a) social obligation
    b) ethics
    c) stakeholder
    d) locus of control
    (p. 129)

16. The first level of moral development is labeled _____ and at this level a person's choice between right or wrong is based on personal consequences.
    a) preconventional
    b) conventional
    c) principled
    d) precognitive
    (p. 130)

17. If a company were selling unsafe, high-tar cigarettes to Third World countries, a manager with high ego strength would be likely to _____.
    a) say he believes that because the cigarettes are unsafe, the company should not sell them, and then actively campaign to persuade the company to stop selling the cigarettes
    b) say he believes that the cigarettes are unsafe and the company should not sell them, but do nothing to encourage the company to stop the practice
    c) not say what he thinks, but informally suggest that the company stop selling the cigarettes
    d) not act to change the company practice even if he believes the cigarettes are unsafe
    (p. 130)

18. People with a(n) _____ believe that they control their own destinies.
    a) low self-esteem
    b) high mach score
    c) internal locus of control
    d) low ego strength
    (p. 131)

19. Research shows that the single most important influence on an individual's decision to act ethically or unethically is the _____.
    a) behavior of managers
    b) written code of ethics
    c) degree of importance attached to the decision
    d) ego strength of the individual
    (p. 131)

20. An organization's formal rules, job descriptions, and written codes of ethics are all part of an organization's _____ that impact ethical behavior.
    a) values
    b) locus of control
    c) culture
    d) structural variables
    (p. 131)

21. You would not open someone's purse and steal money, but you might take home small office supplies without thinking about the ethical implications. This dichotomy is an example of _____ on ethical behavior.
    a) the locus of control
    b) the influence of integrative social contracts
    c) issue intensity
    d) structural variables.
    (p. 132)

22. The _____ makes it illegal for U.S. firms to knowingly corrupt a foreign official.
    a) OECD
    b) Maastricht Treaty
    c) ISO 14001
    d) Foreign Corrupt Practices Act
    (p. 133)

23. At the World Economic Forum in 1999, the United Nations secretary general challenged world business leaders to "embrace and enact" the _____, a document outlining nine principles for doing business globally in the areas of human rights, labor, and the environment.
    a) WTO
    b) Document of Nine
    c) Maastricht Treaty
    d) Global Compact
    (p. 134)

24. Irresponsible and unethical behaviors are _____ in our society.
    a) prevalent
    b) occasional
    c) rare
    d) never seen
    (p. 139)

25. An individual or organization who seeks out opportunities to improve society by using practical, innovative, and sustainable approaches is known as a(n) _____.
    a) industry leader
    b) social entrepreneur
    c) top manager
    d) business entrepreneur
    (p. 142)

## True/False Questions

1. T  F  The classical view of social responsibility states that a manager's social responsibility goes beyond making a profit.
    (p. 116)

2. T  F  The most outspoken critic of the classical view of social responsibility is Nobel laureate Milton Friedman.
    (p. 116)

3. T  F  The classical view of social responsibility is based on the belief that corporations are *not* independent entities responsible only to stockholders.
    (pp. 116-117)

4. T  F  In response to popular demand, McDonald's changed from Styrofoam to paper for packaging its food products. This is an example of social responsiveness. (p. 119)

5. T  F  Social responsibility adds an ethical imperative to do those things that make society better and not to do those that could make it worse. (p. 119)

6. T  F  Evidence shows that when a company takes actions to be more socially responsible it will hurt its long-term economic performance. (p. 122)

7. T  F  Socially responsible mutual stock funds use a type of social screening to apply social criteria to investment decisions. (p. 121)

8. T  F  There is a short list of serious environmental problems, each of which can be easily solved through corporate social obligation. (p. 123)

9. T  F  If a company responds to customer concerns about the environment by producing environmentally friendly products, the company is using a market approach to going green. (p. 124)

10. T  F  If an organization pursues an activist approach to being green, it looks for ways to respect and preserve the earth and its natural resources. (p. 124)

11. T  F  One important purpose of shared values is in building team spirit within the organization. (p. 126)

12. T  F  An organization's stockholders are responsible for establishing and upholding the corporate values they want employees to embrace. (p. 127)

13. T  F  Top-performing companies consciously connect values and the way employees do their work. (p. 127)

14. T  F  If a manager focuses on the personal consequences to a decision, his moral development is probably at the preconventional stage. (p. 130)

15. T    F    People who score high on ego strength are likely to resist impulses to act unethically and instead follow their convictions.
(p. 130)

16. T    F    Locus of control is a personality measure of the strength of a person's convictions.
(p. 131)

17. T    F    People with an external locus of control are less likely to take personal responsibility for the consequences of their behavior and are more likely to rely on external forces.
(p. 131)

18. T    F    A culture that is likely to shape high ethical standards is one that is low in risk tolerance and low in conflict tolerance.
(pp. 131-132)

19. T    F    The level of harm, the degree of consensus, and the probability that an act will cause harm are all elements that determine the issue intensity of an ethical decision.
(p. 132)

20. T    F    Under the Foreign Corrupt Practices Act, certain payments to foreign government officials are legal when such payoffs are an accepted part of doing business in that country.
(p. 133)

21. T    F    The selection process should be viewed as an opportunity to learn about an individual's level of moral development, personal values, ego strength, and locus of control.
(pp. 134-135)

22. T    F    Codes of ethics should be clearly written so that ethical options are specifically identified.
(p. 135)

23. T    F    When a manager uncovers wrongdoing, managers who want to emphasize their commitment to doing business ethically should punish the offender privately and not publicize the wrongdoing.
(p. 136)

24. T    F    Independent social audits evaluate decisions and management practices in terms of the organization's code of ethics and increase the likelihood of detecting unethical practices.
(p. 138)

25. T   F   Whistleblowers are individuals who raise ethical concerns or issues to top management within their organizations.
(pp. 140-141)

## Match Terms with Definitions

a. Ethics
b. Values
c. Ego strength
d. Locus of control
e. Social responsibility
f. Classical view
g. Code of ethics
h. Social obligation

i. Socioeconomic view
j. Social responsiveness
k. Values-based management
l. Whistleblower
m. Social entrepreneur
n. Social screening
o. Social impact management

_____ 1. The view that management's only social responsibility is to maximize profits.
_____ 2. An obligation, beyond that required by the law and economics, for a firm to pursue long-term goals that are good for society.
_____ 3. The obligation of a business to meet its economic and legal responsibilities.
_____ 4. An approach to managing in which managers establish, promote, and practice an organization's shared values.
_____ 5. A formal statement of an organization's primary values and the ethical rules it expects its employees to follow.
_____ 6. The capacity of a firm to adapt to changing societal conditions.
_____ 7. An individual or organization who seeks out opportunities to improve society by using practical, innovative, and sustainable approaches.
_____ 8. The view that management's social responsibility goes well beyond the making of profits to include protecting and improving society's welfare.
_____ 9. Applying social criteria to investment decisions.
_____ 10. Basic convictions about what is right and wrong.
_____ 11. Rules and principles that define right and wrong conduct.
_____ 12. A personality characteristic that measures the strength of a person's convictions.
_____ 13. An approach to managing in which managers examine the social impacts of their decisions and actions.
_____ 14. A personality attribute that measures the degree to which people believe they are masters of their own fate.
_____ 15. Individuals who raise ethical concerns or issues to others inside or outside the organization.

## Essay Questions

1. Compare and contrast the two views of social responsibility.
   (pp. 116-117)

2. What is the relationship between social responsibility and economic performance?
   (pp. 120-122)

3. Describe the factors that affect managerial ethics.
   (pp. 130-132, Exhibit 5-8)

4. Discuss the three stages of moral development.
   (pp. 130, Exhibit 5-9)

5. What are whistleblowers? Should companies protect employees who raise ethical concerns?
   (pp. 140-142)

# Chapter 6   Decision Making: The Essence of the Manager's Job

## Learning Outline

### The Decision-Making Process
- Define decision and the decision-making process.
- Describe the eight steps in the decision-making process.

### The Manager as Decision Maker
- Discuss the assumptions of rational decision making.
- Describe the concepts of bounded rationality, satisficing, and escalation of commitment.
- Explain intuitive decision making.
- Contrast programmed and nonprogrammed decisions.
- Contrast the three decision-making conditions.
- Explain maximax, maximin, and minimax decision choice approaches.
- Describe the four decision-making styles.
- Discuss the twelve decision-making biases managers may exhibit.
- Describe how managers can deal with the negative effects of decision errors and biases.
- Explain the managerial decision-making model.

### Decision Making for Today's World
- Explain how managers can make effective decisions in today's world.
- List the six characteristics of an effective decision-making process.
- Describe the five habits of highly reliable organizations.

---

**A Manager's Dilemma**

Renee Lum, a customer service manager at American Savings Bank, is charged with assessing the effectiveness of the bank's new self-service automated phone system. Answer the following questions and compare your answers to those in **Managers Respond** at the end of the chapter.
1. What was American Savings Bank's objective in setting up the self-service automated phone system?
2. How can Ms. Lum evaluate the effectiveness of the new system?
3. What decision criteria should she use?

---

## Lecture Outline

I. The Decision-Making Process.
   A. Individuals at all levels and in all areas of organizations make decisions.
   B. Eight steps to the Decision-Making Process (Refer to Exhibit 6-1)
      1. Step 1:  Identifying a Problem.
         a. Don't confuse problems with the symptoms of a problem.
         b. Problem identification is subjective.

        c. Importance of authority, information, and resources.

        d. Pressure triggers the decision process.

    2. Step 2: Identifying Decision Criteria.

        a. Determining what's relevant in making a decision.

    3. Step 3: Allocating Weights to the Criteria.

        a. Assignment of weights based on importance of criteria.

        b. Example. (Refer to Exhibit 6-2)

    4. Step 4: Developing Alternatives.

        a. List viable alternatives.

        b. No evaluation of alternatives at this point.

    5. Step 5: Analyzing Alternatives.

        a. Evaluate alternatives based on criteria.

        b. Most decisions by managers involve judgments.

        c. Examples. (Refer to Exhibits 6-3 and 6-4)

    6. Step 6: Selecting an Alternative.

        a. Choose the alternative that generated the highest total in Step 5.

    7. Step 7: Implementing the Alternative.

        a. Concerned with putting the decision into action.

        b. Reassess any changes in the environment.

        c. Convey decision to those affected by it and get their commitment.

    8. Step 8: Evaluating Decision Effectiveness.

        a. Evaluation of outcome to see if the problem has been resolved.

        b. If problem still exists, the manager may need to go back to one of the earlier steps.

  C. Learning Review.

- Define decision and the decision-making process.
- Describe the eight steps in the decision-making process.

  D. Key Words.

    1. Decision – A choice from two or more alternatives.

    2. Decision-making process – A set of eight steps that include identifying a problem, selecting an alternative, and evaluating the decision's effectiveness.

    3. Problem – A discrepancy between an existing and a desired state of affairs.

    4. Decision criteria – Criteria that define what's relevant in a decision.

II. The Manager as Decision Maker.

  A. Decision making is part of all four managerial functions. (Refer to Exhibit 6-5)

  B. Making Decisions: Rationality, Bounded Rationality, and Intuition.

    1. Managers are assumed to make rational decisions.

    2. Assumptions of Rationality. (Refer to Exhibit 6-6)

        a. Clear and unambiguous problem.

        b. Single, well-defined goal.

        c. Known alternatives and consequences.

        d. Clear and consistent preferences.

        e. No time or cost constraints.

        f. Payoff maximization for the organization.

3. Bounded Rationality.
    a. Managers make decisions rationally, but are limited by their ability to process information.
    b. Managers satisfice.
    c. Escalation of commitment.
4. Role of Intuition.
    a. Intuitive decision making.
    b. What is intuition?  (Refer to Exhibit 6-7)
    c. Almost 50 percent of managers emphasized intuition over formal analysis.
C. Types of Problems and Decisions.
    1. Structured Problems and Programmed Decisions.
        a. Structured problems are straightforward and familiar.
        b. Programmed decisions are recurring decisions that can be handled using a routine approach.
        c. Procedure.
            i. Rule.
            ii. Policy.
    2. Unstructured Problems and Nonprogrammed Decisions.
        a. Unstructured problems are new or unusual.
        b. Nonprogrammed decisions are unique and nonrecurring and require custom-made solutions.
    3. Integration.
        a. Difference between programmed and nonprogrammed decisions.  (Refer to Exhibit 6-8)
        b. Problems confronting managers usually become more unstructured as they move up the organizational hierarchy.
        c. Few managerial decisions are either fully programmed or fully nonprogrammed.

---

**Thinking Critically About Ethics**
A friend from college is looking for a job and is minimally qualified for a job for which you are in charge of hiring.  You feel you could find a more qualified candidate if you keep looking.  Consider the following questions as you think about ethics in the workplace.
1.  What factors will influence your hiring decision?
2.  Describe how you could use the steps in the decision-making process to make a decision in this case.

---

D. Decision-Making Conditions.
    1. Certainty.
    2. Risk.
        a. Expected Value for Revenues Example.  (Refer to Exhibit 6-9)
    3. Uncertainty.
        a. Choice of alternative is influenced by the limited amount of information available and the psychological orientation of the decision maker.
        b. Maximax choice – maximizing the maximum payoff.

    c.  Maximin choice – maximizing the minimum payoff.

    d.  Minimax choice – minimizing the maximum regret.

---

**Managing IT: Making Better Decisions with IT**

One of the primary uses for IT can be to help managers make better decisions by sorting through tons of data looking for trends, patterns, and other insights. Consider the following questions as you think about the role of IT in effective management.

1. How can IT help managers make better decisions?
2. How can IT help managers assess the effectiveness of previous decisions?

---

  E.  Decision-Making Styles.
    1.  Two dimensions of decision making.
      a.  Way of thinking – rational vs. intuitive.
      b.  Tolerance for ambiguity.
    2.  Four styles of decision making. (Refer to Exhibit 6-12)
      a.  Directive style.
      b.  Analytic style.
      c.  Conceptual style.
      d.  Behavioral style.
      e.  Most managers display characteristics of more than one style.

---

**The Value of Diversity in Decision Making**

Making good decisions is tough! Drawing upon diverse employees can prove valuable to a manager's decision making. An important decision you must make is what you wish to major in.

1. What are some drawbacks to diversity in decision making?
2. How can you use information about diversity in making important life decisions?

---

  F.  Decision-Making Biases and Errors.
      a.  Heuristics (rules of thumb) simplify decision making.
      b.  Common decision-making errors and biases. (Refer to Exhibit 6-13)
      c.  How to avoid decision-making errors and biases.
  G.  Summing Up Managerial Decision Making. (Refer to Exhibit 6-14)
  H.  Learning Review.
    •  Discuss the assumptions of rational decision making.
    •  Describe the concepts of bounded rationality, satisficing, and escalation of commitment.
    •  Explain intuitive decision making.
    •  Contrast programmed and nonprogrammed decisions.
    •  Contrast the three decision-making conditions.
    •  Explain maximax, maximin, and minimax decision choice approaches.
    •  Describe the four decision-making styles.
    •  Discuss the twelve decision-making biases managers may exhibit.
    •  Describe how managers can avoid the negative effects of decision errors and biases.
    •  Explain the managerial decision-making model.

I.   Key Terms.
   1.  Rational decision making – Describes choices that are consistent and value-maximizing within specified constraints.
   2.  Bounded rationality – Decision-making behavior that's rational, but limited (bounded) by an individual's ability to process information.
   3.  Satisficing – Acceptance of solutions that are "good enough."
   4.  Escalation of commitment – An increased commitment to a previous decision despite evidence that it may have been wrong.
   5.  Intuitive decision making – Making decisions on the basis of experience, feelings, and accumulated judgment.
   6.  Structured problems – Straightforward, familiar, and easily defined problems.
   7.  Programmed decision – A repetitive decision that can be handled by a routine approach.
   8.  Procedure – A series of interrelated sequential steps that can be used to respond to a well-structured problem.
   9.  Rule – An explicit statement that tells managers what they can or cannot do.
   10. Policy – A guideline for making decisions.
   11. Unstructured problems – Problems that are new or unusual and for which information is ambiguous or incomplete.
   12. Nonprogrammed decisions – A unique decision that requires a custom-made solution.
   13. Certainty – A situation in which a manager can make accurate decisions because all outcomes are known.
   14. Risk – A situation in which the decision maker is able to estimate the likelihood of certain outcomes.
   15. Uncertainty – A situation in which a decision maker has neither certainty nor reasonable probability estimates available.
   16. Directive style – A decision-making style characterized by low tolerance for ambiguity and a rational way of thinking.
   17. Analytic style – A decision-making style characterized by a high tolerance for ambiguity and a rational way of thinking.
   18. Conceptual style – A decision-making style characterized by a high tolerance for ambiguity and an intuitive way of thinking.
   19. Behavioral style – A decision-making style characterized by a low tolerance for ambiguity and an intuitive way of thinking.
   20. Heuristics – Rules of thumb that managers use to simplify decision making.
   21. Business performance management (BPM) – IT software which provides key performance indicators to help managers monitor efficiency of projects and employees.

III. Decision Making for Today's World.
   A.  Today's business world revolves around making decisions, usually with incomplete information and intense time pressure.
   B.  Guidelines for decision making.
      1.  Understand cultural differences.
      2.  Know when it's time to call it quits.

3. Use effective decision-making processes.
4. Advice from Karl Weick, an organizational psychologist is to build *highly reliable organizations* which share five habits.
    a. They're not tricked by their success.
    b. They defer to experts on the front line.
    c. They let unexpected circumstances provide the solution.
    d. They embrace complexity.
    e. They anticipate, but also anticipate their limits.

C. Learning Review.
  - Explain how managers can make effective decisions in today's world.
  - List the six characteristics of an effective decision-making process.
  - Describe the five habits of highly reliable organizations.

---

**Focus on Leadership: Cultural Differences in Leaders' Decision-Making Styles**
Cultural differences can and do impact the way managers make decisions. Consider the cultural characteristics identified by GLOBE researchers (see Chapter 4) and how these characteristics might come into play at each step in the managerial decision-making process.

---

## Multiple-Choice Questions

1. A choice between two or more alternatives is a _____.
    a) problem
    b) goal
    c) decision
    d) challenge
    (p. 156)

2. The decision-making process begins with _____.
    a) identification of decision criteria
    b) analysis of alternatives
    c) identification of the problem
    d) allocation of weights to criteria
    (p. 156)

3. A discrepancy between an existing and a desired state of affairs is a _____.
    a) problem
    b) goal
    c) decision
    d) challenge
    (p. 157)

4. Managers can be better at identifying problems if they understand the characteristics of problems. Which of the following is a characteristic of a problem?
a) A discrepancy between their current state and some standard
b) Pressure to act or make a decision
c) Sufficient resources to carry out some necessary action
d) Any of the above
(p. 158)

5. Which of the following is NOT one of the eight steps in the decision-making process?
a) Identifying a problem
b) Maximizing the benefit to the individual
c) Selecting an alternative
d) Allocating weights to criteria
(p. 157, Exhibit 6-1)

6. A manager determines that cost, speed, and enlarging capability are relevant to the decision to purchase a new photocopy machine. The manager is in the _____ phase of the decision-making process.
a) allocating weights to the criteria
b) identifying decision criteria
c) developing alternatives
d) formulating a problem
(p. 158)

7. Larry and Joyce are brainstorming possible solutions to a staffing problem. They are writing their ideas down without assessing their practicality or do-ability. Larry and Joyce are at what stage in the decision-making process?
a) Developing alternatives
b) Analyzing alternatives
c) Setting decision criteria
d) Choosing an alternative solution
(p. 159)

8. Once the alternatives have been identified, the next step a decision maker takes is _____.
a) allocate weights to the criteria
b) identify decision criteria
c) critically analyze each alternative
d) choose an alternative
(p. 159)

9. One of the crucial steps is implementing an alternative in the decision-making process is to _____.
   a) re-assess the environment for any changes
   b) allocate weights to the criteria
   c) identify risks associated with potential alternatives
   d) optimize benefits to the manager
   (p. 160)

10. The control mechanism in the decision-making process is _____.
    a) developing alternatives
    b) in the implementation state
    c) evaluating the decision's effectiveness
    d) setting the criteria weights
    (p. 161)

11. In perfect rationality, decision making _____.
    a) uses a simple model constructed to evaluate and rate criteria
    b) decisions are made in the best economic interest of the organization
    c) requires that the search continues until a satisfactory and sufficient solution is found
    d) All of the above are true.
    (p. 162)

12. Bounded rationality is _____.
    a) conveying a decision to those affected and getting their commitment to it
    b) the withholding by group members of different views in order to appear in agreement
    c) behavior that is rational within the parameters of a simplified model that captures the essential features of a problem
    d) an explicit statement that tells managers what they ought or ought not to do
    (p. 163)

13. When a decision is considered "good enough" rather than the best decision, the result is _____.
    a) bounded rationality
    b) a denial of the use of intuition in the process
    c) a programmed decision
    d) satisficing
    (p. 163)

14. Tammy is thinking through a marketing decision made by her superiors. She continues to favor a decision choice that has proven to be less than effective. Tammy is demonstrating _____.
    a) bounded rationality
    b) satisficing
    c) escalation of commitment
    d) intuitive decision making
    (p. 163)

15. Making decisions on the basis of experience, feelings, and accumulated judgment is

    _____.
    a) rational decision making
    b) escalation of commitment
    c) bounded rationality
    d) intuitive decision making
    (p. 164)

16. Routine repetitive decisions are _____.
    a) nonprogrammed decisions
    b) programmed decisions
    c) poorly structured problems
    d) well-structured problems
    (p. 165)

17. Policies, procedures, and rules are developed to help managers deal with _____.
    a) structured problems
    b) satisficing decisions
    c) bounded rationality
    d) nonprogrammed decisions
    (p. 165)

18. Which of the following is an example of a *procedure* for snack breaks in a production company?
    a) Each production worker is entitled to a snack break in the morning and in the afternoon each workday.
    b) No food is to be taken into the work area. All snacks must be eaten in the break room.
    c) Employees will be given a morning break beginning at 10 a.m. for production line one and continuing at 15-minute intervals until all four production lines have taken a break. Workers should report to the production line after a 15-minute break.
    d) All statements are examples of procedures.
    (p. 165)

19. The manager of a retail clothing store just found out that some "name brand" merchandise was actually brought into the United States illegally. This is an example of _____.
   a) a well-structured problem
   b) satisficing
   c) an unstructured problem
   d) a programmed decision
   (p. 166)

20. Jane can repair a saw at Quality Production, Inc., in two hours whereas it takes Justine five hours to make repairs. Assuming that both workers are present, the manager will always choose Jane to make repairs to the saws. This is a decision under _____.
   a) conditions of certainty
   b) conditions of risk
   c) conditions of uncertainty
   d) escalation of commitment
   (p. 167)

21. A manager has no idea what alternatives are available for new computer support systems and does not know how to determine this information. This is a decision under _____.
   a) conditions of certainty
   b) conditions of risk
   c) conditions of uncertainty
   d) heuristic decision making
   (pp. 168-169)

22. Decision makers with a low tolerance for ambiguity, who are efficient and logical, and focus on the short run use a(n) _____ style of decision making.
   a) directive
   b) analytic
   c) conceptual
   d) behavioral
   (p. 171)

23. A manager with a degree for tolerance for ambiguity, but who wants more information and considers many alternatives before deciding, is exhibiting a(n) _____ style of decision making.
   a) directive
   b) analytic
   c) conceptual
   d) behavioral
   (p. 171)

24. Behavioral style decision makers _____.
    a) have a low tolerance for ambiguity, are very rational and efficient in their decision styles
    b) want information, tolerate ambiguity, and are careful decision makers
    c) take a broad outlook and examine many different alternatives. They focus on the long run
    d) work well with others, are concerned about the achievement of others, and often use meetings to communicate decisions while trying to avoid conflict
    (p. 171)

25. Rules of thumb that managers use to simplify decision making are _____.
    a) heuristics
    b) policies
    c) procedures
    d) strategies
    (p. 172)

## True/False Questions

1.  T   F   A problem is a discrepancy between an existing and a desired state of affairs.
            (p. 156)

2.  T   F   The decision-making process is a set of eight steps that begins with developing alternatives.
            (p. 157, Exhibit 6-1)

3.  T   F   To trigger the decision process, the problem must put pressure on the manager to act.
            (p. 158)

4.  T   F   Decision criteria are rules of thumb that decision makers use to simplify decisions.
            (p. 158)

5.  T   F   Included in the implementation stage of decision making is the conveying of the decision to those affected by it and gaining their commitment.
            (p. 160)

6.  T   F   Evaluating the decision effectiveness may cause managers to return to an earlier step in the decision process.
            (p. 161)

7.  T   F   Rational decision making assumes that all alternatives and consequences are known.
            (pp. 162-163)

8. T  F  Rational decision making assumes that the criteria and preferences can be ranked according to importance.
(pp. 162-163)

9. T  F  Bounded rationality is acceptance of solutions that are "good enough."
(p. 163)

10. T  F  Because they can't possibly analyze all information on all alternatives, managers satisfice, rather than maximize.
(p. 163)

11. T  F  Lewis keeps repairing his car because he doesn't want to admit that his girlfriend was right when she told him not to buy it because it's a lemon. Lewis is guilty of bounded rationality.
(p. 163)

12. T  F  Intuition in decision making almost always reduces the quality of the decision.
(p. 164)

13. T  F  Betty has many years' experience and sometimes makes decisions based on her "gut" feeling. She uses intuitive decision making.
(p. 164)

14. T  F  Most managers assume that decision making is largely intuitive and use a rational approach simply to confirm what they "know" is the right decision.
(p. 164)

15. T  F  Structured problems are usually solved with nonprogrammed decisions.
(p. 165)

16. T  F  A rule is a guideline for making decisions.
(p. 165)

17. T  F  Nonprogrammed decisions are unique, nonrecurring situations.
(p. 166)

18. T  F  Unstructured problems are straightforward and familiar.
(p. 166)

19. T  F  When the decision maker knows the probability of occurrences of alternatives; the decision is made under conditions of uncertainty.
(p. 167)

20. T  F  Decisions when you're not certain about the outcomes and can't even make reasonable probability estimates are termed conditions of uncertainty.
(p. 168)

21. T  F  The psychological orientation of the decision maker affects the level of uncertainty of a decision.
(p. 168)

22. T  F  Acceptance by others is important in the behavioral style of decision making.
(p. 171)

23. T  F  The conceptual style of decision making is characterized by a high tolerance for ambiguity and a rational way of thinking.
(p. 171)

24. T  F  Decision makers with a behavioral style work well with others.
(p. 171)

25. T  F  A decision maker who sees the big picture, looks at many alternatives, and has a long-term focus exhibits a conceptual decision-making style.
(p. 171)

## Match Terms with Definitions

a. Certainty
b. Uncertainty
c. Behavioral style
d. Decision
e. Risk
f. Implementation
g. Directive style
h. Nonprogrammed decision

i. Rational decision making
j. Problem
k. Bounded rationality
l. Policy
m. Procedure
n. Satisficing
o. Rule

_____ 1. A discrepancy between an existing and a desired state of affairs.
_____ 2. Conveying a decision to those affected and getting their commitment to it.
_____ 3. Describes choices that are consistent and value-maximizing within specified constraints.
_____ 4. Those conditions in which the decision maker is able to estimate the likelihood of certain outcomes.
_____ 5. Acceptance of solutions that are "good enough."
_____ 6. A decision style that values time, doesn't tolerate ambiguity well, and makes decisions with minimal information.
_____ 7. A series of interrelated sequential steps that can be used to respond to a structured problem.
_____ 8. The type of decision often faced with unstructured problems. Each solution is unique and nonrecurring.
_____ 9. A guide that establishes parameters for making decisions.
_____ 10. Behavior that is rational within the parameters of a simplified model that captures the essential features of a problem.
_____ 11. A situation in which a manager can make accurate decisions because the outcome of every alternative is known.
_____ 12. An explicit statement that tells managers what they ought or ought not to do.
_____ 13. A situation in which a decision maker has neither certainty nor reasonable estimates available.
_____ 14. A decision style that works well with teams, is receptive to other's ideas, and that tries to avoid conflicts.
_____ 15. A choice from two or more alternatives.

## Essay Questions

1.  Outline the eight steps of the decision-making process, briefly explaining each step. (pp. 156-161, Exhibit 6-1)

2.  What are the basic assumptions underlying rational decision making? (pp. 162-163, Exhibit 6-6)

3.  What is intuition?  What is the role of intuition in decision making? (p. 164, Exhibit 6-7)

4.  What are the various types of decisions managers face, and how do rules, procedures, and policy help them make the decisions? (pp. 165-167)

5.  Discuss the four decision-making styles. (pp. 170-171, Exhibit 6-12)

# Chapter 7  Foundations of Planning

## Learning Outline

**What Is Planning and Why Do Managers Plan?**
- Define planning.
- Differentiate between formal and informal planning.
- Describe the purposes of planning.
- Discuss the conclusions from studies of the relationship between planning and performance.

**How Do Managers Plan?**
- Define goals and plans.
- Describe the types of goals organizations might have.
- Explain why it's important to know an organization's stated and real goals.
- Describe each of the different types of plans.

**Establishing Goals and Developing Plans**
- Discuss how traditional goal setting works.
- Explain the concept of the means-end chain.
- Describe the management by objectives (MBO) approach.
- Describe the characteristics of well-designed goals.
- Explain the steps in setting goals.
- Discuss the contingency factors that affect planning.
- Describe the approaches to planning.

**Contemporary Issues in Planning**
- Explain the criticisms of planning and whether they're valid.
- Describe how managers can effectively plan in today's dynamic environment.

---

**A Manager's Dilemma**

Edina Bukvic owns a small wedding dress shop in Zivinice, Bosnia, and is interested in expanding her business.  Consider the following questions and compare your answers to those in **Managers Respond** at the end of the chapter.
1. What types of plans might Ms. Bukvic need to guide her business as it grows?
2. How has microfinance opened doors for entrepreneurs and small businesses in the Third World and developing countries?

---

## Lecture Outline

I. What Is Planning and Why Do Managers Plan?
    A. Planning involves defining the organization's goals and developing plans to integrate and coordinate organizational work.
        1. Formal Planning.
        2. Informal Planning.

B.  Purposes of Planning.
   1.  Provides direction.
   2.  Reduces uncertainty.
   3.  Minimizes waste and redundancy.
   4.  Establishes goals or standards in controlling.
C.  Planning and Performance.
   1.  Formal planning is associated with positive financial results.
   2.  The quality of the planning process contributes more than the extent of planning.
   3.  The external environment may affect results.
   4.  The planning/performance relationship is influenced by the planning time frame.
D.  Learning Review.
   •  Define planning.
   •  Differentiate between formal and informal planning.
   •  Describe the purposes of planning.
   •  Explain the conclusions from studies of the relationship between planning and performance.
E.  Key Term.
   1.  Planning – Defining the organization's goals, establishing an overall strategy for achieving those goals, and developing plans for organizational work.

II.  How Do Managers Plan?
   A.  Planning is often called the primary management function.
   B.  The Role of Goals and Plans in Planning.
      1.  Types of Goals.
         a.  Goals can be Financial or Strategic. (Refer to Exhibit 7-1)
            (i)     Financial goals are related to financial performance.
            (ii)    Strategic goals are related to other areas of performance.
         b.  Goals can be Real or Stated.
            (i)     Stated goals are official statements.
            (ii)    Real goals are actually pursued by the organization.

---

**Focus on Leadership**

Antonio Villaraigosa, the first Latino mayor of Los Angeles in more than a century, is known for his skill in framing issues in such a way that others can see them the way he does.  Consider the following questions as you think about the characteristics of effective leadership.
1.  What is framing?
2.  Why is framing relevant to leaders today?

---

      2.  Types of Plans.  (Refer to Exhibit 7-2)
         a.  Plans can be described by their breadth.
            (i)     Strategic – covers a longer time-frame and a broader view of the organization.
            (ii)    Operational – specify the details.

      b. Plans can be described by their time frame.
         (i)       Short term – covering one year or less.
         (ii)      Long term – time frame beyond three years.
      c. Plans can be described by their specificity.  (Refer to Exhibit 7-3)
         (i)       Directional – flexible and set general guidelines.
         (ii)      Specific – clearly defined and leave no room for interpretation.
      d. Plans can be described by frequency of use.
         (i)       Single use – meets the needs of a unique situation.
         (ii)      Standing – provide guidance for activities performed repeatedly.

C. Learning Review.
- Define goals and plans.
- Describe the types of goals organizations might have.
- Explain why it's important to know an organization's stated and real goals.
- Describe each of the different types of plans.

D. Key Terms.
1. Goals – Desired outcomes for individuals, groups, or entire organizations.
2. Plans – Documents that outline how goals are going to be met.
3. Stated goals – Official statements of what an organization says, and what it wants its various stakeholders to believe, its goals are.
4. Real goals – Goals that an organization actually pursues, as defined by the actions of its members.
5. Framing – A way to use language to manage meaning.
6. Strategic plans – Plans that apply to the entire organization, establish the organization's overall goals, and seek to position the organization in terms of the environment.
7. Operational plans – Plans that specify the details of how the overall goals are to be achieved.
8. Long-term plans – Plans with a time frame beyond three years.
9. Short-term plans – Plans covering one year or less.
10. Specific plans – Plans that are clearly defined and that leave no room for interpretation.
11. Directional plans – Plans that are flexible and that set out general guidelines.
12. Single-use plan – A one-time plan specifically designed to meet the needs of a unique situation.
13. Standing plans – Ongoing plans that provide guidance for activities performed repeatedly.

III. Establishing Goals and Developing Plans.
  A. Approaches to Establishing Goals.
    1. Traditional goal setting – goals set at the top and then broken down into sub goals.
      a. Problems.
         (i)       Difficulty in translating corporate goals into individual objectives.
         (ii)      Ambiguous goals.  (Refer to Exhibit 7-4)

                    (iii)        Managers apply their own interpretations and biases.
            b.  Means-ends chain means higher-level goals are linked to lower-level
                goals.
            c.  Management by objectives (MBO).  (Refer to Exhibit 7-5)
                    (i)      Goal specificity.
                    (ii)     Participative decision making.
                    (iii)    Explicit time period.
                    (iv)     Performance feedback.
        2.  Six Characteristics of Well-Designed Goals.  (Refer to Exhibit 7-6)
            a.  Written in terms of outcomes.
            b.  Measurable and quantifiable.
            c.  Clear as to a time frame.
            d.  Challenging but attainable.
            e.  Written down.
            f.  Communicated to all necessary organizational members.
        3.  Five Steps in Goal Setting.
            a.  Review the organization's mission.
            b.  Evaluate available resources.
            c.  Determine the goals individually or with input from others.
            d.  Write down the goals and communicate them to all who need to know.
            e.  Review results and whether goals are being met.
    B.  Developing Plans.
        1.  Contingency Factors in Planning.
            a.  Level in the organization.  (Refer to Exhibit 7-7)
            b.  Degree of environmental uncertainty.
            c.  Length of future commitments.
        2.  Approaches to Planning.
            a.  Traditional approach – planning done by top-level managers and formal
                planning departments.
            b.  Another approach - develop plans by organizational members at various
                levels.

---

**Thinking Critically About Ethics**

As concerns about a potential bird-flu pandemic rise, some companies have considered whether or not it makes sense to maintain private stocks of flu vaccine in order to protect employees and maintain business operations during a potential outbreak.  Consider the following questions as you think about ethics.
1.  How ethical would it be for companies to hold supplies to which the general public didn't have access but badly needed?
2.  Would it be unethical for a company to preferentially protect its own employees?
3.  What other alternatives might there be to stockpiling vaccine?

---

    C.  Learning Review.
        •   Discuss how traditional goal setting works.
        •   Explain the concept of the means-end chain.
        •   Describe the management by objectives (MBO) approach.
        •   Describe the characteristics of well-designed goals.

- Explain the steps in setting goals.
- Discuss the contingency factors that affect planning.
- Describe the approaches to planning.

D. Key Terms.
1. Traditional goal setting – An approach to setting goals in which goals are set at the top level of the organization and then broken into subgoals for each level of the organization.
2. Means-ends chain – An integrated network of goals in which the accomplishment of goals at one level serves as the means for achieving the goals, or ends, at the next level.
3. Management by objectives – A process of setting mutually agreed-upon goals and using those goals to evaluate employee performance.
4. Mission – The purpose of an organization.
5. Commitment concept – Plans should extend far enough to meet those commitments made today.
6. Formal planning department – A group of planning specialists whose sole responsibility was helping to write various organizational plans.

IV. Contemporary Issues in Planning.
A. Six Criticisms of Planning.
1. Planning may create rigidity.
2. Plans can't be developed for a dynamic environment.
3. Formal plans can't replace intuition and creativity.
4. Planning focuses managers' attention on today's competition, not on tomorrow's survival.
5. Formal planning reinforces success, which may lead to failure.
6. Just planning isn't enough.
B. Effective Planning in Dynamic Environments.
1. External environment is constantly changing.
2. Managers want to develop plans that are specific but flexible.
3. Effective planning means flattening the organizational hierarchy.
C. Learning Review.
- Explain the criticisms of planning and whether they're valid.
- Describe how managers can effectively plan in today's dynamic environment.

## Multiple-Choice Questions

1. Which of the following is a characteristic of formal planning, but not informal planning?
   a) Little or no sharing of goals within the organization
   b) Planning is general
   c) Specific actions programs exist for goal achievement
   d) Concerned with ends.
   (p. 184)

2. Which of the following is one of the four reasons for planning?
   a) Planning automatically increases flexibility.
   b) Planning reduces uncertainty.
   c) Planning is always of value even when inaccurate.
   d) Planning is very difficult and requires significant training in order to do it properly.
   (p. 185)

3. _____ are desired outcomes for individuals, groups, or entire organizations.
   a) Plans
   b) Goals
   c) Strategies
   d) Policies
   (p. 186)

4. _____ are official statements of what an organization says, and what it wants its stakeholders to believe, its goals are.
   a) Real goals
   b) Stated goals
   c) MBO objectives
   d) Directional plans
   (p. 187)

5. Which of the following is NOT an example of a financial goal?
   a) Bigger cash flows
   b) Higher dividends
   c) Stronger bond and credit ratings
   d) A bigger market share
   (p. 187)

6. _____ establish the overall goals of the organization, while _____ specify how those objectives are to be achieved.
   a) Strategic plans; operational plans
   b) Long-term plans; short-term plans
   c) Specific plans; directional plans
   d) Standing plans; single-use plans
   (p. 189)

7. Long-term plans are those with a time frame _____.
   a) covering less than one year
   b) covering more than one year
   c) beyond two years
   d) beyond three years
   (p. 189)

8. Short-term plans are those with a time frame covering _____.
   a) one year or less
   b) two years or less
   c) three years or less
   d) four years or less
   (p. 189)

9. Flexible plans that set out general guidelines are _____.
   a) operational
   b) strategic
   c) specific
   d) directional
   (p. 190)

10. When environmental uncertainty is high, _____ are preferable.
    a) strategic plans
    b) directional plans
    c) operational plans
    d) standing plans
    (p. 190)

11. A plan specifically designed to meet the needs of a unique situation and created in response to unprogrammed decisions is a _____ plan.
    a) short-term
    b) specific
    c) directional
    d) single-use
    (p. 190)

12. _____ plans are ongoing plans that provide guidance for activities performed repeatedly.
    a) Directional
    b) Standing
    c) Operational
    d) Single-use
    (p. 191)

13. In _____, goals are set at the top level and then broken down into subgoals.
    a) a strategic process
    b) traditional goal setting
    c) a series of single-use plans
    d) directional goal setting
    (p. 191)

14. In traditional goal setting _____.
    a) goals are jointly set by an employee and her manager
    b) managers set an integrated network of goals
    c) goals are set at the top of the organization and then broken into subgoals for each organizational level
    d) only financial objectives are set by management
    (p. 191)

15. When the hierarchy of organizational goals is clearly defined, it forms an integrated network of goals, or a(n) _____.
    a) means-end chain.
    b) organizational chart.
    c) strategic plan.
    d) contingency plan.
    (p. 192)

16. _____ is a management system in which specific performance goals are jointly determined by employees and their managers.
    a) Management by objectives (MBO)
    b) Critical event analysis
    c) Total quality management (TQM)
    d) Zero-based budgeting
    (pp. 192-193)

17. Management by objectives (MBO) has four elements. Which of the following is NOT one of those four objectives?
    a) Goal specificity
    b) Participative decision making
    c) An implicit time period
    d) Performance feedback
    (p. 193)

18. Research shows that an important condition for an MBO program to succeed is _____.
    a) a team-based workforce
    b) reliance on lower-level management
    c) top management commitment
    d) use of means-end chains
    (p. 193)

19. Which of the following is a characteristic of well-designed goals?
    a) Measurable and quantifiable
    b) Challenging yet attainable
    c) Written down
    d) All of the above
    (p. 193, Exhibit 7-6)

20. The organization's _____ is the purpose of the organization.
    a) real goals
    b) stated goals
    c) commitment concept
    d) mission
    (p. 195)

21. The goal-setting process is a five-step process. What is the first step in this process?
    a) Determine the goals individually or with input from others.
    b) Review the organization's mission.
    c) Evaluate available resources.
    d) Review results and whether goals are being met.
    (p. 195)

22. The more that current plans affect future plans, the longer the time frame for which managers should plan. This effect is called _____.
    a) the commitment concept
    b) environmental uncertainty
    c) standing planning
    d) contingency planning
    (p. 196)

23. In the traditional approach, planning was done entirely by _____.
    a) first-line managers
    b) employees and their managers
    c) middle management
    d) top-level management
    (p. 197)

24. Sometimes planning is criticized for _____.
    a) being too intuitive and creative
    b) focusing on the future at the expense of today's needs
    c) creating rigidity
    d) All of the above
    (pp. 198-199)

25. Planning _____.
    a) guarantees success
    b) can lead to failure by encouraging repetition of past behaviors
    c) works well in a dynamic environment
    d) can replace creativity and intuition in a stable environment
    (pp. 198-199)

## True/False Questions

1. T  F  Planning is concerned with desired "ends," but not "means."
(p. 184)

2. T  F  Without planning, departments and individuals might work at cross-purposes, preventing the organization from moving efficiently toward its goals.
(p. 185)

3. T  F  Generally speaking, formal planning is associated with higher profits, higher return on assets, and other positive financial results.
(p. 185)

4. T  F  In those research studies where formal planning has not led to higher performance, the external environment was typically the culprit.
(p. 185)

5. T  F  Goals are often called the foundation of planning.
(p. 186)

6. T  F  Plans are desired outcomes for individuals, groups, or entire organizations.
(p. 186)

7. T  F  An example of a *financial goal* is "Lower costs relative to key competitors."
(p. 187)

8. T  F  Focusing only on a single goal such as profit can lead to unethical practices because managers and employees will ignore other important parts of their jobs in order to look good in that one measure.
(p. 186)

9. T  F  An organization's real goals are generally identical to its stated goals.
(p. 189)

10. T  F  Operational plans tend to cover a longer time frame and a broader view of the organization.
(p. 189)

11. T  F  Long-term plans are those with a time frame beyond two years.
(p. 189)

12. T  F  Specific plans are clearly defined and leave no room for interpretation.
(p. 190)

13. T  F  When uncertainty is high, it is preferable to use directional plans instead of specific plans.
(p. 190)

14. T  F  Single-use plans provide managers with guidance for activities performed repeatedly within the organization.
(p. 191)

15. T  F  In a means-ends chain the higher-level goals are linked to lower-level goals, which serve as a means for their accomplishment.
(p. 192)

16. T  F  Studies of actual MBO programs have not confirmed that MBO programs increase employee performance and organizational productivity.
(p. 193)

17. T  F  MBO programs tend to be more effective in times of dynamic environmental change.
(p. 193)

18. T  F  Well-designed goals should be challenging but attainable.
(p. 193, Exhibit 7-6)

19. T  F  It's important to review the mission statement before writing goals because the goals should reflect what the mission statement says.
(p. 195)

20. T  F  For the most part, operational planning dominates managers' planning efforts at lower levels.
(p. 195)

21. T  F  As managers rise in the hierarchy, their planning becomes more operational.
(p. 196, Exhibit 7-7)

22. T  F  The commitment concept means that plans should extend for at least the long term, three years or longer.
(p. 196)

23. T  F  A formal planning department is a group of planning specialists whose sole responsibility is to help write the various organizational plans.
(p. 197)

24. T  F  Visions have a tendency to become less formalized as they evolve.
(p. 198)

25. T  F  An important weakness of planning is its tendency to focus on the future to the neglect of today's issues.
(p. 198)

## Match Terms with Definitions

a. Traditional goal setting
b. MBO
c. Commitment concept
d. Directional plans
e. Long-term plans
f. Short-term plans
g. Specific plans
h. Strategic plans

i. Operational goals
j. Single-use plans
k. Standing plans
l. Goals
m. Stated goals
n. Means-ends chain
o. Real goals

_____ 1. Plans should extend far enough to see through current commitments.
_____ 2. Plans that cover less than one year.
_____ 3. Plans that are clearly defined and leave no room for interpretation.
_____ 4. Flexible plans that set out general guidelines.
_____ 5. Plans that are organization-wide, establish overall objectives, and position an organization in terms of its environment.
_____ 6. A one-time plan that's specifically designed to meet the needs of a unique situation and is created in response to unprogrammed decisions that managers make.
_____ 7. Objectives that an organization actually pursues as defined by the actions of its members.
_____ 8. Ongoing plans that provide guidance for activities repeatedly performed in the organization and that are created in response to programmed decisions that managers make.
_____ 9. Plans that extend beyond three years.
_____ 10. A system in which specific performance objectives are jointly determined by subordinates and their superiors, progress toward objectives is periodically reviewed, and rewards are allocated on the basis of this progress.
_____ 11. An integrated network of organizational objectives in which higher-level objectives are linked to lower-level objectives, which serve as the means for their accomplishment.
_____ 12. Desired outcomes for individuals, groups, or entire organizations.
_____ 13. Goals are set at the top and then broken down into subgoals for each level in an organization.
_____ 14. Official statements of what an organization says, and what it wants various publics to believe, are its objectives.
_____ 15. Plans that specify details on how overall objectives are to be achieved.

## Essay Questions

1. Discuss the relationship between planning and performance.
   (p. 195)

2. Discuss the various types of plans that managers can use. (Hint, classify plans by breadth, time frame, specificity, and frequency of use.)
   (pp. 189-191, Exhibit 7-2)

3. Explain management by objectives (MBO). What are the steps in a typical MBO program?
   (pp. 192-193, Exhibit 7-5)

4. Identify and describe the steps in goal setting.
   (p. 195)

5. What is the relationship between a manager's level in the organization and the type of planning done?
   (pp. 195-196, Exhibit 7-7)

# Chapter 8   Strategic Management

## Learning Outline

### The Importance of Strategic Management
- Define strategic management, strategy, and business model.
- Explain why strategic management is important.

### The Strategic Management Process
- List the six steps in the strategic management process.
- Describe what managers do during external and internal analyses.
- Explain the role of resources, capabilities, and core competencies.
- Describe strengths, weaknesses, opportunities, and threats.

### Types of Organizational Strategies
- Describe the three major types of corporate strategies.
- Discuss the BCG matrix and how it's used.
- Describe the role of competitive advantage in business strategies.
- Explain Porter's five forces model.
- Describe Porter's three generic competitive strategies and the rule of three.

### Strategic Management in Today's Environment
- Explain why strategic flexibility is important.
- Describe strategies applying e-business techniques.
- Explain what strategies organizations might use to become more customer oriented and to be more innovative.


## Lecture Outline

---

**A Manager's Dilemma**

Kevin Plank's company, Under Armor, dominates the market for men's performance sportswear and is actively working to expand it's product line to include women and children. As you read the Manager's Dilemma, think about the following question and compare your thoughts to **Managers Respond** at the end of the chapter.

1. How could SWOT analysis help Under Armor as it expands its consumer base by offering products tailored to women and children?

---

I. The Importance of Strategic Management.
   A. What Is Strategic Management?
      1. Organizations vary in how well they perform because of differences in their strategic and competitive abilities.
      2. An important task of managers that entails all of the basic management functions.
      3. Two Focuses of a Company's Business Model.
         a. Whether customers will value what the company is providing.
         b. Whether the company can make any money doing that.

B.  Why Is Strategic Management Important?
    1.  It makes a difference in how well an organization performs.
    2.  Organizations face continually changing situations.
    3.  Organizations are composed of diverse units that need to be coordinated.
    4.  Strategic management is involved in many of the decisions that managers make.
    5.  Strategic management now includes not-for-profit organizations.
C.  Learning Review.
    •  Define strategic management, strategy, and business model.
    •  Explain why strategic management is important.
D.  Key Terms.
    1.  Strategic management – What managers do to develop the organization's strategies.
    2.  Strategies – The decisions and actions that determine the long-run performance of an organization.
    3.  Business model – A strategic design for how a company intends to profit from its strategies, processes, and activities.

II.  The Strategic Management Process.  (Refer to Exhibit 8-1)
A.  Step 1:  Identifying the Organization's Current Mission, Goals, and Strategies
    1.  Every organization needs a mission.
    2.  Typical components of a mission statement. (Refer to Exhibit 8-2)
    3.  Goals provide measurable performance targets.
B.  Step 2:  Doing an External Analysis.
    1.  External environment is a constraint on a manager's actions.
    2.  Managers must assess opportunities and threats.
C.  Step 3:  Doing an Internal Analysis.
    1.  Both resources and core competencies can determine the organization's competitive weapons.
    2.  Identify organizational strengths and weaknesses.
    3.  An understanding of organizational culture is often overlooked.
    4.  After completing the SWOT analysis, managers are ready to formulate appropriate strategies.

---

**Thinking Critically About Ethics**

Many company Web sites have information that is available for anyone to read.  In competitive industries, survival and success is difficult.  After reading the scenario presented, respond to the following questions.
1.  Is lying to improve the competitive edge over others acceptable?
2.  Do you feel it is acceptable for companies to give false or misleading information about their products or services?
3.  Identify some form of information you have obtained that was not truthful.  Did you make decisions based on this information?

---

D.  Step 4:  Formulating Strategies.
E.  Step 5:  Implementing Strategies.
F.  Step 6:  Evaluating Results.

| Managing IT: IT's Role in Company Strategy |
|---|
| IT systems can be wonderful assets and tools. When the IT system isn't working as it is supposed to, however, it can create serious problems. Consider the following questions as you think about the role of IT in company strategy. |
| 1. How can IT complement a company's strategy? |
| 2. What should companies do in cases when the IT system doesn't work as it is supposed to? |

    G. Learning Review.
- List the six steps in the strategic management process.
- Describe what managers do when they do external and internal analysis.
- Explain the role of resources, capabilities, and core competencies.
- Define strengths, weaknesses, opportunities, and threats.

    H. Key Terms.
1. Strategic management process – A six-step process that encompasses strategic planning, implementation, and evaluation.
2. Mission – A statement of the purpose of an organization.
3. Opportunities – Positive trends in external environmental factors.
4. Threats – Negative trends in external environmental factors.
5. Resources – An organization's assets that are used to develop, manufacture, and deliver products or services to its customers.
6. Capabilities – An organization's skills and abilities for doing the work activities needed in its business.
7. Core competencies – The organization's major value-creating skills and capabilities that determine its competitive weapons.
8. Strengths – Any activities the organization does well or any unique resources that it has.
9. Weaknesses – Activities the organization does not do well or resources it needs but does not possess.
10. SWOT analysis – An analysis of the organization's strengths, weaknesses, opportunities, and threats.

III. Types of Organizational Strategies.
    A. Corporate Strategy.
        1. Growth Strategy – seeks to increase the organization's business.
            a. Growth through concentration – increase in number of products or markets served in its primary business.
            b. Growth through vertical integration – increase control of supply or distribution chains.
                1. Backward vertical integration – control of inputs
                2. Forward vertical integration – control of outputs.
            c. Growth through horizontal integration – combining with other organizations in the same industry.

  d. Growth through diversification.
    (i)    Related diversification – growth by merging with or acquiring firms in different, but related, industries.
    (ii)   Unrelated diversification – growth by merging with or acquiring firms in different and unrelated industries.
 2. Stability Strategy – characterized by an absence of significant change.
  a. Examples of stability strategy.
  b. Reasons for pursuing a stability strategy.
 3. Renewal Strategy – addresses organizational weaknesses that are leading to performance declines.
  a. Retrenchment strategy – short-run renewal strategy for less serious performance problems.
  b. Turnaround strategy – for use when performance problems are more critical.
 4. Corporate Portfolio Analysis.
  a. BCG matrix. (Refer to Exhibit 8-5)
  b. A business is placed in one of four categories.
    (i)    Cash cows – low growth, high market share.
    (ii)   Stars – high growth, high market share.
    (iii)   Question marks – high growth, low market share.
    (iv)   Dogs – low growth, low market share.
B. Business or Competitive Strategy
 1. Seeks to determine how an organization should compete in each of its businesses.
 2. Strategic business units allow different businesses within a parent organization to be independent and formulate their own strategies.
 3. The Role of Competitive Advantage – an organization's distinctive edge, resulting from its core competencies.
 4. Quality as a Competitive Advantage.
 5. Sustaining Competitive Advantage.
 6. Competitive Strategies.
  a. Michael Porter's Competitive Strategies Framework.
  b. Five competitive forces dictate the rules of competition.  (Refer to Exhibit 8-6)
    (i)    Threat of new entrants.
    (ii)   Threat of substitutes.
    (iii)   Bargaining power of buyers.
    (iv)   Bargaining power of suppliers.
    (v)   Current rivalry.
  c. Three generic competitive strategies.  (Refer to Exhibit 8-7)
    (i)    Cost leadership strategy.
    (ii)   Differentiation strategy.
    (iii)   Focus strategy.
 7. The Rule of Three
  a. In many industries, three major players emerge to dominate the market.
  b. The three major players are "full-line generalists."

      c.  Other firms may be successful in the industry as "super niche players."

      d.  Other firms that can't specialize are "ditch dwellers."

C.  Functional Strategy.

    1.  Functional strategies support the business strategy.

D.  Learning Review.

- Describe the three major types of corporate strategies.
- Discuss the BCG matrix and how it's used.
- Describe the role of competitive advantage in business strategies.
- Explain Porter's five forces model.
- Describe Porter's three generic competitive strategies and the rule of three.

E.  Key Terms.

1.  Corporate strategy – An organizational strategy that determines what businesses a company should be in or wants to be in, and what it wants to do with those businesses.

2.  Growth strategy – A corporate strategy that's used when an organization wants to grow and does so by expanding the number of products offered or markets served, either through its current business(es) or through new business(es).

3.  Related diversification – When a company grows by combining with firms in different, but related, industries.

4.  Unrelated diversification – When a company grows by combining with firms in different and unrelated industries.

5.  Stability strategy – A corporate strategy characterized by an absence of significant change in what the organization is currently doing.

6.  Renewal strategy – A corporate strategy designed to address organizational weaknesses that are leading to performance declines.

7.  Retrenchment strategy – A short-run renewal strategy.

8.  Turnaround strategy – A renewal strategy for situations in which the organization's performance problems are more serious.

9.  BCG matrix – A strategy tool that guides resource allocation decisions on the basis of market share and growth rate of SBUs.

10.  Business or competitive strategy – An organizational strategy that focuses on how the organization will compete in each of its businesses.

11.  Strategic business units (SBUs) – The single businesses of an organization in several different businesses that are independent and formulate their own strategies.

12.  Competitive advantage – What sets an organization apart; its distinctive edge.

13.  Cost leadership strategy – A business strategy in which the organization competes on the basis of having the lowest costs in the industry.

14.  Differentiation strategy – A business strategy in which a company offers unique products that are widely valued by customers.

15.  Focus strategy – A business strategy in which a company pursues a cost or differentiation advantage in a narrow industry segment.

16.  Stuck in the middle – A situation where an organization hasn't been able to develop either a low cost or a differentiation competitive advantage.

17. Functional strategy – The strategies used by an organization's various functional departments to support the business or competitive strategy.

IV. Strategic Management in Today's Environment.
   A. Managers in all kinds of organizations face increasingly intense global competition and high performance expectations by investors and customers.
   B. Strategic Flexibility.
      1. The key for managers is to respond quickly when it becomes obvious that the strategy isn't working.
      2. Suggestions for developing strategic flexibility.  (Refer to Exhibit 8-7)

---
**Focus on Leadership**

By definition, upper-level managers are ultimately responsible for every decision and action of every organizational employee.  Consider the following questions as you think about leadership in the workplace.
1.  What does it take to be an effective strategic leader?
2.  What differentiates strategic versus nonstrategic leadership?

---

   C. New Directions in Organizational Strategies.
      1. E-Business Strategies.
         a. Managers can formulate e-business strategies that contribute to the development of a sustainable competitive advantage.
      2. Customer Service Strategies.
         a. Giving customers what they want.
         b. Effective customer communication system.
         c. Importance of organization's culture.
      3. Innovation Strategies.
         a. Innovation strategies can include the application of existing technology to new uses.
         b. Innovation emphasis.
            (i)     Basic scientific research.
            (ii)    Product development.
            (iii)   Process development.
         c. Innovation timing.
            (i)     First-mover advantages and disadvantages.  (Refer to Exhibit 8-8)
   D. Learning Review.
      • Explain why strategic flexibility is important.
      • Describe e-business strategies.
      • Explain what strategies organizations might use to become more customer oriented and to be more innovative.
   E. Key Terms.
      1. Strategic flexibility – The ability to recognize major external environmental changes, to quickly commit resources, and to recognize when a strategic decision was a mistake.
      2. First mover – An organization that's first to bring a product innovation to the market or to use a new process innovation.

## Multiple-Choice Questions

1. Which of the following is NOT true about strategic management?
   a) Strategic management is an important task of managers and entails all of the basic management functions.
   b) Strategic management is involved in many of the decisions that managers make.
   c) Strategic management is important for profit-making organizations, but less important for not-for-profit and governmental organizations.
   d) Strategic management has been linked to higher performance levels.
   (pp. 208-210)

2. _____ is a six-step process that encompasses strategic planning, implementation, and evaluation.
   a) The strategic management process
   b) SWOT analysis
   c) The BCG matrix
   d) Cost-volume-profit analysis
   (p. 210)

3. A mission statement should have all of the following components EXCEPT _____.
   a) products or service
   b) market
   c) concern for employees
   d) concern for competitors
   (p. 211, Exhibit 8-2)

4. _____ are positive trends in external environmental factors.
   a) Opportunities
   b) Threats
   c) Weaknesses
   d) SBUs
   (p. 212)

5. Core competencies are determined in the _____ step of the strategic management process.
   a) implementing strategies
   b) external analysis
   c) internal analysis
   d) formulating strategies
   (p. 212)

6. _____ is (are) the organization's major value-creating skills, capabilities, and resources that determine its competitive weapons.
   a) A mission statement
   b) Core competencies
   c) Cash cows
   d) Competitive strategies
   (p. 212)

7. When analyzing an organization's strengths and weaknesses, firms often overlook _____.
   a) the impact of management on a company's strengths
   b) the part employees play in building an organization's strengths
   c) the negative effect, or weaknesses created, by weak upper management
   d) the organization's culture and its effect
   (p. 213)

8. In a SWOT analysis an organization's opportunities come at the juncture of _____.
   a) overcoming environmental threats and the empowerment of employees
   b) the organization's mission and choice of functional strategy
   c) the organization's resources/abilities and opportunities in the environment
   d) the company's choice of management and mission
   (p. 214)

9. _____ is the strategy that determines what business a company is in, or wants to be in, and what it wants to do with that business.
   a) Corporate strategy
   b) Business strategy
   c) Competitive strategy
   d) Functional strategy
   (p. 217)

10. There are three main corporate strategies: growth, stability, and _____.
    a) low cost
    b) renewal
    c) market leader
    d) profit maximization
    (p. 217)

11. A firm that chooses to enlarge its operations by acquiring similar businesses in the same industry is pursuing a corporate strategy of _____.
    a) growth
    b) stability
    c) retrenchment
    d) combination
    (p. 218)

12. When a firm acquires another company in a different industry the firm is pursuing a
_____.
    a) growth through unrelated diversification strategy
    b) differentiation strategy
    c) stability through merger
    d) combination of core competencies strategy
    (p. 218)

13. A _____ strategy is a corporate strategy characterized by an absence of significant
change.
    a) growth
    b) retrenchment
    c) related diversification
    d) stability
    (p. 219)

14. A _____ strategy is a short-run strategy designed to address organizational
weaknesses that are leading to performance declines.
    a) growth
    b) stability
    c) retrenchment
    d) combination
    (p. 220)

15. There are two main types of renewal strategies, retrenchment strategy and _____
strategy.
    a) turnaround
    b) growth
    c) restructuring
    d) stability
    (p. 220)

16. Which product category in the BCG matrix has low growth and high market share?
    a) Cash cow
    b) Question mark
    c) Star
    d) Dog
    (p. 221, Exhibit 8-5)

17. In the BCG matrix, the _____ are businesses in an attractive industry that hold a small
market share percentage (high growth, low market share).
    a) cash cows
    b) stars
    c) question marks
    d) dogs
    (p. 221, Exhibit 8-5)

18. The suggested strategy for products that fit into the _____ category of the BCG matrix is to use them to generate funds so that investments can be made in other products.
    a) cash cow
    b) question mark
    c) star
    d) dog
    (p. 221)

19. Business strategy seeks to answer which question?
    a) How do we support the selected strategy?
    b) In what set of businesses should we be involved?
    c) How should we compete in each of our businesses?
    d) What business are we in?
    (p. 221)

20. _____ is what sets an organization apart; that is, its distinct edge.
    a) Strategic plan
    b) Monopolistic advantage
    c) First-mover advantage
    d) Competitive advantage
    (p. 222)

21. _____ management focuses on customers and continuous improvement.
    a) Leadership
    b) Quality
    c) Functional
    d) Differential
    (p. 222)

22. The concept of competitive strategies comes from the work of _____.
    a) Miles and Snow
    b) Mary Parker Follett
    c) Chester Barnard
    d) Michael Porter
    (p. 223)

23. What is the competitive strategy that involves a cost advantage or a differentiation advantage in a narrow segment?
    a) Focus
    b) Leadership
    c) Market hole
    d) Stuck in the middle
    (p. 224)

24. Evidence suggests that competitive forces in an industry, if kept relatively free of government interference or other special circumstances, will inevitably create a situation where _____ companies dominate any given market.
    a) five
    b) four
    c) three
    d) two
    (p. 225)

25. A functional strategy _____.
    a) plans to integrate operations of three product areas.
    b) pinpoints consumers between the ages of 25 and 35 as the target customer group
    c) involves the selection of two primary product areas for focus of operations
    d) supports the business strategy
    (p. 226)

## True/False Questions

1. T  F  Strategic management is part of many of the decisions managers make.
          (p. 208)

2. T  F  A company's business model is a strategic design for how a company intends to profit from its strategies, work processes, and work activities.
          (p. 209)

3. T  F  The first step in the strategic management process involves identifying the organization's current mission, objectives, and strategies.
          (p. 210)

4. T  F  Weaknesses are negative trends in external environmental factors.
          (p. 213)

5. T  F  An organization's culture is always a strength when it comes to strategic planning.
          (p. 213)

6. T  F  Corporate strategy seeks to answer the question: How should we compete in each of our businesses?
          (p. 217)

7. T  F  Growth strategy seeks to decrease the level of the organization's operations.
          (p. 217)

8.  T   F   A firm may implement a growth strategy through either related or unrelated diversification.
(pp. 218-219)

9.  T   F   A corporate strategy that seeks to reduce size or diversity of the organization operations is called a stability strategy.
(p. 219)

10. T   F   The BCG matrix is a strategy tool that guides resource allocation decisions on the basis of market share and growth rate of SBUs.
(p. 220)

11. T   F   The location of a product on the BCG matrix is determined by a company's market share and anticipated market growth.
(p. 221, Exhibit 8-5)

12. T   F   According to the BCG matrix, cash cows have low market share and low anticipated market growth.
(p. 221, Exhibit 8-5)

13. T   F   Strategic business units are businesses within an organization that are independent and formulate their own strategies.
(p. 222)

14. T   F   Constant improvement in the quality and reliability of an organization's products or services may result in a competitive advantage that can't be taken away.
(p. 222)

15. T   F   According to Michael Porter, understanding industry competitive factors is not essential in developing strategic alternatives.
(p. 223)

16. T   F   The profit maximizing strategy is a business strategy in which the organization is the lowest-cost producer in its industry.
(p. 224)

17. T   F   A differentiation strategy is a business strategy in which a company offers unique products that are widely valued by customers.
(p. 224)

18. T   F   A focus strategy is a cost-leadership or differentiation strategy that has been developed for a specific market.
(p. 224)

19. T  F  The premise of the Rule of Three is that successful companies have three levels of management.
(p. 225)

20. T  F  The Rule of Three says that most markets evolve in a cyclical fashion and describes how that evolution occurs.
(p. 225)

21. T  F  Functional strategies support the business strategy.
(p. 226)

22. T  F  Strategic flexibility involves recognizing major external environmental changes, quickly committing resources, and recognizing when a strategic decision isn't working.
(p. 227)

23. T  F  Managers can formulate strategies using e-business techniques that contribute to the development of a sustainable competitive advantage.
(p. 228)

24. T  F  One disadvantage of being a first-mover is a lack of customer loyalty.
(p. 230, Exhibit 8-8)

25. T  F  One advantage of being a first-mover is control over scarce resources and keeping competitors from having access to them.
(p. 230, Exhibit 8-8)

# Match Terms with Definitions

a. Stability strategy
b. BCG matrix
c. Unrelated diversification
d. Business strategy
e. SWOT analysis
f. Weaknesses
g. Threats
h. Strategic management process

i. Growth strategy
j. Related diversification
k. Strategic business unit (SBU)
l. Retrenchment strategy
m. Core competencies
n. Opportunities
o. Corporate strategy

_____ 1. A corporate strategy characterized by an absence of significant change in what the organization is currently doing.

_____ 2. Focuses on how a corporation should compete in each of its businesses.

_____ 3. Activities the organization does not do well or resources it needs but does not possess.

_____ 4. Analysis of an organization's strengths and weaknesses and its environmental opportunities and threats.

_____ 5. A short-run renewal strategy.

_____ 6. The organization's major value-creating skills and capabilities that determine the organization's competitive weapons.

_____ 7. Positive trends in external environmental factors.

_____ 8. Seeks to determine what businesses a company should be in.

_____ 9. A single business or collection of businesses that is independent and formulates its own strategy.

_____ 10. A corporate strategy that's used when an organization wants to grow and does so by expanding the number of products offered or market served, either through its current business(es) or through new business(es).

_____ 11. A way that companies choose to grow that involves combining with firms in different, but related industries.

_____ 12. A six-step process encompassing strategic planning, implementation, and evaluation.

_____ 13. Negative trends in external environmental factors.

_____ 14. A way that companies choose to grow that involves combining with firms in different and unrelated industries.

_____ 15. Strategy tool to guide resource allocation decisions based on market share and growth of SBUs.

**Essay Questions**

1. Why is strategic management important?
   (pp. 208-210)

2. Outline the six-step strategic management process, briefly explaining each step.
   (pp. 210-216, Exhibit 8-1)

3. What are the three main corporate strategies?  Briefly explain each one.
   (pp. 217-220)

4. Draw and explain the BCG matrix.  Be sure to label each axis and each quadrant.
   (pp. 220-221, Exhibit 8-5)

5. Today's environment has required new directions in organizational strategies.
   Explain strategies for applying e-business techniques, customer service strategies, and
   innovation strategies.
   (pp. 228-230)

# Chapter 9  Planning Tools and Techniques

## Learning Outline

### Techniques for Assessing the Environment
- List the different approaches to assess the environment.
- Explain what competitor intelligence is and ways that managers can do it legally and ethically.
- Describe how managers can improve the effectiveness of forecasting.
- List the steps in the benchmarking process.

### Techniques for Allocating Resources
- List the four techniques for allocating resources.
- Describe the different types of budgets.
- Explain what a Gantt chart and a load chart do.
- Describe how PERT network analysis works.
- Understand how to compute a breakeven point.
- Describe how managers can use linear programming.

### Contemporary Planning Techniques
- Explain why flexibility is so important to today's planning techniques.
- Describe project management.
- List the steps in the project planning process.
- Discuss why scenario planning is an important planning tool.

---

**A Manager's Dilemma**

As CEO of the zoological society of San Diego, Paula Brock's emphasis on the budget-and-planning process helped the San Diego Zoo protect its avian population from an outbreak of exotic Newcastle Disease while still making the organization's bottom line. Consider the following question and compare your response to **Managers Respond** at the end of the chapter.

1. How should Ms. Brock go about educating the zoo's professional scientists and animal keepers about the importance of updating budgets throughout the year and encourage them to be more involved in the budgeting process?

---

## Lecture Outline

I. Techniques for Assessing the Environment.
   A. Environmental Scanning.
      1. Likely to reveal issues and concerns that could affect current or planned activities.
      2. Competitor Intelligence.
         a. The process of gathering information about competitors.
         b. Ways of gathering information.
         c. Reverse engineering.
         d. Legal and ethical concerns.

      3. Global Scanning.
         a. Value of global scanning.
         b. Sources of information.
B. Forecasting.
    1. Forecasting Techniques. (Refer to Exhibit 9-1)
       a. Quantitative Forecasting.
       b. Qualitative Forecasting.
       c. Collaborative Forecasting.
    2. Forecasting Effectiveness.
       a. Goal of forecasting is to provide managers with information that facilitates decision making.
       b. Mixed success with forecasting.
       c. Ways to improve effectiveness of forecasting.
          (i)     Techniques are most effective when the environment isn't changing rapidly.
          (ii)    Forecasting is relatively ineffective at predicting nonseasonal events.
          (iii)   Use simple methods.
          (iv)   Involve more people in the process.
          (v)    Compare every forecast with "no change."
          (vi)   Use rolling forecasts.
          (vii)  Don't rely on a single forecasting method.
          (viii) Don't assume you can accurately identify turning points in a trend.
          (ix)   Forecasting is a managerial skill and can be practiced and improved.
    3. Benchmarking.
       a. Benchmarking is a search for best practices.
       b. Steps in Benchmarking. (Refer to Exhibit 9-2)
          (i)     Form a planning team.
          (ii)    Team collects data.
          (iii)   Analyze data.
          (iv)   Prepare and implement Action Plan.
C. Learning Review.
- List the different approaches to assessing the environment.
- Explain what competitor intelligence is and ways that managers can do it legally and ethically.
- Describe how managers can improve the effectiveness of forecasting.
- List the steps in the benchmarking process.

116

D. Key Terms.
   1. Environmental scanning – The screening of large amounts of information to anticipate and interpret changes in the environment.
   2. Competitor intelligence – Environmental scanning activity by which organizations gather information about competitors.
   3. Forecasts – Predictions of outcomes.
   4. Quantitative forecasting – Forecasting that applies a set of mathematical rules to a series of past data to predict outcomes.
   5. Qualitative forecasting – Forecasting that uses the judgment and opinions of knowledgeable individuals to predict outcomes.
   6. Benchmarking – The search for the best practices among competitors or noncompetitors that lead to their superior performance.

II. Techniques for Allocating Resources.
   A. Types of resources include financial, physical, human, intangible, and structural/cultural.
   B. Budgeting
      1. Budget is a numerical plan for allocating resources.
      2. Types of budgets. (Refer to Exhibit 9-3)
         a. Revenue budget.
         b. Expense budget.
         c. Profit budget.
         d. Cash budget
      3. Suggestions for improving budgeting. (Refer to Exhibit 9-4)
   C. Scheduling.
      1. Gantt Charts. (Refer to Exhibit 9-5)
         a. Developed by Henry Gantt.
         b. Visually shows when tasks are supposed to be done and compares that with actual progress.
         c. Manager can see deviations from plan.
      2. Load Charts. (Refer to Exhibit 9-6)
         a. Modified Gantt Chart.
         b. Allows managers to plan and control capacity utilization.
      3. PERT Network Analysis. (Refer to Exhibit 9-7)
         a. Flowchart diagram for organizing large, complex projects.
         b. Four important terms:
            (i)    Events.
            (ii)   Activities.
            (iii)  Slack time.
            (iv)   Critical path.
         c. Manager must identify all key activities, rank them in order of occurrence, and estimate completion time.
         d. Example of PERT network. (Refer to Exhibits 9-8 and 9-9)
   D. Breakeven Analysis.
      1. A widely used resource allocation technique.

2. Manager must know unit price of the product, variable cost per unit, and total fixed costs.
3. Example of breakeven analysis. (Refer to Exhibit 9-10)
E. Linear Programming.
   1. Can't be applied to all resource allocation problems.
   2. Conditions when linear programming is useful.
   3. Kinds of problems that can be solved with linear programming.
   4. Example of linear programming. (Refer to Exhibit 9-11)
      a. Objective function.
      b. Constraints.
      c. Graphical solution. (Refer to Exhibit 9-12)
      d. Feasibility region.
F. Learning Review.
   - List the four techniques for allocating resources.
   - Describe the different types of budgets.
   - Explain what a Gantt chart and a load chart do.
   - Describe how PERT network analysis works.
   - Understand how to compute a breakeven point.
   - Describe how managers can use linear programming.
G. Key Terms.
   1. Resources – The assets of the organization including financial, physical, human, intangible, and structural/cultural.
   2. Budget – A numerical plan for allocating resources to specific activities.
   3. Scheduling – Detailing what activities have to be done, the order in which they are to be completed, who is to do each, and when they are to be completed.
   4. Gantt chart – A scheduling chart developed by Henry Gantt that shows actual and planned output over a period of time.
   5. Load chart – A modified Gantt chart that schedules capacity by entire departments or specific resources.
   6. PERT network – A flowchart diagram showing the sequence of activities needed to complete a project and the time or cost associated with each.
   7. Events – End points that represent the completion of major activities in a PERT network.
   8. Activities – The time or resources needed to progress from one event to another in a PERT network.
   9. Slack time – The amount of time an individual activity can be delayed without delaying the whole project.
   10. Critical path – The longest sequence of activities in a PERT network.
   11. Breakeven analysis – A technique for identifying the point at which total revenue is just sufficient to cover total costs.
   12. Linear programming – A mathematical technique that solves resource allocation problems.

III. Contemporary Planning Techniques.
  A. Today's environment is dynamic and complex and managers need planning techniques that emphasize flexibility.
  B. Project Management.
    1. Project is a one-time-only set of activities that has a definite beginning and ending point in time.
    2. Project Management Process. (Refer to Exhibit 9-13)
      a. Define project goals.
      b. Identify activities and resources.
      c. Determine the sequence of completion.
      d. Develop an overall project schedule.
    3. The Role of the Project Manager.
  C. Scenario Planning.
    1. A scenario is a consistent view of what the future is likely to be.
    2. Developing scenarios can also be described as contingency planning.
    3. Intent is to reduce uncertainty.
    4. Difficult to forecast random events.
    5. Scenario planning can help prepare for unexpected events. (Refer to Exhibit 9-14)
  D. Learning Review.
    - Explain why flexibility is so important to today's planning techniques.
    - Describe project management.
    - List the steps in the project planning process.
    - Discuss why scenario planning is an important planning tool.
  E. Key Terms.
    1. Project – A one-time-only set of activities that has a definite beginning and ending point in time.
    2. Project management – The task of getting a project's activities done on time, within budget, and according to specifications.
    3. Scenario – A consistent view of what the future is likely to be.

## Multiple-Choice Questions

1. _____ is the screening of large amounts of information to anticipate and interpret changes in the environment.
   a) Competitor intelligence
   b) Environmental scanning
   c) Corporate espionage
   d) Forecasting
   (p. 238)

2. The fastest growing area of environmental scanning is _____.
   a) competitor intelligence
   b) for governmental intelligence
   c) for global competition
   d) concerning the changing nature of the workplace
   (p. 239)

3. The process of buying competitors' products and having your own engineers study them to learn about new technical innovations is called _____.
   a) competitor intelligence
   b) corporate espionage
   c) illegal competition
   d) reverse engineering
   (p. 239)

4. The value of global scanning to managers _____.
   a) is greater than environmental scanning
   b) is usually less than environmental scanning
   c) is impossible to calculate
   d) is dependent on the extent of the organization's global activities
   (p. 240)

5. Which of the following is an example of qualitative forecasting technique?
   a) Regression model
   b) Substitution effect
   c) Customer evaluation
   d) Time series analysis
   (p. 241, Exhibit 9-1)

6. Which quantitative forecasting technique predicts one variable on the basis of known or assumed other variables?
   a) Time series analysis
   b) Regression models
   c) Econometric models
   d) Substitution effect
   (p. 241, Exhibit 9-1)

7. _____ is a method that allows managers to improve performance by analyzing and then copying the methods of major competitors.
   a) Environmental scanning
   b) Forecasting
   c) Benchmarking
   d) Budgeting
   (p. 243)

8. One way that managers can make their forecasting more effective is to _____.
   a) understand that forecasting techniques are most accurate when the environment is not rapidly changing
   b) involve fewer people in the process
   c) use more complex methods
   d) stick to a single forecasting method
   (p. 242)

9. The first step in the benchmarking process is to _____.
   a) identify the companies against which to benchmark
   b) gather internal data
   c) form a planning team
   d) scan the environment to determine the major threats
   (p. 243, Exhibit 9-2)

10. A _____ is a numerical plan for allocating resources to specific activities.
   a) forecast
   b) budget
   c) benchmark
   d) quantitative forecast
   (p. 244)

11. The _____ budget lists primary activities and allocates dollar amounts to each.
   a) expense
   b) cash
   c) profit
   d) revenue
   (p. 244, Exhibit 9-3)

12. The _____ budget forecasts cash on hand and how much will be needed.
   a) cash
   b) fixed
   c) variable
   d) revenue
   (p. 244, Exhibit 9-3)

13. What scheduling technique uses a bar graph to illustrate planned activities and their completion over a period of time?
   a) Load chart
   b) Gantt chart
   c) PERT network
   d) Simulation
   (p. 246)

14. The _____ is used to track whole departments or resources rather than activities. This tool allows managers to plan and control for capacity.
    a) load chart
    b) Gantt chart
    c) PERT network
    d) simulation
    (p. 246)

15. A flowchart diagram showing the sequence of activities needed to complete a project and the time or cost associated with each is a _____.
    a) load chart
    b) critical path
    c) Gantt chart
    d) PERT network
    (p. 247)

16. The _____ marks the longest time through the network for a PERT project.
    a) activity path
    b) critical path
    c) serious of events
    d) PERT network
    (p. 247)

17. When using PERT to track the work in constructing an office building, digging a subterranean garage in six weeks is an example of a(n) _____.
    a) activity
    b) critical path
    c) event
    d) load factor
    (p. 247, Exhibit 9-8)

18. _____ is a planning technique for identifying the point at which total revenue is just sufficient to cover total costs.
    a) A PERT diagram
    b) A profit budget
    c) Breakeven analysis
    d) Linear programming
    (p. 249)

19. Crosstick Company wants to know how many units it must sell to break even. Crosstick has the following financial information: fixed costs are $25,000, variable costs per unit are $4, selling price per unit is $9. Breakeven point in units is:
a) 10,000 units.
b) 8,000 units.
c) 7,500 units.
d) 5,000 units.
(p. 249)

20. Which of the following mathematical techniques can be used to solve resource allocation problems?
a) Linear programming
b) Breakeven analysis
c) PERT diagram
d) Revenue budget
(p. 249)

21. A candy company produces two kinds of candy using the same ingredients and has the following available this week: 500 pounds of chocolate, 300 pounds of sugar, and 100 pounds of nuts. Managers must know these values to write the _____ for the linear programming problem.
a) constraints
b) feasibility region
c) objective function
d) revenue budget
(p. 252)

22. Two planning techniques appropriate for dynamic and complex environments are project management and _____.
a) linear programming
b) breakeven theory analysis
c) scenario planning
d) probability theory
(p. 252)

23. A _____ is a one-time-only set of activities that has a definite beginning and ending point in time.
a) probability factor
b) project
c) simulation
d) project management process
(p. 253)

24. The task of getting a project's activities done on time, within budget, and according to specifications is called _____.
    a) probability theory
    b) marginal analysis
    c) project management
    d) queuing theory
    (p. 253)

25. Developing scenarios of what the future is likely to be is also described as _____.
    a) capital budgeting
    b) project management
    c) marginal analysis
    d) contingency planning
    (p. 254)

## True/False Questions

1. T  F  Companies that use environmental scanning generally have higher performance.
    (p. 238)

2. T  F  The Economic Espionage Act makes it legal to steal trade secrets in the United States.
    (p. 240)

3. T  F  The value of global scanning to managers is largely independent of the extent of the organization's global activities.
    (p. 240)

4. T  F  Econometric models use a set of regression equations to simulate segments of the economy.
    (p. 241, Exhibit 9-1)

5. T  F  Benchmarking is a quality tool that even small companies find of value.
    (p. 243)

6. T  F  Studies have shown that companies using benchmarking have achieved faster growth and greater productivity than companies that don't use benchmarking.
    (p. 243)

7. T  F  Resources of the organization include financial, physical, human, intangibles, and structural/cultural.
    (p. 244)

8. T  F  Forecasts are numerical plans for allocating resources to specific activities.
    (p. 244)

9.  T  F  All budgets are essentially fixed budgets because they don't change once set.
          (p. 244, Exhibit 9-3)

10. T  F  A revenue budget projects future sales.
          (p. 244, Exhibit 9-3)

11. T  F  Fixed budgets assume all costs are fixed.
          (p. 244, Exhibit 9-3)

12. T  F  Budgets are a planning technique used mostly by top-level managers.
          (p. 245)

13. T  F  Gantt charts, load charts, and PERT network analysis are all types of useful
          scheduling devices.
          (p. 246)

14. T  F  A modified Gantt chart that schedules capacity by workstations is called a
          PERT diagram.
          (p. 246)

15. T  F  PERT network analysis is most useful when the activities scheduled are few in
          number and independent of each other.
          (p. 247)

16. T  F  The critical path is the shortest sequence of activities in a PERT network.
          (p. 247)

17. T  F  Fixed costs are fixed per unit but vary in total as volume changes.
          (p. 249)

18. T  F  At the breakeven point, the difference between price and variable costs, when
          multiplied by the number of units sold, equals the fixed costs.
          (p. 249)

19. T  F  Selecting transportation routes that minimize shipping costs and allocating a
          limited advertising budget among various product brands are two uses for
          linear programming technology.
          (p. 250)

20. T  F  Limited resources act as *constraints* in solving a linear programming problem.
          (p. 251)

21. T  F  Scheduling is the task of getting a project's activities done on time, within
          budget, and according to specifications.
          (p. 253)

22. T  F  A project is a one-time-only set of activities with a definite beginning and ending point in time.
(p. 253)

23. T  F  Project management begins with a clear definition of the project's goals.
(p. 253)

24. T  F  The final step in the project management process is comparing the outcomes with the initial objectives.
(p. 253, Exhibit 9-13)

25. T  F  A scenario is a consistent view of what the future is likely to be.
(p. 254)

## Match Terms with Definitions

a. Environmental scanning
b. Competitor intelligence
c. Scenario
d. Forecasts
e. Quantitative forecasting
f. Qualitative forecasting
g. Benchmarking
h. Resources

i. Budget
j. Gantt chart
k. PERT
l. Load chart
m. Scheduling
n. Critical path
o. Breakeven analysis

_____ 1. A numerical plan for allocating resources to specific activities.
_____ 2. A technique for scheduling complicated projects comprising many activities, some of which are interdependent.
_____ 3. The assets of the organization including financial, physical, human, intangible, and structural/cultural.
_____ 4. The longest sequence of activities in a PERT network.
_____ 5. A consistent view of what the future is likely to be.
_____ 6. Applies a set of mathematical rules to a series of past data to predict future outcomes.
_____ 7. The search for the best practices among competitors or noncompetitors that led to their superior performance.
_____ 8. Environmental scanning activity by which organizations gather information about competitors.
_____ 9. A listing of necessary activities, their order of accomplishment, who is to do each, and time needed to complete them.
_____ 10. The screening of large amounts of information to anticipate and interpret changes in the environment.
_____ 11. Uses the judgment and opinions of knowledgeable individuals to predict outcomes.
_____ 12. A modified Gantt chart that schedules capacity by entire departments or specific resources.
_____ 13. A technique for identifying the point at which total revenue is just sufficient to cover total costs.
_____ 14. Predictions of outcomes.
_____ 15. A scheduling chart that shows actual and planned output over a period of time.

## Essay Questions

1. Discuss three techniques available to managers for assessing the environment.
   (pp. 238-243)

2. What is benchmarking and what is its value for businesses?
   (p. 243)

3. Identify the various kinds of budgets used by managers. What information does each type budget provide?
   (pp. 244-245, Exhibit 9-3)

4. Discuss PERT network analysis and diagram a PERT network for a project you are working on this semester.
   (pp. 247-249)

5. What is project management? List the steps in the project management process.
   (p. 253, Exhibit 9-13)

# Chapter 10 Organizational Structure and Design

## Learning Outline

### Defining Organizational Structure
- Discuss the traditional and contemporary views of work specialization, chain of command, and span of control.
- Describe each of the five forms of departmentalization.
- Explain cross-functional teams.
- Differentiate authority, responsibility, and unity of command.
- Tell what factors influence the amount of centralization and decentralization.
- Explain how formalization is used in organizational design.

### Organizational Design Decisions
- Contrast mechanistic and organic organizations.
- Explain the relationship between strategy and structure.
- Tell how organizational size affects organizational design.
- Discuss Woodward's findings on the relationship of technology and structure.
- Explain how environmental uncertainty affects organizational design.

### Common Organizational Designs
- Contrast the three traditional organizational designs.
- Explain team-based, matrix, and project structures.
- Discuss the design of virtual, network, and modular organizations.
- Describe the characteristics of a learning organization.

---

**A Manager's Dilemma**

When Penny Baker founded National Bankcard Systems, he wanted it to be as friendly as possible. As the business grew, however, his friendly, laid-back management style lead to certain problems. Consider the following questions and compare your answers to **Managers Respond** at the end of the chapter.

1. What kinds of problems did Mr. Baker encounter as a result of his management style?
2. How did these problems arise?
3. How should he structure his organization so that he can be a "nice boss who encourages employees to have fun, but keeps them at arm's length"?

---

## Lecture Outline

I. Defining Organizational Structure
   A. Traditional approaches are being questioned.
      1. Organizing is the process through which managers design an organization's structure.
         a. Purposes of organizing. (Refer to Exhibit 10-1)
      2. Organizational structure.
      3. Organizational design.

B. Work Specialization.
   1. Degree to which activities in an organization are divided into separate jobs.
   2. Henry Ford's application to the assembly line.
   3. Entire job is broken down into steps, each done by a different employee.
   4. View in first half of the 20th century.
   5. View in the 1960s.
   6. View today.

---

**Thinking Critically About Ethics**
Changes in technology have produced a great impact on employees' skills. After reading the summary, respond to the following questions.
1. What ethical obligation do organizations have to assist workers whose skills have become obsolete?
2. What about employees? Do they have an obligation to keep their skills from becoming obsolete?
3. What ethical guidelines might you suggest for dealing with employee skill obsolescence?

---

C. Departmentalization.
   1. The basis by which jobs are grouped together.
   2. Five common forms of specialization. (Refer to Exhibit10-2)
      a. Functional departmentalization – groups jobs by functions performed.
      b. Product departmentalization – groups jobs by product line.
      c. Geographical departmentalization – groups jobs on basis of territory.
      d. Process departmentalization – groups jobs on the basis of product or customer flow.
      e. Customer departmentalization – groups jobs on the basis of customers with common needs or problems.
   3. Popular trends in departmentalization.
      a. Customer departmentalization.
      b. Cross-functional teams – experts in various specialties work together.
D. Chain of Command.
   1. The continuous line of authority that extends from upper organizational levels to the lowest levels.
   2. Authority.
   3. Responsibility.
   4. Unity of command.
      a. One of Fayol's 14 principles of management.
      b. Helps preserve the concept of a continuous line of authority.
   5. Less relevant today due to information technology and the use of self-managed and cross-functional teams.
E. Span of Control
   1. The number of employees a manager can efficiently and effectively manage.
   2. All things being equal, the wider or larger the span, the more efficient the organization. (Refer to Exhibit 10-3)
   3. Many factors influence the appropriate span of control.

4. Recent trend is toward larger spans of control.
F. Centralization and Decentralization.
1. Centralization – the degree to which decision making is concentrated at a single point in the organization.
2. Decentralization – the degree to which lower-level employees provide input or actually make decisions.
3. Factors that influence the amount of centralization and decentralization. (Refer to Exhibit 10-4)
4. Trend toward decentralized decision making.
5. Employee empowerment – increasing the decision-making discretion of employees.
G. Formalization.
1. Refers to the degree to which jobs within the organization are standardized and the extent to which employee behavior is guided by rules and procedures.
2. High formalization means employees have little discretion, there are explicit job descriptions, numerous rules, and clearly defined procedures.
3. Low formalization means that job behaviors are relatively unstructured and employees have a great deal of freedom.
4. Degree of formalization varies between organizations and even within organizations.
H. Learning Review.
- Discuss the traditional and contemporary views of work specialization, chain of command, and span of control.
- Describe each of the five forms of departmentalization.
- Explain cross-functional teams.
- Differentiate authority, responsibility, and unity of command.
- Tell what factors influence the amount of centralization and decentralization.
- Explain how formalization is used in organizational design.
I. Key Terms.
1. Organizing – Arranging and structuring work to accomplish the organization's goals.
2. Organizational structure – The formal arrangement of jobs within an organization.
3. Organizational design – Developing or changing an organization's structure.
4. Work specialization – Dividing work activity into separate job tasks.
5. Departmentalization – The basis by which jobs are grouped together.
6. Functional departmentalization – Groups jobs by functions performed.
7. Product departmentalization – Groups jobs by product line.
8. Geographical departmentalization – Groups jobs on the basis of geographical region.
9. Process departmentalization – Groups jobs on the basis of product or customer flow.
10. Customer departmentalization – Groups jobs on the basis of specific and unique customers who have common needs.
11. Cross-functional teams – Work teams composed of individuals from various functional specialties.

12. Chain of command – The line of authority extending from upper organizational levels to the lowest level, which clarifies who reports to whom.
13. Authority – The rights inherent in a managerial position to tell people what to do and to expect them to do it.
14. Responsibility – The obligation to perform any assigned duties.
15. Unity of command – The management principle that each person should report only to one manager.
16. Span of control – The number of employees a manager can efficiently and effectively manage.
17. Centralization – The degree to which decision making is concentrated in upper levels of the organization.
18. Decentralization – The degree to which lower-level employees provide input or actually make decisions.
19. Employee empowerment – Giving employees more authority (power) to make decisions.
20. Formalization – How standardized an organization's jobs are and the extent to which employee behavior is guided by rules and procedures.

II. Organizational Design Decisions.
   A. Mechanistic and Organic Organizations. (Refer to Exhibit 10-5)
      1. Mechanistic organizations.
         a. Rigid and tightly controlled structure.
         b. Characterized by high specialization, rigid departmentalization, narrow spans of control, high formalization, limited information network, and little participation in decision making.
         c. This design tries to minimize impact of differing personalities, judgments, and ambiguities.
      2. Organic organizations.
         a. Highly adaptive and flexible.
         b. Flexibility allows rapid change.
         c. Employees are highly trained and empowered to handle diverse job activities.
   B. Contingency Factors.
      1. Strategy and Structure.
         a. Structure should facilitate achievement of goals.
         b. Structure should follow strategy.
         c. Current strategy frameworks focus on three dimensions.
            (i)      Innovation.
            (ii)     Cost minimization.
            (iii)    Imitation.
      2. Size and Structure.
         a. Size affects structure.
         b. Large organizations tend to have more specialization, centralization, and departmentalization.

3. Technology and Structure.
   a. Every organization has some form of technology to convert its inputs into outputs.
   b. Joan Woodward studied the relationship between structural design elements and organizational success. (Refer to Exhibit 10-6)
     1. Unit production.
     2. Mass production.
     3. Process production.
   c. Organizations adapt their structure to their technology.
   d. The more routine the technology, the more mechanistic the structure can be.
4. Environmental Uncertainty and Structure.
   a. Uncertainty threatens organizational effectiveness and managers want to minimize it.
   b. Environmental uncertainty can be reduced through adjustments in the organization's structure.
   c. The greater the uncertainty, the more an organization needs the flexibility of an organic design.
   d. Today's managers are restructuring organizations to be lean, fast, and flexible.

C. Learning Review.
- Contrast mechanistic and organic organizations.
- Explain the relationship between strategy and structure.
- Tell how organizational size affects organizational design.
- Discuss Woodward's findings on the relationship of technology and structure.
- Explain how environmental uncertainty affects organizational design.

D. Key Terms.
1. Mechanistic organization – An organizational design that's rigid and tightly controlled.
2. Organic organization – An organizational design that's highly adaptive and flexible.
3. Unit production – The production of items in units or small batches.
4. Mass production – The production of items in large batches.
5. Process production – The production of items in continuous processes.

III. Common Organizational Designs.
  A. Traditional Organizational Designs. (Refer to Exhibit 10-7)
    1. Simple Structure.
      a. Low departmentalization, wide spans of control, authority centralized in a single person and little formalization.
      b. Commonly used by small businesses in which owner and manager are the same person.
    2. Functional Structure.
      a. Groups similar or related occupational specialties together.

3. Divisional Structure.
    a. Made up of separate business units or divisions.
    b. Each unit has limited autonomy, with the parent corporation overseeing and coordinating various divisions.
B. Contemporary Organizational Designs. (Refer to Exhibit 10-8)
    1. Traditional designs aren't appropriate for increasingly dynamic and complex environments.
    2. Team Structures.
        a. Entire organization is made up of work groups or teams.
        b. Employee empowerment is crucial.
        c. In large organizations, team structure complements a functional or divisional structure.
    3. Matrix and Project Structures.
        a. Matrix Structure
            (i)     Assigns specialists from different functional departments to work on one or more projects. (Refer to Exhibit 10-9)
            (ii)    Dual chain of command.
        b. Project Structure.
            (i)     Employees continuously work on projects.
            (ii)    All work is performed by teams of employees.
            (iii)   Tend to be fluid and flexible.
    4. The Boundaryless Organization
        a. Design is not defined by, or limited to, the horizontal, vertical, or external boundaries imposed by a predefined structure.
        b. Term coined by Jack Welch, former chairman of General Electric.
        c. Internal vs. external boundaries.
        d. Virtual organization.
        e. Network organization.
C. Today's Organizational Design Challenges.
    1. Keeping Employees Connected.
        a. Employers must keep widely dispersed and mobile employees connected to the organization.
    2. Building a Learning Organization
        a. Doesn't involve a specific organizational design.
        b. Learning organization has developed the capacity to continuously learn, adapt, and change.
        c. Members share information and collaborate on work activities throughout the entire organization.
        d. Empowered employees work in teams, while managers serve as facilitators, supporters, and advocates.
    3. Managing Global Structural Issues
        a. The structure and strategies of organizations worldwide are similar, while the behavior within them is reflective of cultural characteristics.
    4. A Final Thought.
        a. Design should help employees do their work in the most efficient and effective way they can.

D. Learning Review.
- Contrast the three traditional organizational designs.
- Explain team, matrix, and project structure.
- Discuss the design of virtual and network organizations.
- Discuss the organizational design challenges facing managers today.

E. Key Terms.
1. Simple structure – An organizational design with low departmentalization, wide spans of control, centralized authority, and little formalization.
2. Functional structure – An organizational design that groups similar or related occupational specialties together.
3. Divisional structure – An organizational structure made up of separate semi-autonomous units or divisions.
4. Team structure – An organizational structure in which the entire organization is made up of work groups or teams.
5. Matrix structure – An organizational structure that assigns specialists from different functional departments to work on one or more projects.
6. Project structure – An organizational structure in which employees continuously work on projects.
7. Boundaryless organization – An organization whose design is not defined by, or limited to, the horizontal, vertical, or external boundaries imposed by a predefined structure.
8. Virtual organization – An organization that consists of a small core of full-time employees and that temporarily hires outside specialists to work on opportunities that arise.
9. Network organization – An organization that uses its own employees to do some work activities and networks of outside suppliers to provide other needed product components or work processes.
10. Learning organizations – An organization that has developed the capacity to continuously learn, adapt, and change.
11. Organizational chart – A visual drawing of an organization's structure.

## Multiple-Choice Questions

1. The formal arrangement of jobs within an organization is _____.
   a) organizational design
   b) organizational structure
   c) departmentalization
   d) work specialization
   (p. 266)

2. During the first half of the twentieth century, managers viewed _____ as an unending source of increased productivity, but by the 1960s, it had become evident that a good thing could be carried too far.
   a) centralization
   b) employee empowerment
   c) work specialization
   d) departmentalization
   (p. 267)

3. A fast-food organization that maintains a central office for marketing, accounting, and personnel uses _____ departmentalization.
   a) product
   b) customer
   c) functional
   d) process
   (pp. 268-269, Exhibit 10-2)

4. A telephone company that has several divisions, such as cellular service, domestic calling, and international calling uses _____ departmentalization.
   a) product
   b) customer
   c) functional
   d) geographic
   (pp. 268-269, Exhibit 10-2)

5. The rights inherent in a managerial position to tell people what to do and to expect them to do it is _____.
   a) authority
   b) responsibility
   c) chain of command
   d) management
   (p. 270)

6. Fayol insisted that a person should report to only one manager. This is known as _____.
   a) division of labor
   b) span of control
   c) unity of control
   d) centralization
   (p. 270)

7. Susan decides that she can manage more people and creates several new departments in her chain of command. She is utilizing the organizational principle of _____.
   a) unity of command
   b) division of labor
   c) span of control
   d) centralization
   (p. 271)

8. An organization where decision making is concentrated in the hands of a few upper managers and little if any input is sought from employees has a(n) _____.
   a) matrix or project structure
   b) organic structure
   c) formal structure
   d) centralized structure
   (p. 272)

9. As organizations become more flexible and responsive, there's been a distinct trend toward _____.
   a) increased formalization
   b) mass production
   c) centralized decision making
   d) decentralized decision making
   (p. 273)

10. Another term for increased decentralization is _____, which is increasing the decision-making discretion of employees.
    a) formalization
    b) employee empowerment
    c) cross-functional teams
    d) organic organization
    (p. 273)

11. A(n) _____ organization is highly adaptive and flexible with highly trained and empowered employees.
    a) organic
    b) mechanistic
    c) matrix
    d) centralized
    (p. 275)

12. A company with high specialization, narrow spans of control, and a high degree of formal structure would be a _____ structure.
   a) matrix
   b) mechanistic
   c) decentralized
   d) simple
   (p. 275, Exhibit 10-5)

13. Historically, the size of an organization _____.
   a) has had little affect on its structure
   b) significantly affects organization structure
   c) determines organizational structure
   d) has forced simpler, more organic structures on organizations as they grow
   (p. 276)

14. In her research on technology and organizational structure, Joan Woodward determined that _____.
   a) there is one best way to organize a business
   b) mass production technology was most effective when matched with a mechanistic structure
   c) process production technology was most effective when matched with a mechanistic structure
   d) there was no significant relationship between a technology and structure
   (p. 277, Exhibit 10-6)

15. According to Joan Woodward, the most effective structure for unit and process production is _____.
   a) bureaucracy
   b) mechanistic
   c) organic
   d) indeterminate
   (p. 277, Exhibit 10-6)

16. A functional structure _____.
   a) groups similar or related occupational specialties together
   b) is strong in helping management keep sight of its best interests in the pursuit of functional goals
   c) is inherently organic in structure
   d) clearly assigns responsibilities for outcomes
   (p. 279)

17. A weakness of the _____ is the duplication of activities and resources, increase in costs, and reduction in efficiency.
    a) functional structure
    b) simple structure
    c) divisional structure
    d) All of the above
    (p. 278, Exhibit 10-7)

18. The Montreal office of Sun Life Assurance of Canada has organized its customer representatives into groups of eight who are trained to handle all customers' requests. The company is using a _____ structure.
    a) divisional
    b) team-based structure
    c) project or matrix
    d) simple
    (pp. 279-280, Exhibit 10-8)

19. When the Kellogg Company temporarily brings together people who have expertise in product design, food research, marketing, finance, and manufacturing to plan and design new cereals, it represents which of these structures?
    a) Boundaryless organization
    b) Divisional structure
    c) Project structure
    d) Bureaucratic structure
    (pp. 280-281)

20. If a company wants an organizational structure that eliminates the chain of command, creates limitless spans of control, and introduces empowered teams, its best choice of structure would be _____.
    a) simple and mechanistic
    b) a virtual company
    c) a boundaryless structure
    d) a matrix or project structure
    (p. 282)

21. A _____ is an organization that consists of a small core of full-time employees that temporarily hires outside specialists to work on opportunities that arise.
    a) project structure
    b) boundaryless organization
    c) virtual organization
    d) matrix organization
    (p. 282)

22. The horizontal boundaries imposed by work specialization and departmentalization and the boundaries which separate employees into organizational levels and hierarchies are collectively known as _____.
    a) bureaucratic boundaries
    b) internal boundaries
    c) environmental boundaries
    d) external boundaries
    (p. 282)

23. A _____ uses its own employees to do some work activities and networks outside suppliers to provide other needed product components or work processes.
    a) boundaryless organization
    b) network organization
    c) learning organization
    d) mechanistic organization
    (p. 282)

24. Which of the following contemporary organizational designs would not be feasible if we didn't have current communication technology?
    a) Matrix structure
    b) Bureaucratic structure
    c) Learning organizations
    d) All of the above
    (p. 283)

25. This type of organization is characterized by continuous learning, adaptation, and change.
    a) Divisional organization
    b) Simple organization
    c) Learning organization
    d) Boundaryless organizational
    (p. 284)

## True/False Questions

1. T   F   Most managers today see work specialization as an unending source of increased productivity.
           (p. 267)

2. T   F   Setting up departments by separating engineering, accounting, manufacturing, personnel, and marketing departments is functional departmentalization.
           (p. 268)

3. T  F  One disadvantage of geographic departmentalization is poor communication across functional areas.
(p. 269, Exhibit 10-2)

4. T  F  With cross-functional teams, power is centralized and not shared.
(pp. 268-269)

5. T  F  The rights inherent in a managerial position to give orders and expect them to be followed is called responsibility.
(p. 270)

6. T  F  The wider or larger the span of control, the more efficient the organization.
(p. 271)

7. T  F  The trend in recent years has been toward larger spans of control, which are consistent with managers' efforts to reduce costs and speed up decision making.
(p. 271)

8. T  F  The degree to which jobs within an organization are standardized is the degree of centralization in an organization.
(p. 272)

9. T  F  If a job is highly formalized, then the person doing that job has little discretion as to what is to be done, when it's to be done, and how he or she does it.
(p. 273)

10. T  F  Organic organizational structures tend to be efficiency machines and rely heavily on rules, regulations, standardized tasks, and similar controls.
(p. 275)

11. T  F  Structure should follow strategy.
(p. 276)

12. T  F  Large organizations tend to have more specialization, departmentalization, centralization, and rules and regulations than do small organizations.
(p. 276)

13. T  F  There is no real relationship between environmental uncertainty and organizational structure.
(p. 277)

14. T  F  Because mechanistic organizations are not equipped to respond to rapid environmental change and environmental uncertainty, we're seeing organizations designed to be more organic.
(p. 277)

15. T   F   Mechanistic design options include simple, matrix, network, task force, and committee structures.
(p. 278)

16. T   F   Companies naturally progress from simple to bureaucratic structure as they grow.
(p. 278)

17. T   F   The simple structure is the most widely practiced in small businesses in which the manager and the owner are one and the same.
(p. 278)

18. T   F   If a company has separate decentralized autonomous business units, each with its own products, clients, competitors, and profit goals, the company has a divisional structure.
(p. 279)

19. T   F   Employee empowerment is crucial in a team structure because there is no line of managerial authority from top to bottom.
(p. 279)

20. T   F   The matrix structure breaks the unity of command principle.
(p. 281)

21. T   F   In a project structure, employees return to their formal departments at the completion of a project.
(p. 281)

22. T   F   A boundaryless organization has the same structure as a virtual organization.
(p. 282)

23. T   F   The network organization approach allows organizations to concentrate on what they do best and contract out other activities to companies that can do those activities best.
(p. 282)

24. T   F   The modular organization is a boundaryless option for managers that uses outside suppliers to provide product components which are then assembled into final products.
(p. 282)

25. T   F   A learning organization is characterized by the ability to adapt and change.
(p. 284)

# Match Terms with Definitions

a. Organic organization
b. Organizational structure
c. Learning organization
d. Formalization
e. Centralization
f. Organizational design
g. Unity of command
h. Authority

i. Chain of command
j. Span of control
k. Work specialization
l. Departmentalization
m. Cross-functional team
n. Matrix organization
o. Mechanistic organization

_____ 1. The ability to adapt and change with the environment characterizes this type of organization.
_____ 2. The number of subordinates a manager can supervise efficiently and effectively.
_____ 3. The development or changing of an organization's structure.
_____ 4. The degree to which an organization relies on rules and procedures to direct the behavior of employees.
_____ 5. The rights inherent in a managerial position to give orders and expect them to be obeyed.
_____ 6. The concentration of decision-making authority to upper levels in an organization.
_____ 7. The flow of authority from the top to the bottom of an organization.
_____ 8. A structure that is adaptive and flexible.
_____ 9. The degree to which tasks are divided into separate jobs; the division of labor within an organization.
_____ 10. An organization's framework as expressed by its degree of complexity, formalization, and centralization.
_____ 11. An organizational arrangement in which a hybrid grouping of individuals who are experts in various specialties (or functions) work together.
_____ 12. The principle that a subordinate should have one and only one superior to whom he or she is directly responsible.
_____ 13. An organizing approach that assigns specialists from different functional departments to work on one or more projects that are led by a project manager.
_____ 14. A structure that is high in complexity, formalization, and centralization.
_____ 15. The process of grouping individuals into separate units or departments to accomplish organizational goals.

## Essay Questions

1. Describe the five common forms of departmentalization.
   (pp. 268-270, Exhibit 10-2)

2. Explain the concepts of chain of command, authority, and responsibility.
   (p. 270)

3. What are the factors that influence the amount of centralization and decentralization that is appropriate for an organization?
   (p. 272, Exhibit 10-4)

4. Compare and contrast the mechanistic organization and the organic organization.
   (p. 275, Exhibit 10-5)

5. What are the strengths and weaknesses of the simple structure, functional structure, divisional structure?
   (p. 278, Exhibit 10-7)

# Chapter 11  Communication and Information Technology

## Learning Outline

### Understanding Communication
- Explain why effective communication is important for managers.
- Define communication.
- Differentiate between interpersonal and organizational communication.
- Discuss the functions of communication.

### Interpersonal Communication
- Explain all the components of the communication process.
- List the communication methods managers might use
- Describe nonverbal communication and how it takes place.
- Explain the barriers to effective interpersonal communication and how to overcome them.

### Organizational Communication
- Contrast formal and informal communication.
- Explain how communication can flow in an organization.
- Describe the three common communication networks.
- Discuss how managers should handle the grapevine.

### Understanding Information Technology
- Describe how technology affects managerial communication.
- Define e-mail, instant messaging, blogs and wikis, voice-mail, fax, EDI, teleconferencing, videoconferencing, web conferencing, intranet, and extranet.
- Explain how information technology affects organizations.

### Communication Issues in Today's Organizations
- Discuss the challenges of managing communication in an Internet world.
- Explain how organizations can manage knowledge.
- Describe why communicating with customers is an important managerial issue.
- Explain how political correctness is affecting communication.

---

**A Manager's Dilemma**

The NFL is considered financially the best-run professional sports league.  As the chief financial officer of the NFL, Kim Williams must communicate regularly with the owners regarding all financial issues.  Consider the following questions and compare your answer to **Managers Respond** at the end of the chapter.

1. Why is effective communication with team owners important for Ms. Williams?
2. What can Ms. Williams do to improve the effectiveness of her communications with team owners?

---

# Lecture Outline

I.  Understanding Communication.
    A.  Everything a manager does involves communicating, and ineffective communication skills can lead to problems for the manager.
    B.  What Is Communication?
        1.  The transfer and understanding of meaning.
        2.  Effective communication does not equal agreement.
        3.  Communication encompasses both interpersonal communication and organizational communication.
    C.  Functions of Communication.
        1.  Four major functions of communication.
            a.  Control.
            b.  Motivation.
            c.  Emotional expression.
            d.  Information.
    D.  Learning Review.
        *   Explain why effective communication is important for managers.
        *   Define communication.
        *   Differentiate between interpersonal and organizational communication.
        *   Discuss the functions of communication.
    E.  Key Terms.
        1.  Communication – The transfer and understanding of meaning.
        2.  Interpersonal communication – Communication between two or more people.
        3.  Organizational communication – All the patterns, networks, and systems of communication within an organization.

II. Interpersonal Communication.
    A.  The Interpersonal Communication Process.  (Refer to Exhibit 11-1)
        1.  Communication source.
        2.  Message.
        3.  Encoding
        4.  Channel.
        5.  Decoding.
        6.  Receiver.
        7.  Feedback.
        8.  Noise interferes with transmission, receipt, or feedback of a message.
    B.  Methods of Communicating Interpersonally.
        1.  Managers have a wide variety of communication methods.
            a.  Examples of methods include face-to-face, telephone, group meetings, formal presentations, memos, and many others.
        2.  Managers can use 12 questions to evaluate the various communication methods.
        3.  Comparison of various communication methods on the 12 criteria.  (Refer to Exhibit 11-2)
    C.  Nonverbal communication – transmitted without words.

1. Body language.
2. Verbal intonation.

D. Barriers to Effective Interpersonal Communication.
1. Continual potential for distortion.
2. Filtering.
   a. The deliberate manipulation of information to make it appear more favorable to the receiver.
   b. Extent of filtering tends to be a function of the number of vertical levels in the organization and the organizational culture.
   c. Organizational culture encourages or discourages filtering by the behavior it rewards.
3. Emotions.
   a. Extreme emotions hinder effective communication.
   b. It's best to avoid reacting to a message when you're upset.

---

**Managing Workforce Diversity: The Communication Styles of Men and Women**
Deborah Tannen's work shows that the gender differences in communication can pose critical problems. After reading the scenario presented, respond to the following questions.
1. What can be done to combat this problem?
2. Identify an example of a communication problem between you and a member of the opposite sex.

---

4. Information Overload.
   a. The information we have to work with exceeds our processing capacity.
   b. When faced with information overload, people tend to select out, ignore, pass over, or forget information.
5. Defensiveness.
   a. When people feel that they're being threatened, they tend to react in ways that reduce their ability to achieve mutual understanding.
6. Language.
   a. Words mean different things to different people because of diverse backgrounds and jargon.
7. National Culture.
   a. Interpersonal communication is conducted differently around the world.
   b. Individualistic cultures compared to collectivist cultures.
   c. Cultural differences affect the way a manager chooses to communicate.
E. Overcoming the Barriers.
1. Most individuals must hear new information seven times before they understand.
2. Use Feedback.
   a. Feedback reduces misunderstanding and inaccuracies.
   b. Feedback can be verbal or nonverbal.
3. Simplify Language.
4. Listen Actively.

      a.   Listening is an active search for meaning.

      b.   Active listening is enhanced by developing empathy with the sender.

      c.   Active listening behaviors. (Refer to Exhibit 11-3)

   5.  Constrain Emotions.

   6.  Watch Nonverbal Cues.

F. Learning Review.

- Explain all the components of the communication process.
- List the communication methods managers might use.
- Discuss the criteria that help managers evaluate the various communication methods.
- Describe nonverbal communication and how it takes place.
- Explain the barriers to effective interpersonal communication.
- Discuss the ways to overcome the barriers.
- List the active listening barriers.

G. Key Terms.

1. Message – A purpose to be conveyed.
2. Encoding – Converting a message into symbols.
3. Channel – The medium a message travels along.
4. Decoding – Retranslating a sender's message.
5. Communication process – The seven elements involved in transferring meaning from one person to another.
6. Noise – Any disturbances that interfere with the transmission, receipt, or feedback of a message.
7. Nonverbal communication – Communication transmitted without words.
8. Body language – Gestures, facial expressions, and other movements of the body that convey meaning.
9. Verbal intonation – An emphasis given to words or phrases that convey meaning.
10. Filtering – The deliberate manipulation of information to make it appear more favorable to the receiver.
11. Selective perception – When people selectively interpret what they see or hear on the basis of their interests, background, experience, and attitudes.
12. Information overload – The information we have to work with exceeds our processing capacity.
13. Jargon – Specialized terminology or technical language that members of a group use to communicate among themselves.
14. Active listening – Listening for full meaning without making premature judgments or interpretations.

III. Organizational Communication.

A. Formal Versus Informal Communication.

1. Formal communication – any communication that takes place within prescribed organizational work arrangements.

2. Informal communication is not defined by the organization's hierarchy.

      a.   Purposes of informal communication.

         (i)       Satisfy employees' need for social interaction.

(ii)    Improve organizational performance.
B.  Direction of Communication Flow.
   1.  Downward communication.
      a.  Any communication that flows downward from manager to employee.
      b.  Used to inform, direct, coordinate, and evaluate employees.
   2.  Upward communication.
      a.  Communication that flows from employees to managers.
      b.  Gives managers ideas on how things can be improved.
      c.  Extent of upward communication depends on organizational culture.
   3.  Lateral communication
      a.  Communication between employees on the same organizational level.
      b.  Saves time and facilitates coordination.
      c.  Cross-functional teams rely heavily on lateral communication.
   4.  Diagonal communication.
      a.  Communication that cuts across both work areas and organizational levels.
      b.  Facilitated by e-mail.
C.  Organizational Communication Networks.  (Refer to Exhibit 11-4)
   1.  Types of Communication Networks.
      a.  Chain network – Communication flows according to the formal chain of command.
      b.  Wheel network – Communication flows between a leader and a work group
      c.  All-channel network – Communication flows freely among all members of work teams.
      d.  Preferred channel depends on goal.
   2.  The Grapevine
      a.  The informal organizational communication network.
      b.  Grapevine acts as a filter and a feedback mechanism.
      c.  Rumors can never be eliminated entirely.
D.  Learning Review.
   • Contrast formal and informal communication.
   • Explain how communication can flow in an organization.
   • Describe the three common communication networks.
   • Discuss how managers should handle the grapevine.
E.  Key Terms.
   1.  Formal communication – Communication that follows the official chain of command or is required to do one's job.
   2.  Informal communication – Communication that is not defined by the organization's structural hierarchy.
   3.  Downward communication – Communication that flows downward from a manager to employees.
   4.  Upward communication – Communication that flows upward from employees to managers.
   5.  Lateral communication – Communication that takes place among any employees on the same organizational level.

6.  Diagonal communication – Communication that cuts across work areas and organizational levels
7.  Communication networks – The variety of patterns of vertical and horizontal flows of organizational communication.
8.  Grapevine – The informal organizational communication network.

IV. Understanding Information Technology.
    A. Technology is changing the way we live and work.
       1.  Changing technology is a source of environmental uncertainty as well as a source of increased efficiency and effectiveness.
    B. How Technology Affects Managerial Communication.
       1.  Improved manager's ability to monitor individual or team performance.
       2.  Provided information and opportunities for employees.
       3.  Increased accessibility.

---

**Thinking Critically About Ethics**

Internet distractions can prove to be very costly to organizations. After reading the information provided, respond to the following questions.
1.  Do you feel employees should have Internet access at work for personal use? Why or why not?
2.  How can organizations prevent abuse of Internet use in the workplace?

---

       4.  Networked Computer Systems – organization links its computers creating an organizational network.
          a.  E-mail.
          b.  Instant messaging (IM).
          c.  Blogs and wikis.
          d.  Voice mail.
          e.  Fax.
          f.  Electronic data interchange (EDI).
          g.  Teleconferencing, videoconferencing, and Web conferencing.
          h.  Intranet and extranet.
       5.  Wireless Capabilities.
          a.  Networked computer systems require organizations to be connected by wires.
          b.  Wireless communication depends on signals sent through air or space without any physical connection.
    C. How Information Technology Affects Organizations.
       1.  Communication is no longer constrained by geography or time.
       2.  Psychological costs are associated with constant accessibility.
    D. Learning Review.
       • Describe how technology affects managerial communication.
       • Define e-mail, instant messaging, blogs and wikis, voice mail, fax, EDI, teleconferencing, videoconferencing, Web conferencing, intranet, and extranet.
       • Explain how information technology affects organizations.

E. Key Terms.
1. E-mail – The instantaneous transmission of written messages on computers that are linked together.
2. Instant messaging (IM) – Interactive real-time communication that takes place among computer users logged on the computer network at the same time.
3. Blog – An online journal that usually focuses on a particular subject.
4. Wiki – A type of Web site that allows anyone visiting it to add, remove, or otherwise edit the content.
5. Voice mail – A communication system that digitizes a spoken message, transmits it over a network, and stores the message on disk for the receiver to retrieve later.
6. Fax – Communication through machines that allow the transmission of documents containing both text and graphics over ordinary telephone lines.
7. Electronic data interchange (EDI) – A way for organizations to exchange standard business transaction documents using direct computer-to-computer networks.
8. Teleconferencing – Communication system that allows a group of people to confer simultaneously using telephone or e-mail group communications software.
9. Videoconferencing – A simultaneous communication conference where participants can see each other.
10. Web conferencing – Holding group meetings or live presentations over the Internet.
11. Intranet – An organizational communication network that uses Internet technology and is accessible only by organizational employees.
12. Extranet – An organizational communication network that uses Internet technology and allows authorized users inside the organization to communicate with certain outsiders.

V. Communication Issues in Today's Organizations.
  A. Effective communicators are connected to employees, customers, and other stakeholders.
  B. Managing Communication in an Internet World.
    1. New technology has created special communication challenges.
      a. Legal and security issues.
      b. Lack of personal interaction.
  C. Managing the Organization's Knowledge Resources.
    1. Managers need to make it easy for employees to communicate and share their knowledge.
    2. Organizations can build online information databases that employees can access.

3. Organizations can create communities of practice.
   a. Group must actually meet on a regular basis and use information to improve.
   b. It's important to maintain strong human interactions through communication.
   c. These groups face the same communication problems that individuals face.
D. The Role of Communication in Customer Service.
   1. What communication takes place and how it takes place can have significant impact on a customer's satisfaction with the service and the likelihood of being a repeat customer.
   2. Managers need to make sure that employees communicate appropriately with customers.
   3. Three components in any service delivery process.
      a. Customer.
      b. Service organization.
      c. Individual service provider.
   4. Organizations with a strong service culture already value taking care of customers.
   5. The quality of interpersonal interaction between the customer and a contact employee does influence customer satisfaction.
E. "Politically Correct" Communication.
   1. Politically correct vocabulary.
   2. Politically correct language restricts communication clarity.
F. Learning Review.
   • Discuss the challenges of managing communication in an Internet world.
   • Explain how organizations can manage knowledge.
   • Describe why communicating with customers is an important managerial issue.
   • Explain how political correctness is affecting communication.
G. Key Term.
   1. Communities of practice – Groups of people who share a concern, a set of problems, or a passion about a topic, and who deepen their knowledge and expertise in that area by interacting on an ongoing basis.

## Multiple-Choice Questions

1. Communication involves all of the following EXCEPT _____.
   a) information
   b) transfer of meaning
   c) agreement
   d) understanding
   (p. 293)

2. Which of the following is NOT one of the four major functions of communication listed in your text?
   a) Control
   b) Power
   c) Motivation
   d) Emotional expression
   (p. 294)

3. The communication source, the message, encoding, decoding, and the channel are all elements of the _____.
   a) feedback loop
   b) departmentalization
   c) filtering process
   d) communication process
   (p. 294, Exhibit 11-1)

4. Some examples of _____ include background sounds, phone static, and illegible print.
   a) decoding
   b) noise
   c) message enhancers
   d) filtering
   (p. 295)

5. Four conditions influence the effectiveness of an encoded message. Which of the following is one of those conditions?
   a) The skills of the sender
   b) The attitudes and knowledge of the sender
   c) The social-cultural system
   d) All of the above
   (p. 295)

6. The best-known types of nonverbal communication are body language and _____.
   a) verbal intonation
   b) the grapevine
   c) filtering
   d) e-mails
   (p. 298)

7. A college professor who releases the class early after noticing the students' eyes are glassed over and that they are yawning is being alert to _____.
   a) the students' nonverbal communications
   b) the verbal intonation of the class
   c) the selective perception process
   d) the impact of time-space constraint
   (p. 298)

8.  Hand motions, facial expressions, and gestures can convey meaning.  They are
    referred to as _____.
    a)  jargon
    b)  feedback
    c)  body language
    d)  filtering
    (p. 298)

9.  When an employee tells his or her manager exactly what the manager wants to hear,
    the employee is _____ the information.
    a)  encoding
    b)  filtering
    c)  communicating
    d)  decoding
    (p. 298)

10. After completing an employee's performance appraisal, a manager may want to
    convey the findings through multiple channels in order to decrease the potential for
    _____.
    a)  distortion
    b)  filtering
    c)  employee dissatisfaction
    d)  feedback
    (p. 298)

11. When people feel that they're being threatened, they tend to react in ways that reduce
    their ability to achieve mutual understanding.  This is known as _____.
    a)  perceptual screening
    b)  jargon
    c)  defensiveness
    d)  encoding
    (p. 299)

12. One effective method to overcome barriers to communication is _____.
    a)  never to allow jargon to be used
    b)  to use only upward communication methods
    c)  to form isolated work teams
    d)  to utilize the feedback loop
    (pp. 301-303)

13. All of the following are specific behaviors that active listeners demonstrate EXCEPT
    _____.
    a) make eye contact
    b) be sympathetic
    c) don't overtalk
    d) ask questions
    (p. 302, Exhibit 11-3)

14. Which type of communication is NOT defined by the organization's structural hierarchy?
    a) Informal communication
    b) Upward communication
    c) Diagonal communication
    d) Formal communication
    (p. 303)

15. _____ communication is communication that cuts across both work areas and organizational levels.
    a) Horizontal
    b) Diagonal
    c) Formal
    d) Downward
    (p. 305)

16. The _____ network represents communication that flows between a strong leader and others in a work group or team.
    a) wheel
    b) all-channel
    c) grapevine
    d) chain
    (p. 305)

17. The choice of which network to use is contingent on the goal you are attempting to achieve. For example, if you are concerned with high member satisfaction, the _____ network has proven to work best.
    a) ball and chain
    b) wheel
    c) all-channel
    d) grapevine
    (p. 305, Exhibit 11-4)

18. According to the results of a survey described in your text, 63 percent of employees hear about matters through the _____.
    a) windmill
    b) human resources department
    c) chief information officer
    d) grapevine
    (p. 306)

19. _____ is interactive real-time communication that takes place among computer users logged onto the network at the same time.
    a) Voice mail
    b) Instant messaging
    c) E-mail
    d) Electronic data interchange (EDI)
    (p. 307)

20. _____ is a way for organizations to exchange standard business transaction documents using computer-to-computer networks.
    a) Electronic data interchange (EDI)
    b) Teleconferencing
    c) The intranet
    d) Videoconferencing.
    (p. 308)

21. Examples of communication applications of a network system include _____.
    a) teleconferencing
    b) filtering
    c) state and local laws
    d) digital television
    (p. 308)

22. A(n) _____ is a type of Web site that allows anyone visiting it to add, remove, or otherwise edit the content.
    a) intranet
    b) blog
    c) wiki
    d) extranet
    (p. 308)

23. \_\_\_\_\_ are groups of people who share a concern, a set of problems, or a passion about a topic, and who deepen their knowledge and expertise in that area by interacting on an ongoing basis.
    a) Chat rooms
    b) Focus groups
    c) Communication channels
    d) Communities of practice
    (p. 312)

24. Which of the following is NOT one of the three components of any service delivery process?
    a) Feedback system
    b) Customer
    c) Service organization
    d) Individual service provider
    (p. 312)

25. One of the problems with politically correct language is that \_\_\_\_\_.
    a) it purposefully offends a group of people
    b) it restricts communication clarity
    c) it adds words to our vocabulary
    d) the grapevine doesn't understand it
    (p. 313-314)

## True/False Questions

1. T  F  Everything a manager does involves communicating.
        (p. 292)

2. T  F  Perfect communication would be when a transmitted thought or idea was received and understood by the receiver exactly as it was envisioned by the sender.
        (p. 293)

3. T  F  For many employees, their work group is a primary source of social interaction. The function met by this communication is to control member behavior.
        (p. 294)

4. T  F  Encoding is the transfer and understanding of the intended message.
        (p. 295)

5. T  F  Disturbances that interfere with the transmission, receipt, or feedback of a message are called noise.
        (pp. 294-295)

6.  T  F  The attitudes and knowledge of the sender do not influence the effectiveness of the encoded message.
(p. 295)

7.  T  F  Feedback returns the message to the sender and provides a check on whether understanding has been achieved.
(p. 295)

8.  T  F  Managers should ask questions prior to choosing a communication method. When they assess *complexity capacity* they are asking how many different messages can be transmitted with this message.
(p. 296)

9.  T  F  Some of the most meaningful communications are neither spoken nor written.
(p. 298)

10. T  F  Verbal intonation refers to the emphasis someone gives to words or phrases that conveys meaning.
(p. 298)

11. T  F  The deliberate manipulation of information to make it appear more favorable to the receiver is called filtering.
(p. 298)

12. T  F  Extreme emotions are likely to hinder effective communication.
(p. 299)

13. T  F  When individuals experience information overload, they tend to select out, ignore, pass over, or forget information.
(p. 299)

14. T  F  When people feel they are being threatened, they become defensive and engage in behaviors such as verbally attacking others, making sarcastic remarks, and questioning others' motives.
(pp. 299-300)

15. T  F  Collectivist countries employ a more formal manner of interpersonal contact.
(p. 301)

16. T  F  Good feedback means getting only yes-and-no answers.
(p. 301)

17. T  F  Jargon can facilitate understanding when it is used within a group who all know what it means.
(p. 302)

18. T    F    Active listening involves listening for full meaning without making premature judgments or interpretations.
(p. 302)

19. T    F    Formal communication refers to communication that follows the official chain of command or is part of the communication required to do one's job.
(p. 303)

20. T    F    Lateral communication is used to inform, direct, coordinate, and evaluate employees.
(p. 304)

21. T    F    In today's often chaotic and rapidly changing environment, lateral communications are frequently needed to save time and facilitate coordination.
(p. 304)

22. T    F    Of the three common organizational communication networks, the all-channel network provides the highest member satisfaction.
(p. 305, Exhibit 11-4)

23. T    F    Technology, and more specifically information technology, has radically changed the way organizational members communicate.
(p. 307)

24. T    F    In instant messaging (IM), information on transactions is transmitted from one organization's computer system to another through a telecommunications network.
(p. 307)

25. T    F    The intranet is an organizational communication network that uses Internet technology and is accessible only by organizational employees.
(p. 309)

## Match Terms with Definitions

a. Jargon
b. Filtering
c. Nonverbal communication
d. Communication process
e. Message
f. Communication
g. Noise
h. Body language
i. Verbal intonation
j. Grapevine
k. Electronic data interchange
l. Informal communication
m. Active listening
n. Communication networks
o. Intranet
p. Extranet
q. Instant messaging
r. Interpersonal communication
s. Channel
t. Formal communication

_____ 1. Any disturbances that interfere with the transmission, receipt, or feedback of a message.

_____ 2. Listening for full meaning without making premature judgments or interpretations.

_____ 3. Gestures, facial configurations, and other movements of the body that convey meaning.

_____ 4. An emphasis given to words or phrases that conveys meaning.

_____ 5. A purpose to be conveyed.

_____ 6. An organizational communication network that uses Internet technology and is accessible only by organizational employees.

_____ 7. The seven elements involved in transferring meaning from one person to another.

_____ 8. The deliberate manipulation of information to make it appear more favorable to the receiver.

_____ 9. The informal organizational communication network.

_____ 10. A way for organizations to exchange standard business transaction documents using direct computer-to-computer networks.

_____ 11. Communication transmitted without words.

_____ 12. Interactive real-time communication that takes place among computer users logged onto the computer network at the same time.

_____ 13. The transfer and understanding of meaning.

_____ 14. Communication that is not defined by the organization's structural hierarchy.

_____ 15. Specialized terminology or technical language that members of a group use to communicate among themselves.

_____ 16. The variety of patterns of vertical and horizontal flows of organizational communication.

_____ 17. An organizational communication network that uses Internet technology and allows authorized users inside the organization to communicate with certain outsiders.

_____ 18. Communication between two or more people.

_____ 19. The medium a message travels along.

_____ 20. Communication that follows the official chain of command or is required to do one's job.

## Essay Questions

1. Draw and label a diagram of the interpersonal communication process. (pp. 294-295, Exhibit 11-1)

2. List and explain barriers to effective interpersonal communication. (pp. 299–301)

3. The work of Deborah Tannen suggests that men and women have different communication styles. Explain the characteristics of the styles and give examples. (p. 300, Managing Workforce Diversity)

4. Explain active listening and list active listening behaviors. (p. 302, Exhibit 11-3)

5. Describe three common communication networks and evaluate each in terms of speed, accuracy, emergence of leader, and member satisfaction. (p. 305, Exhibit 11-4)

# Chapter 12  Human Resource Management

## Learning Outline

### Why Human Resource Management Is Important; The Human Resource Management Process

- Explain how an organization's human resources can be a significant source of competitive advantage.
- List the eight activities necessary for staffing the organization and sustaining high employee performance.
- Discuss the environmental factors that most directly affect the HRM process.

### Human Resource Planning; Recruitment/Decruitment; Selection; Orientation; Training

- Contrast job analysis, job description, and job specification.
- Discuss the major sources of potential job candidates.
- Describe the different selection devices and which work best for different jobs.
- Tell what a realistic job preview is and why it's important.
- Explain why orientation is so important.
- Describe the different types of training and how that training can be provided.

### Employee Performance Management; Compensation/Benefits; Career Development

- Describe the different performance appraisal methods.
- Discuss the factors that influence employee compensation and benefits.
- Describe skill-based and variable pay systems.
- Describe career development for today's employees.

### Current Issues in Human Resource Management

- Explain how managers can manage downsizing.
- Discuss how managers can manage workforce diversity.
- Explain what sexual harassment is and what managers need to know about it.
- Describe how organizations are dealing with work-life balance issues.
- Discuss how organizations are controlling HR costs.

---

**A Manager's Dilemma**

Rick Waugh, president and CEO of Toronto-based Bank of Nova Scotia, expects that about half of the bank's senior managers will retire in the next 5 to 10 years.  Consider the following questions and compare your answers to **Managers Respond** at the end of the chapter.

1. What can Mr. Waugh do to ensure that his organization maintains a high quality workforce?
2. What can he do to ensure that he has enough people to fill important management roles as others retire?

# Lecture Outline

I. Why Human Resource Management Is Important.
   A. All managers must engage in some HR activities.
   B. Studies have concluded that an organization's human resources can be a significant source of competitive advantage.
   C. Achieving competitive success involves working with and through people and seeing them as partners.
   D. High performance work practices lead to both high individual and high organizational performance. (Refer to Exhibit 12-1)

II. The Human Resource Management Process.
   A. Eight activities of the HRM process. (Refer to Exhibit 12-2)
      1. The first three activities concern identifying and selecting employees.
      2. The next two activities concern orientation and training.
      3. The final three activities concern retention and sustaining high performance.
   B. HRM process is influenced by the external environment.
      1. Factors in the external environment include employee labor unions and governmental laws and regulations, and demographic trends.
         a. Labor union represents workers and seeks to protect their interests through collective bargaining.
         b. Laws and regulations that influence HRM. (Refer to Exhibit 12-3)
            (i)   Hiring and promotion decisions must be made without regard to race, sex, religion, age, color, national origin, or disability.
            (ii)  Affirmative action programs seek to enhance the status of members of protected groups.
            (iii) Managers are not completely free to choose, promote, or fire and need to be aware of the laws.
         c. Demographic trends.
   C. Learning Review.
      • Explain how an organization's human resources can be a significant source of competitive advantage.
      • List the eight activities necessary for staffing the organization and sustaining high employee performance.
      • Discuss the environmental factors that most directly affect the HRM process.
   D. Key Terms.
      1. High-performance work practices – Work practices that lead to both high individual and high organizational performance.
      2. Human resource management process – Activities necessary for staffing the organization and sustaining high employee performance.
      3. Labor union – An organization that represents workers and seeks to protect their interests through collective bargaining.
      4. Affirmative action – Programs that enhance the organizational status of members of protected groups.

III. Human Resource Planning.
    A. Planning can help avoid sudden talent shortages and surpluses.
    B. HR planning can be condensed into two steps.
        1. Assessing current human resources.
        2. Assessing future human resource needs and developing a program to meet those needs.
    C. Current Assessment.
        1. Human resource inventory is derived from forms filled out by employees.
        2. Job analysis defines jobs and behaviors necessary to perform them.
            a. Information is used to prepare a job description that describes job content, environment, and conditions of employment.
            b. Minimum qualifications for a job are given in the job specification.
    D. Meeting Future Human Resource Needs.
        1. Determined by the organization's mission, goals, and strategies.
        2. Demand for employees is a result of demand for the organization's products or services.
        3. Managers identify HR shortages and overstaffing.

IV. Recruitment and Decruitment.
    A. Recruitment.
        1. The process of locating, identifying, and attracting capable applicants.
        2. Evaluation of major sources of potential job candidates. (Refer to Exhibit 12-4)
        3. Web-based recruiting or e-recruiting has become popular.
        4. Employee referrals generally produce the best candidates.
    B. Decruitment.
        1. Reducing the size of the workforce is not a pleasant task.
        2. Decruitment options. (Refer to Exhibit 12-5)

V. Selection.
    A. Selection is the process of screening applicants to ensure that the most appropriate candidates are hired.
    B. Errors in hiring can have far-reaching implications.
    C. What Is Selection?
        1. Selection seeks to predict which applicants will be successful if hired.
        2. Any selection decision can result in four possible outcomes. (Refer to Exhibit 12-6)
            a. A decision is correct if we hire successful applicants or reject unsuccessful applicants.
            b. Problems arise when we reject candidates who would have been successful (reject errors) or accept those who ultimately perform poorly (accept errors).
    D. Validity and Reliability.
        1. Validity is the proven relationship between a selection device and some relevant criterion.
        2. Reliability indicates that the device measures the same thing consistently.

E.  Types of Selection Devices.  (Refer to Exhibit 1-7)
   1.  Application Forms.
   2.  Written Tests.
      a.  Typical  written tests include tests of intelligence, aptitude, ability, and interest.
      b.  Other tests include personality, behavioral, and aptitude tests.
      c.  Legal challenges have been successful when these tests are not job related.
   3.  Performance-Simulation Tests.
      a.  Made up of actual job behaviors.
      b.  Work sampling presents applicant with a set of tasks that are central to the job.
      c.  Assessment centers evaluate managerial potential through job simulation activities.
   4.  Interviews.
      a.  An almost universal selection device.
      b.  May not be the most useful selection device due to interviewer bias and judgment.
      c.  Suggestions to make interviews more valid and reliable.  (Refer to Exhibit 12-8)
      d.  Certain interview questions are illegal.  (See Exhibit 12-9)
      e.  Situational interviews have candidates role play in mock scenarios.
   5.  Background Investigations.
      a.  Two types of background investigations are verifications of application data and reference checks.
         (i)     Verifications of application data are associated with lower employee turnover.
         (ii)    Reference checks are essentially worthless since they tend to be almost universally positive.
   6.  Physical Examination.
      a.  Only a small number of jobs have physical requirements.
      b.  Mostly used for insurance purposes.
F.  What Works Best and When?
   1.  Many selection devices are of limited value to managers.  (Refer to Exhibit 12-10)
   2.  Realistic job preview includes both positive and negative information about a job and company.
   3.  Applicants who have been given a realistic job preview hold lower and more realistic job expectations.

VI. Orientation.
    A.  Orientation is introduction to a new job and organization.
    B.  Two types of orientation.
        1.  Work unit orientation familiarizes the employee with the goals of the work unit, clarifies how the job contributes to the unit's goals and introduces employee to coworkers.
        2.  Organizational orientation informs the new employee about the organization's objectives, history, philosophy, procedures, and rules.
        3.  Managers have an obligation to make the integration of the new employee as smooth and as free of anxiety as possible.
        4.  Successful orientation lowers the likelihood of poor work performance and reduces the probability of a surprise resignation.

VII. Employee Training.
    C.  Employee training is an important HRM activity.
    D.  As job demands change, employee skills have to be altered and updated.
    E.  Types of Training.  (Refer to Exhibit 12-11)

    F.  Training Methods.  (Refer to Exhibit 12-12)
        1.  Traditional methods include on-the-job training, job rotation, mentoring and coaching, experiential exercises, workbooks and manuals, or classroom lectures.
        2.  Technology-based training methods are becoming more widely used because of their accessibility, lower cost, and ability to deliver information.

G. Learning Review.
- Contrast job analysis, job description, and job specification.
- Discuss the major sources of potential job candidates.
- Describe the different selection devices and which work best for different jobs.
- Tell what a realistic job preview is and why it's important.
- Explain why orientation is so important.
- Describe the different types of training and how that training can be provided.

H. Key Terms.
1. Human resource planning – Ensuring that the organization has the right number and kinds of capable people in the right places and at the right times.
2. Job analysis – An assessment that describes a job.
3. Job description – A written statement of what a jobholder does, how it is done, and why it is done.
4. Job specification – A statement of the minimum qualifications that a person must possess to perform a given job successfully.
5. Recruitment – Locating, identifying, and attracting capable applicants.
6. Decruitment – Reducing an organization's workforce.
7. Selection – Screening job applicants to ensure that the most appropriate candidates are hired.
8. Validity – The proven relationship that exists between a selection device and some relevant job criterion.
9. Reliability – The ability of a selection device to measure the same thing consistently.
10. Work sampling – A type of job tryout in which applicants perform a task or set of tasks that are central to it.
11. Assessment centers – Places evaluating managerial potential through job simulation activities.
12. Realistic job preview (RJP) – A preview of a job that provides both positive and negative information about the job and the company.
13. Orientation – Introducing a new employee to his or her job and the organization.

VII. Employee Performance Management.
A. Performance management systems establish performance standards that are used to evaluate employee performance.
B. Performance Appraisal Methods. (Refer to Exhibit 12-13)
1. Written Essays.
2. Critical Incidents.
   a. Evaluator focuses on behaviors that separate effective from ineffective job performance.
   b. Only specific behaviors, not vaguely defined personality traits, are cited.
3. Graphic Rating Scales.
   a. One of most popular performance appraisal methods.
   b. Evaluator rates employee on performance factors using an incremental scale.

4. Behaviorally Anchored Rating Scales
   a. Combine major elements from the critical incident and graphic rating scale approaches.
5. Multiperson Comparisons.
6. Objectives
   a. MBO is also a mechanism for appraising performance.
7. 360-Degree Feedback.
   a. Utilizes information from the full circle of people with whom the manager interacts.
   b. Not appropriate for determining pay, promotion, or terminations, but can be effective for career coaching and helping a manager recognize his or her strengths and weaknesses.

VIII. Compensation and Benefits.
   A. An effective and appropriate compensation system can help attract and retain competent and talented individuals.
   B. Organizational compensation can include many different types of rewards and benefits.
   C. Factors that influence compensation and benefits. (Refer to Exhibit 12-14)
   D. Skill-based pay systems reward employees for job skills and competencies.
   E. Variable pay systems reward employees based on performance.

---

**Managing IT: HR and IT**

E-learning has had many benefits for the firms that use it in their training programs. What are some of the ways that the use of IT has improved the delivery of knowledge, skills, and attitudes to new employees?

---

IX. Career Development.
   A. The term career has several meanings.
   B. The Way It Was.
   C. You and Your Career Today.
      1. Boundaryless career is one in which individuals have increased personal responsibility.
      2. The optimum career choice is one that offers the best match between what you want out of life and your interests, abilities, and market opportunities.
      3. Top 10 important job factors for college graduates. (Refer to Exhibit 12-15)
      4. Suggestions for a successful management career. (Refer to Exhibit 12-16)
   D. Learning Review.
     • Describe the different performance appraisal methods.
     • Discuss the factors that influence employee compensation and benefits.
     • Describe skill-based and variable pay systems.
     • Describe career development for today's employees.
   E. Key Terms.
      1. Performance management system – Establishes performance standards that are used to evaluate employee performance.

2. Written essay – Appraising performance through a written description.
3. Critical incidents – Appraising performance by focusing on critical job behaviors.
4. Graphic rating scales – Appraising performance using a rating scale on a set of performance factors.
5. Behaviorally anchored rating scales (BARS) – Appraising performance using a rating scale on examples of actual job behavior.
6. Multiperson comparisons – Appraising performance by comparing it with others' performance.
7. 360-degree feedback – Appraising performance using feedback from supervisors, employees, and coworkers.
8. Skill-based pay – A pay system that rewards employees for the job skills they can demonstrate.
9. Variable pay – A pay system in which an individual's compensation is contingent on performance.
10. Career – A sequence of positions held by a person during his or her lifetime.

X. Current Issues in Human Resource Management.
   A. Managing Downsizing.
      1. Downsizing is the planned elimination of jobs.
      2. Open and honest communication is critical.
      3. Downsizing is as stressful for the survivors as it is for the victims.
   B. Managing Workforce Diversity.
      1. Recruitment.
         a. Managers need to widen their recruiting net.
         b. Employee referrals tend to produce candidates who are similar to present employees.
      2. Selection.
         a. Selection process should not discriminate.
         b. Applicants should be made comfortable with the organization's culture.
      3. Orientation and Training.
         a. Outsider-insider transition is often more challenging for women and minorities.
         b. Many organizations provide diversity awareness workshops.
      4. Sexual Harassment.
         a. Any unwanted activity of a sexual nature that affects an individual's employment.
         b. Charges are made by both men and women.
         c. Creates an unpleasant work environment and undermines employees' ability to perform their jobs.
         d. Organization needs to educate employees to protect itself.
         e. Workplace Romances.
            (i) Organizations should have clear policies regarding workplace dating and discourage supervisor-subordinate relationships.

5. Work-Family Life Balance.
   a. An organization hires a person who has a personal life outside the office, personal problems, and family commitments.
   b. Family-friendly benefits are offered by many organizations.
   c. Segmentation vs. integration of family and work.
6. Controlling HR Costs.
   a. Controlling health care costs.
   b. Employee pension plans.
C. Learning Review.
   • Explain how managers can manage downsizing.
   • Discuss how managers can manage workforce diversity.
   • Tell what sexual harassment is and what managers need to know about it.
   • Describe how organizations are dealing with work-family life balance issues.
   • Discuss how organizations are controlling HR costs.
D. Key Terms.
   1. Downsizing – The planned elimination of jobs in an organization.
   2. Sexual harassment – Any unwanted activity of a sexual nature that explicitly or implicitly affects an individual's employment, performance, or work environment.
   3. Family-friendly benefits – Benefits which accommodate employees' needs for work-life balance.

## Multiple-Choice Questions

1. Which of the following would be an example of a high-performance work practice?
   a) The use of self-directed work teams
   b) Implementation of employee suggestions
   c) Job rotation
   d) All of the above
   (p. 323, Exhibit 12-1)

2. The human resource management process consists of eight activities necessary for staffing the organization and sustaining high performance. Which of the following is NOT one of those eight activities?
   a) Recruitment
   b) Orientation
   c) Compensation and Benefits
   d) Outplacement
   (p. 324, Exhibit 12-2)

3. _____ is an organization that represents workers and seeks to protect their interests through collective bargaining.
   a) Affirmative action
   b) A labor union
   c) Human resource management
   d) An employment agency
   (p. 323)

4. Affirmative action programs seek to balance _____.
   a) the employment, upgrading, and retention of members from protected groups such as minorities and females
   b) individual goals over organizational goals
   c) the enormous financial costs involved with HRM
   d) laws and regulations
   (p. 324)

5. A(n) _____ is created from forms filled out by employees with information such as name, education, training, and prior employment.
   a) human resource inventory
   b) assessment center
   c) job analysis
   d) pay system
   (p. 326)

6. In setting up operations for a new production company, the personnel manager and area managers have developed a list of jobs needed and behaviors that are necessary to perform those jobs. This is an example of a _____.
   a) job analysis
   b) job specification
   c) human resource inventory
   d) job description
   (p. 326)

7. A statement of the minimum qualifications that a person must possess to perform a given job successfully is a _____.
   a) job specification
   b) job description
   c) job analysis
   d) job definition
   (p. 326)

8. The process of locating, identifying, and attracting capable applicants is called _____.
   a) decruitment
   b) orientation
   c) recruitment
   d) selection
   (p. 327)

9. If an organization has a surplus of employees, management might want to reduce the organization's workforce through _____.
   a) recruitment
   b) decruitment
   c) job analysis
   d) leadership
   (p. 328)

10. Which of the following is a decruitment option?
    a) Employee referrals
    b) Company Web site
    c) Internet
    d) Early retirement
    (p. 328, Exhibit 12-5)

11. Which of the follow decruitment options involves not filling openings created by voluntary resignations or normal retirements?
    a) Firing
    b) Layoffs
    c) Attrition
    d) Job sharing
    (p. 328, Exhibit 12-5)

12. After the recruiting effort has developed a pool of candidates, the next step in the HRM process is to determine who is best qualified for the job. This step is called _____.
    a) attrition
    b) decruitment
    c) selection
    d) orientation
    (p. 329)

13. In selection, when a job candidate is selected but performs poorly, there is _____.
    a) validity
    b) an accept error
    c) reliability
    d) a reject error
    (p. 329, Exhibit 12-6)

14. A reject error occurs when _____.
    a) a candidate is accepted who ultimately performs poorly
    b) a candidate is rejected who would have performed successfully on the job
    c) a candidate is accepted who ultimately performs successfully on the job
    d) a candidate is rejected who would have performed poorly on the job
    (p. 329)

15. A selection device has _____ if there is a proven relationship between the selection device and some relevant job criterion.
    a) validity
    b) reliability
    c) verifiability
    d) authority
    (p. 329)

16. The ability of a selection device to measure the same thing consistently is termed

    _____.
    a) validity
    b) reliability
    c) verifiability
    d) authority
    (p. 330)

17. A strength of a(n) _____ is that it has some validity for jobs with certain physical requirements.
    a) application form
    b) background investigation
    c) physical examination
    d) written test
    (p. 331, Exhibit 12-7)

18. When upper-level candidates are put through two to four days of exercises that simulate real problems they will face during the selection process, these candidates are experiencing _____.
    a) sensitivity training
    b) process consultation
    c) a simulation
    d) an assessment center
    (p. 330)

19. Which of the following is a question that a manager may *not* ask a job candidate?
    a) What is your date of birth?
    b) Would you provide a list of references we can check?
    c) How long were you employed in your last position?
    d) Why did you leave your last position?
    (p. 332, Exhibit 12-9)

20. The most effective selection tool in hiring middle and lower-level managers is _____.
    a) the interview
    b) an assessment center
    c) written tests
    d) the application form
    (p. 333, Exhibit 12-10)

21. Boatwear, Inc., wants to make sure that applicants understand the job's positive and negative aspects. They should include a _____ during the interview.
    a) realistic job preview (RJP)
    b) formal orientation
    c) work sample
    d) written test
    (p. 333)

22. A compensation system can include a number of components including _____.
    a) a job analysis
    b) base wages and incentive payments
    c) a clear promotional track
    d) All of the above
    (p. 339)

23. The factors that influence the design of a compensation system include _____.
    a) stockholders' attitudes towards compensation
    b) highly centralized management
    c) state and local laws
    d) an employee's tenure and performance
    (p. 339, Exhibit 12-14)

24. Which of the following is true regarding sexual harassment?
    a) It is on the decline as companies and employees wise up to the problem.
    b) Employers cannot be held responsible if they have a policy in place and communicated.
    c) It can occur between members of the opposite sex or of the same sex.
    d) It must involve touching to be considered sexual harassment.
    (p. 344)

25. In HRM issues, work-life balance concerns include _____.
    a) multiperson comparisons
    b) critical incidents
    c) family friendly benefits
    d) sexual harassment
    (pp. 345-347)

## True/False Questions

1. T  F  Regardless of an organization's HR policies and practices, every manager should be concerned about human resource decisions in his/her unit.
   (p. 322)

2. T  F  High-performance work practices can lead to both high individual and high organizational performance.
   (p. 323)

3. T  F  The entire HRM process is influenced by the external environment.
   (p. 323)

4. T  F  Affirmative action programs require that all applicants be treated equally.
   (p. 324)

5. T  F  Human resource planning can be condensed in two parts: assessing current human resources and assessing future human resource needs and developing a program to meet those needs.
   (p. 326)

6. T  F  Demand for employees is a result of demand for the organization's products or services.
   (p. 326)

7. T  F  Decruitment is the process of talking applicants out of applying for key positions because they aren't qualified.
   (p. 328)

8. T  F  Selection is a process for screening job applicants to ensure that the most appropriate candidates are hired.
   (p. 328)

9. T  F  Validity refers to the ability of a selection device to measure the same thing consistently.
   (p. 329)

10. T  F  The law prohibits managers from using a test score as a selection device unless there is clear evidence that once on the job, individuals with high scores on this test outperform individuals with low test scores.
    (p. 329)

11. T  F  Work sampling is a personnel selection device in which job applicants are presented with a miniature replica of a job and are allowed to perform tasks central to that job.
    (p. 330)

12. T   F   An interviewer can't ask the question, "Have you ever been arrested?"
(p. 332, Exhibit 12-9)

13. T   F   Reference checks have proven to be essentially worthless in evaluating candidates.
(p. 332)

14. T   F   Studies have shown that application forms and the information they provide are the best indicators for predicting the success of the job candidate.
(p. 333, Exhibit 12-10)

15. T   F   The best selection tool for hiring senior management is an assessment center.
(p. 333, Exhibit 12-10)

16. T   F   The realistic job preview provides positive, but not negative, information about the job and the company to the applicant.
(p. 333)

17. T   F   There are two types of orientation: work unit orientation and organization orientation.
(p. 334)

18. T   F   Job rotation is a type of on-the-job training.
(p. 336, Exhibit 12-12)

19. T   F   A performance appraisal technique which appraises an employee on examples of actual job behavior is the behaviorally anchored rating scale.
(p. 337)

20. T   F   Critical incident is a performance appraisal technique in which an evaluator writes out a description of an employee's strengths and weaknesses, past performance, and potential.
(p. 337)

21. T   F   360-degree feedback is a method that utilizes feedback information from the full circle of people with whom the manager interacts.
(p. 338)

22. T   F   An employee's compensation can be influenced by several factors: the kind of job, the business/industry the company is in, and the degree to which the company is labor or capital intensive.
(p. 339, Exhibit 12-14)

23. T   F   The most important job factor for college graduates is pay and benefits.
(p. 341, Exhibit 12-15)

24. T   F   Acquiring a mentor is suggested for managers who aspire to climb to the top of the career ladder.
(p. 341, Exhibit 12-16)

25. T   F   Sexual harassment is a legal issue that can only be found in U.S. corporations. Other countries are not affected with or by this issue.
(p. 344)

## Match Terms with Definitions

a.  Job rotation
b.  Orientation
c.  Sexual harassment
d.  Skill-based pay
e.  Affirmative action programs

f.  Job analysis
g.  Job description
h.  Job specification
i.  Recruitment
j.  Decruitment

k.  Validity
l.  Reliability
m.  Assessment centers
n.  Realistic job preview
o.  Behaviorally anchored rating scale

_____ 1.  A written statement that describes a job.
_____ 2.  The ability of a selection device to measure the same thing consistently.
_____ 3.  A statement of the minimum acceptable qualifications that an incumbent must possess to perform a given job successfully.
_____ 4.  Locating, identifying, and attracting capable applicants.
_____ 5.  Programs that enhance the organizational status of members of protected groups.
_____ 6.  Evaluating managerial potential through job simulation activities.
_____ 7.  A pay system that rewards employees for the job skills they can demonstrate.
_____ 8.  Introducing a new employee to his or her job and the organization.
_____ 9.  Reducing an organization's workforce.
_____ 10.  Any unwanted activity of a sexual nature that explicitly or implicitly affects an individual's employment, performance, or work environment.
_____ 11.  A preview of a job that provides both positive and negative information about the job and the company.
_____ 12.  An assessment that defines jobs and the behaviors necessary to perform them.
_____ 13.  The proven relationship that exists between a selection device and some relevant criterion.
_____ 14.  On-the-job training in which employees work at different jobs in an area.
_____ 15.  Appraising performance using a rating scale on examples of actual job behaviors.

## Essay Questions

1. Describe the key components of the human resource management process.
   (p. 324, Exhibit 12-2)

2. Explain decruitment and decruitment options.
   (p. 328, Exhibit 12-5)

3. Explain validity and reliability and the importance of each in choosing employee selection devices.
   (pp. 329-330)

4. An interviewer must be careful to ask only legal questions of applicants. Give examples of questions an interviewer can't ask and examples of questions that can be asked.
   (p. 332, Exhibit 12-9)

5. Give the advantages and disadvantages of the following performance appraisal methods: critical incidents, behaviorally anchored rating scales, and 360-degree appraisals.
   (p. 337, Exhibit 12-13)

# Chapter 13 Managing Change and Innovation

## Learning Outline

### Forces for Change; Two Views of the Change Process
- Discuss the external and internal forces for change.
- Contrast the calm waters and white-waters rapids metaphors of change.
- Explain Lewin's three-step model of the change process.
- Discuss the environment that managers face today.

### Managing Organizational Change
- Define organizational change.
- Contrast using internal and external change agents.
- Describe how managers might change structure, technology, and people.
- Explain why people resist change and how resistance might be managed.

### Contemporary Issues in Managing Change
- Explain why changing organizational culture is so difficult and how managers can do it.
- Describe employee stress and how managers can help employees deal with stress.
- Discuss what it takes to make change happen successfully.

### Stimulating Innovation
- Explain why innovation isn't just creativity.
- Explain the systems view of innovation.
- Describe the structural, cultural, and human resource variables that are necessary for innovation.
- Explain what idea champions are and why they're important to innovation.

---

**A Manager's Dilemma**

Alex Lee, president of OXO, is responsible for and guides the company's design process. OXO's design approach is based on the concepts and principles of "universal design." Consider the following questions and compare your answers to **Managers Respond** at the end of the chapter.
1. What is "universal design"?
2. How can Mr. Lee ensure that creativity and innovation continue to thrive in his organization?

---

## Lecture Outline

I. Forces for Change.
   A. External Forces.
      1. Marketplace.
      2. Governmental laws and regulations.
      3. Technology.
      4. Labor markets.
      5. Economic changes.

B.  Internal Forces.
    1.  Strategy.
    2.  Workforce.
    3.  New equipment.
    4.  Employee attitudes.

II.  Two Views of the Change Process.
    A.  The Calm Waters Metaphor.
        1.  Change is seen as an occasional disruption in the normal flow of events.
        2.  Lewin's three-step description of the change process.  (Refer to Exhibit 13-1)
           a.  Unfreeze the status quo.
               (i)        Preparing for needed change.
               (ii)       Can be achieved by increasing the driving forces, by decreasing the restraining forces, or both.
           b.  Change to a new state.
           c.  Refreeze to make the change permanent.
               (i)        Object of refreezing is to stabilize the new situation by reinforcing the new behaviors.
        3.  Calm waters environment isn't what most managers face today.
    B.  White-Water Rapids Metaphor.
        1.  Change is an expected and natural state, and managing change is a continual process.
        2.  Consistent with uncertain and dynamic environments and with a world that's increasingly dominated by information, ideas, and knowledge.
        3.  Flexibility is essential to survival.
    C.  Putting the Two Views in Perspective.
        1.  Not every manager faces constant and chaotic change, but the number who don't is dwindling.
        2.  Change is not an occasional disturbance and managers must be ready to deal with it.
    D.  Learning Review.
        •  Discuss external and internal forces for change.
        •  Contrast the calm waters and white-water rapids metaphors of change.
        •  Explain Lewin's three-step model of the change process.
        •  Discuss the environment that managers face today.

III.  Managing Change.
    A.  What Is Organizational Change?
        1.  Any alteration of workplace people, structure, or technology.
        2.  Outside consultants vs. internal managers as change agents.
        3.  Initiating change involves identifying what types of changes might be needed and putting the change process in motion.

B. Types of Change.
1. The manager's options fall into three categories. (Refer to Exhibit 13-2)
   a. Changing Structure.
      (i) Changing conditions or changing strategies bring about the need to make structural changes.
      (ii) Organization's structure is defined in terms of work specialization, departmentalization, chain of command, span of control, centralization and decentralization, and formalization.
      (iii) Managers can alter structural components.
      (iv) Another option is to make major changes in structural design.
   b. Changing Technology.
      (i) Most early studies dealt with efforts aimed at technological change.
      (ii) Competitive factors require managers to introduce new equipment, tools, or operating methods.
      (iii) Automation.
      (iv) Computerization.
   c. Changing People. (Refer to Exhibit 13-3)
      (i) Changing attitudes, expectations, perceptions, and behaviors.
      (ii) Organizational development focuses on programs to change people and the nature and quality of interpersonal work relationships.
   d. Global OD.
      (i) Some techniques that work for U.S. organizations are inappropriate elsewhere.
      (ii) Managers must take into account cultural characteristics.
C. Managing Resistance to Change.
1. Why People Resist Change.
   a. Uncertainty.
   b. Habit.
   c. Concern over personal loss.
   d. Belief that the change is not in the organization's best interest.
2. Techniques for Reducing Resistance.
   a. Seven actions to deal with resistance. (Refer to Exhibit 13-4)
      (i) Education and communication.
      (ii) Participation.
      (iii) Facilitation and support.
      (iv) Negotiation.
      (v) Manipulation and co-optation.
      (vi) Coercion.
      (vii) Selecting people who accept change.
D. Learning Review.
   • Define organizational change.
   • Contrast using internal and external change agents.
   • Explain how managers might change structure, technology, and people.
   • Explain why people resist change and how resistance might be managed.

E.  Key Terms.
   1.  Organizational change – Any alteration of people, structure, or technology in an organization.
   2.  Change agent – Someone who acts as a catalyst and assumes the responsibility for managing the change process.
   3.  Organizational development (OD) – Techniques or programs to change people and the nature and quality of interpersonal work relationships.

IV. Contemporary Issues in Managing Change.
   A.  Changing Organizational Culture.
      1.  Strong cultures are resistant to change because employees have become committed to them.
      2.  It takes time to change organizational culture.
      3.  Understanding the Situational Factors.
         a.  Cultural change is most likely to take place when:
            (i)  A dramatic crisis occurs.
            (ii) Leadership changes hands.
            (iii)The organization is young and small.
            (iv)The culture is weak.
      4.  How Can Cultural Change Be Accomplished?
         a.  There needs to be a comprehensive and coordinated strategy for managing cultural change.  (Refer to Exhibit 13-5)
         b.  Managers must be patient because change will be slow.

---

**Managing Diversity: The Paradox of Diversity**
Organizations hire diverse individuals because of their unique strengths, yet their diverse behaviors and strengths are likely to diminish in strong cultures as people attempt to fit in.  Consider this paradox of diversity as you think about the roles of diversity and organizational culture in the workplace.

---

   B.  Handling Employee Stress.
      1.  Organizational change causes stress.
      2.  What Is Stress?
         a.  Stress is not necessarily bad.
         b.  Functional stress helps performance.
         c.  Stress is usually associated with constraints and demands.
         d.  Two conditions are necessary for potential stress to become actual stress.
            (i)          Uncertainty over the outcome.
            (ii)         Outcome must be important.
      3.  Causes of Stress.  (Refer to Exhibit 13-6)
         a.  Can be related personal or job-related factors.
         b.  Change of any kind has the potential to cause stress.
      4.  Symptoms of Stress.  (Refer to Exhibit 13-7)
         a.  Physical.
         b.  Physiological.
         c.  Behavioral.

5. Reducing Stress.
   a. Organizational efforts:
      (i)     Begin with employee selection.
      (ii)    Realistic job preview.
      (iii)   Improve communication.
      (iv)    Performance planning program.
      (v)     Job redesign.
   b. Stress in personal life.
      (i)     Manager must consider ethics of intruding.
      (ii)    Employee counseling.
      (iii)   Time management program.
      (iv)    Wellness programs.

---

**Thinking Critically About Ethics**

Although numerous organizations offer stress reduction programs, many employees choose not to participate because they don't want to be perceived as being unable to handle the demands of their job.

1. How can organizations assist employees in being receptive to seeking help with stress management?
2. What ethical responsibilities does an organization have to assist employees with handling stress?

---

C. Making Change Happen Successfully.
   1. Change is a global challenge.
   2. Managers at all organizational levels are involved in the change process.
   3. Managers can increase the likelihood of making change happen successfully.
      a. Help make the organization ready for change. (Refer to Exhibit 13-8)
      b. Understand the manager's role in the process.
      c. Increase the role of individual employees.

---

**Focus on Leadership: Championing Change**

Surviving in an increasingly competitive business environment requires managers to be change leaders. Consider the following question as you think about the role of leadership in the workplace.

1. What can a leader do to ensure that change happens successfully?

---

D. Learning Review.
   - Explain why changing organizational culture is so difficult and how managers can do it.
   - Describe employee stress and how managers can help employees deal with stress.
   - Discuss what it takes to make change happen successfully.
E. Key Term.
   1. Stress – The adverse reaction of people to excessive pressure placed on them from extraordinary demands, constraints, or opportunities.

V. Stimulating Innovation.
  A. Creativity Versus Innovation.
    1. An organization that stimulates creativity develops unique ways to work or novel solutions to problems.
    2. An innovative organization is characterized by its ability to channel creativity into useful outcomes.
  B. Stimulating and Nurturing Innovation.
    1. Systems view of innovation. (Refer to Exhibit 13-10)
    2. Structural variables that stimulate innovation. (Refer to Exhibit 13-11)
      a. Organic structures positively influence innovation.
      b. Easy availability of plentiful resources provides a key building block for innovation.
      c. Frequent interunit communication helps break down barriers to innovation.
      d. Innovative organizations try to minimize extreme time pressures on creative activities.
      e. When an organization's structure provided explicit support for creativity, an employee's creative performance was enhanced.
    3. Cultural Variables.
      a. Acceptance of ambiguity.
      b. Tolerance of the impractical.
      c. Low external controls.
      d. Tolerance of risk.
      e. Tolerance of conflict.
      f. Focus on ends rather than means.
      g. Open-system focus.
      h. Positive feedback.
    4. Human Resource Variables.
      a. Characteristics of innovative organizations.
        (i) Actively promote the training and development of members.
        (ii) Offer high job security.
        (iii) Encourage individuals to become idea champions.
      b. Idea champions have common personality characteristics.
      c. Idea champions display characteristics associated with dynamic leadership.
  C. Learning Review.
    • Explain why innovation isn't just creativity.
    • Explain the systems view of innovation.
    • Describe the structural, cultural, and human resource variables that are necessary for innovation.
    • Explain what idea champions are and why they're important to innovation.
  D. Key Terms.
    1. Creativity – The ability to combine ideas in a unique way or to make unusual associations between ideas.
    2. Innovation – Taking creative ideas and turning them into useful products or work methods.

184

3. Idea champion – Individuals who actively and enthusiastically support new ideas, build support, overcome resistance, and ensure that innovations are implemented.

## Multiple-Choice Questions

1. An example of an internal force for change is _____.
   a) employee attitudes
   b) laws and regulations
   c) technology
   d) economic changes
   (p. 357)

2. External forces for change come from various sources. Which of the following is NOT an external force for change?
   a) Governmental laws and regulations
   b) Labor markets
   c) Strategy
   d) Economic changes
   (p. 356)

3. An example of the _____ part of Lewin's model of change is a worker who accepts the new equipment he uses as the best approach to his job.
   a) change
   b) refreeze
   c) driving force
   d) unfreeze
   (p. 358)

4. A worker attends a seminar related to the use of computer technology in production. This seminar causes the worker to investigate how the technology could be used in his company. The part of Lewin's model that includes this action is _____.
   a) change
   b) refreeze
   c) driving force
   d) unfreeze
   (p. 358)

5. Unfreezing can be achieved by either increasing the driving forces or by _____.
   a) decreasing the restraining forces
   b) maintaining the status quo
   c) governmental regulation
   d) redefining strategy
   (p. 358)

6. The metaphor consistent with uncertain and dynamic environments is _____.
   a) calm waters
   b) sinking ships
   c) white-water rapids
   d) lazy river
   (p. 358)

7. When an outside consultant is hired as the agent for change _____.
   a) external forces have little influence on the organization
   b) he/she is more prone to initiate more drastic changes
   c) he/she is seldom a catalyst for change
   d) he/she usually needs a primary change consultant to lead the change effort
   (p. 361)

8. Tony manages a group of office workers and has decided that he wishes to change their attitudes, expectations, perceptions, and behavior. Which category of change is this?
   a) Structure
   b) Technology
   c) Group
   d) People
   (p. 361, Exhibit 13-2)

9. A technique for managing change that involves changing the attitudes, stereotypes, and perceptions that work groups have of each other is _____.
   a) sensitivity training
   b) process consultation
   c) work redesign
   d) intergroup development
   (p. 363, Exhibit 13-3)

10. People resist change for a number of reasons including _____.
    a) a fear of personal loss
    b) a belief that change emphasizes individual goals over organizational goals
    c) the enormous financial costs involved
    d) All of the above
    (p. 364)

11. A method for reducing resistance to change is _____.
    a) education and communication
    b) negotiation
    c) support and facilitation
    d) All of the above
    (p. 365, Exhibit 13-4)

12. When managers employ direct threats or force on an employee to reduce resistance to change, they are engaging in _____.
    a) coercion
    b) participation
    c) negotiation
    d) manipulation and cooptation
    (p. 365, Exhibit 13-4)

13. A manager who wishes to manage change by changing the organization's culture can choose from a number of techniques, including _____.
    a) sensitivity training
    b) automation or computerization
    c) appoint new leadership with a new vision
    d) process consultation
    (p. 368, Exhibit 13-5)

14. The methods of accomplishing cultural change include _____.
    a) maintaining a narrow span of control
    b) utilizing a group of flexible processes
    c) increasing vertical differentiation
    d) conducting a cultural analysis
    (p. 368, Exhibit 13-5)

15. Which of the following situational factors facilitate cultural change?
    a) The culture is strong.
    b) Leadership remains in the same hands for a long period.
    c) A dramatic crisis occurs.
    d) The organization is large and well-established.
    (p. 367)

16. Which of the following is true about stress?
    a) Personality is the primary cause of stress.
    b) It is not necessarily bad in and of itself.
    c) Potential stress always turns into actual stress.
    d) All of the above are true.
    (p. 369)

17. Symptoms of _____ can be physical, psychological, or behavioral.
    a) stress
    b) organizational dysfunction
    c) technology change
    d) structural change
    (p. 370, Exhibit 13-7)

18. When dealing with employee stress, it is best if managers _____.
    a) minimize communication in order to reduce anxiety
    b) do not provide assistance to those employees
    c) offer employee counseling
    d) discourage employees from talking about their feelings to avoid unethical intrusion
    (p. 370)

19. Stress can be reduced in a number of ways, including _____.
    a) job redesign
    b) the selection process
    c) the use of a realistic job preview
    d) All of the above
    (p. 370)

20. Characteristics of change-capable organizations include all of the following EXCEPT _____.
    a) link the past with the present
    b) make learning a way of life
    c) ensure diverse teams
    d) integrate technology
    (p. 371, Exhibit 13-8)

21. An organization that stimulates creativity is characterized by _____.
    a) developing unique ways of doing work and novel solutions to problems
    b) highly centralized management
    c) a dependence on people change techniques
    d) a high-stress environment due to its ambiguity
    (p. 374)

22. The outcomes of the creative process need to be turned into useful products, services, or work methods, which is defined as _____.
    a) technology
    b) innovation
    c) a learning organization
    d) idea championing
    (p. 374)

23. Innovative organizations are characterized by structural variables that include _____.
    a) emphasis on time pressures and deadlines
    b) limited communication
    c) high formalization and work specialization
    d) the use of cross-functional teams and task forces

    (p. 374, Exhibit 13-11)

24. Innovative organizations are characterized by cultural variables that include _____.
   a) mechanistic structures
   b) centralization of authority
   c) acceptance of ambiguity
   d) a low degree of uncertainty
   (p. 374, Exhibit 13-11)

25. The phenomenon of idea championship is an example of what type of variable that fosters innovation in organizations?
   a) Structural
   b) Technological
   c) Cultural
   d) Human resource
   (p. 376)

## True/False Questions

1. T  F  Fluctuations in labor markets constitute a source of external change.
         (p. 356)

2. T  F  The introduction of new equipment represents an internal force for change.
         (p. 357)

3. T  F  According to Kurt Lewin, successful change involves unfreezing the old behavior and attempting a new behavior.
         (p. 358)

4. T  F  Generally, only upper management is able to act as a change agent in the organization.
         (p. 361)

5. T  F  As change agents, managers should be motivated to initiate change because they are committed to improving their organization's performance.
         (p. 361)

6. T  F  Automation is a technological change that replaces certain tasks done by people with machines.
         (p. 362)

7. T  F  OD techniques that work for U.S. organizations are never appropriate for organizational divisions based in other countries.
         (p. 364)

8. T  F  People resist change because of uncertainty, concern over personal loss, and the belief that the change is not in the organization's best interest.
         (p. 364)

189

9.  T  F  Change replaces the known with ambiguity and uncertainty.
(p. 364)

10. T  F  Cooptation is covert attempts to influence such as twisting or distorting facts,
withholding damaging information, or creating false rumors.
(p. 365, Exhibit 13-4)

11. T  F  Coercion is using direct threats or force.
(p. 365, Exhibit 13-4)

12. T  F  The fact that an organization's culture is made of relatively stable and
permanent characteristics tends to make the culture very resistant to change.
(p. 366)

13. T  F  If, over time, a certain culture becomes inappropriate to an organization and a
handicap to management, there might be little a manager can do to change it,
especially in the short run.
(p. 367)

14. T  F  If a manager wants to make cultural change, she can initiate a reorganization,
introduce new stories and rituals, and appoint new leadership.
(p. 368, Exhibit 13-5)

15. T  F  Any type of stress is considered detrimental and must be eliminated
completely to ensure optimum employee work performance.
(p. 369)

16. T  F  Stress comes from personal factors and/or job-related factors.
(p. 369)

17. T  F  Job-related dissatisfaction, tension, anxiety, irritability, boredom, and
procrastination are psychological symptoms of stress.
(p. 370, Exhibit 13-7)

18. T  F  Behavioral symptoms of stress include changes in metabolism, increased heart
and breathing rates, and headaches.
(p. 370, Exhibit 13-7)

19. T  F  Change-capable organizations continue change efforts in order to exploit new
opportunities.
(p. 371)

20. T  F  An organization that stimulates creativity develops unique ways to work or
novel solutions to problems.
(p. 374)

21. T  F  Organic structures negatively influence innovation.
        (p. 375)

22. T  F  Time pressures spur people to work harder and cause them to be more
        creative.
        (p. 375)

23. T  F  Organizations that foster innovation are intolerant of employee risk taking.
        (p. 375)

24. T  F  An organization's cultural variables that create an acceptance of innovation
        include acceptance of ambiguity, tolerating the impractical, and low external
        controls.
        (pp. 375-376)

25. T  F  Idea champions have common personality characteristics such as extremely
        high self-confidence, persistence, energy, and a tendency toward risk-taking.
        (p. 376)

## Match Terms with Definitions

a.  Idea champion                     e.  Organizational change
b.  Organizational development        f.  Change agents
c.  Creativity                        g.  Stress
d.  Innovation

_____ 1. Techniques to change people and the quality of interpersonal work
          relationships.
_____ 2. The process of taking a creative idea and turning it into a useful product,
          service, or method of operation.
_____ 3. People who act as catalysts and manage the change process.
_____ 4. A dynamic condition in which an individual is confronted with an
          opportunity, constraint, or demand related to what he or she desires and for
          which the outcome is perceived to be both uncertain and important.
_____ 5. Individuals who actively and enthusiastically support new ideas, build
          support, overcome resistance, and ensure that innovations are implemented.
_____ 6. Any alterations in people, structure, or technology.
_____ 7. The ability to combine ideas in a unique way or to make unusual associations
          between ideas.

## Essay Questions

1. What external and internal forces shape an organizational change effort?
   (pp. 356-357)

2. List and explain the reasons people resist change.
   (pp. 364-365)

3. Discuss managerial actions that can reduce resistance to change.
   (p. 365, Exhibit 13-4)

4. What are the conditions within an organization that facilitate cultural change?
   (pp. 367-368)

5. Describe how to handle employee stress, reviewing what it means, its causes, and its signs.
   (pp. 368-370)

# Chapter 14 Foundations of Behavior

## Learning Outline

### Why Look at Individual Behavior?
- Explain why the concept of an organization as an iceberg is important to understanding organizational behavior.
- Describe the focus and the goals of organizational behavior.
- Define the six important employee behaviors that managers want to explain, predict, and influence.

### Attitudes
- Describe the three components of an attitude.
- Discuss the three job-related attitudes.
- Describe the impact job satisfaction has on employee behavior.
- Explain how individuals reconcile inconsistencies between attitudes and behavior.

### Personality
- Contrast the MBTI and the Big Five Model of personality.
- Describe the five personality traits that have proved to be the most powerful in explaining individual behavior in organizations.
- Explain how emotions and emotional intelligence impact behavior.

### Perception
- Explain how an understanding of perception can help managers better understand individual behavior.
- Describe the key elements of attribution theory.
- Discuss how the fundamental attribution error and self-serving bias can distort attributions.
- Name three shortcuts used in judging others.

### Learning
- Explain how operant conditioning helps managers understand, predict, and influence behavior.
- Describe the implications of social learning theory for managing people at work.
- Discuss how managers can shape behavior.

### Contemporary OB Issues
- Describe the challenges managers face in managing Gen Y workers.
- Explain what managers can do to deal with workplace misbehavior.

Orascom Telecom targets markets where populations are large but telephone service and use historically are low. Some of these areas are quite risky, both for the company and for employees themselves. Consider the following questions and compare your answers to **Managers Respond** at the end of the chapter.

1. What characteristics should Naguib Sawiris, CEO of Orascom Telecom, look for in potential employees?
2. How can Mr. Sawiris ensure that his company hires employees with these characteristics?

## Lecture Outline

I. Why Look at Individual Behavior?
   A. Organizational behavior specifically addresses how people behave at work.
   B. Organizational behavior can be likened to an iceberg: a small dimension visible and a much larger portion hidden. (Refer to Exhibit 14-1)
   C. Focus of Organizational Behavior.
      1. Individual behavior.
         a. Based predominantly on contributions from psychologists.
         b. Includes topics such as attitudes, personality, perception, learning, and motivation.
      2. Group behavior.
         a. Based on work of sociologists and social psychologists.
         b. Includes topics such as norms, roles, team building, leadership, and conflict.
   D. Goals of Organizational Behavior.
      1. To explain, predict, and influence behavior.
      2. Six important employee behaviors.
         a. Employee productivity.
         b. Absenteeism.
         c. Turnover.
         d. Organizational citizenship behavior (OCB).
         e. Job satisfaction.
         f. Workplace misbehavior.
   E. Learning Review.
      • Explain why the concept of an organization as an iceberg is important to understanding organizational behavior.
      • Describe the focus and goals of organizational behavior.
      • Define the six important employee behaviors that managers want to explain, predict, and influence.
   F. Key Terms.
      1. Behavior – How people act.
      2. Organizational behavior – The study of how people act at work.
      3. Employee productivity – A performance measure of both efficiency and effectiveness.

4. Absenteeism – The failure to report to work.
5. Turnover – The voluntary and involuntary permanent withdrawal from an organization.
6. Organizational citizenship behavior – Discretionary behavior that is not part of an employee's formal job requirements, but that promotes the effective functioning of the organization.
7. Job satisfaction – An employee's general attitude toward his or her job.
8. Workplace misbehavior – Any form of intentional behavior that has negative consequences for the organization or individuals within the organization.

II. Attitudes.
  A. Made up of three components.
    1. Cognitive component.
    2. Affective component.
    3. Behavioral component.
  B. Three most widely known job-related attitudes:
    1. Job satisfaction.
    2. Job involvement.
    3. Organizational commitment.
  C. Job Satisfaction.
    1. Most people are satisfied with their jobs, although rates of satisfaction are declining.
    2. Job satisfaction tends to increase as income increases.
    3. Global Job Satisfaction.
    4. Satisfaction and Productivity.
       a. Strong correlation between satisfaction and productivity.
       b. Organizations with more satisfied employees tend to be more effective.
    5. Satisfaction and Absenteeism.
       a. Satisfied employees have lower levels of absenteeism, but the correlation isn't strong.
    6. Satisfaction and Turnover.
       a. Satisfied employees have lower levels of turnover while dissatisfied employees have higher levels of turnover.
       b. The employee's level of performance is an important moderator of the satisfaction-turnover relationship.
    7. Job Satisfaction and Customer Satisfaction.
       a. Satisfied employees increase customer satisfaction and loyalty.
       b. Dissatisfied customers can increase an employee's job dissatisfaction.
    8. Job Satisfaction and Workplace Misbehavior.
       a. Dissatisfied employees will respond somehow to their dissatisfaction, but responses vary.
  D. Job Involvement and Organizational Commitment.
    1. Job involvement.
       a. Employees with a high level of job involvement strongly identify with and really care about the kind of work they do.
       b. High levels are related to fewer absences and lower resignation rates.

    2. Organizational Commitment.
      a. Identifying with your employing organization.
      b. Less important than once was.
    3. Perceived organizational support.
      a. High levels of perceived organizational support lead to increased job satisfaction and lowered turnover.
E. Attitudes and Consistency.
    1. People seek consistency among their attitudes.
    2. People seek consistency between their attitudes and behavior.
F. Cognitive Dissonance Theory.
    1. Seeks to explain the relationship between attitudes and behavior.
    2. Individuals seek stability with a minimum of dissonance.
    3. Desire to reduce dissonance is determined by three factors.
      a. Importance of the issue.
      b. The degree of influence that individuals believe they have.
      c. The rewards involved in dissonance.
G. Attitude Surveys.
    1. Example of attitude survey. (Refer to Exhibit 14-2)
    2. Regular use of attitude surveys can alert managers to potential problems early enough to do something about them.
H. Implications for Managers.
    1. Attitudes give warnings of potential problems and influence behavior.
    2. Managers should focus on those factors conducive to high levels of employee satisfaction that are likely to help employees be more productive.
    3. Employees will try to reduce dissonance.
      a. Pressure to reduce dissonance is minimized when employee perceives that it is externally imposed and uncontrollable.
      b. Pressure is also decreased if rewards are significant enough to offset the dissonance.
I. Learning Review.
- Describe the three components of an attitude.
- Explain the three job-related attitudes.
- Describe the impact job satisfaction has on employee behavior.
- Discuss how individuals reconcile inconsistencies between attitudes and behavior.
J. Key Terms.
    1. Attitudes – Evaluative statements - either favorable or unfavorable - concerning objects, people, or events.
    2. Cognitive component – That part of an attitude that's made up of the beliefs, opinions, knowledge, or information held by a person.
    3. Affective component – That part of an attitude that's the emotional or feeling part.
    4. Behavioral component – That part of an attitude that refers to an intention to behave in a certain way.

5. Job involvement – The degree to which an employee identifies with his or her job, actively participates in it, and considers his or her job performance to be important to self-worth.
6. Organizational commitment – An employee's orientation toward the organization in terms of his or her loyalty to, identification with, and involvement in the organization.
7. Perceived organizational support – Employees' general belief that their organization values their contribution and cares about their well-being.
8. Cognitive dissonance – Any incompatibility or inconsistency between attitudes or between behavior and attitudes.
9. Attitude surveys – Surveys that ask employees how they feel about their jobs, work groups, supervisors, or the organization.

III. Personality.
   A. Most often described in terms of measurable traits that a person exhibits.
   B. Myers Briggs Type Indicator (MBTI).  (See Exhibit 14-3)
      1. Four dimensions.
         a. Social interaction.
            (i)        Extrovert.
            (ii)       Introvert.
         b. Preference for gathering data.
            (i)        Sensing.
            (ii)       Intuitive.
         c. Preference for decision making.
            (i)        Feeling.
            (ii)       Thinking.
         d. Style of making decisions.
            (i)        Perceptive.
            (ii)       Judgmental.
         e. Implications for managers.
   C. The Big Five Model.
      1. Validated by research.
      2. Five personality traits.
         a. Extraversion.
         b. Agreeableness.
         c. Conscientiousness.
         d. Emotional stability.
         e. Openness to experience.
      3. Research supports a relationship between personality dimensions and job performance.
   D. Additional Personality Insights.
      1. Five other personality traits that have proved to explain individual behavior in organizations.
         a. Locus of control.
            (i)        Internal.
            (ii)       External.

      b. Machiavellianism.

      c. Self-esteem.

         (i)        High SEs.

         (ii)       Low SEs.

      d. Self-monitoring.

      e. Risk taking.

E. Personality Types in Different Cultures.

   1. Five personality factors in the Big Five Model appear in almost all cross-cultural studies.

   2. There are no common personality types for a given country.

   3. A country's culture influences the dominant personality characteristics of its people.

---

**Focus on Leadership**

Studies have indicated that emotional intelligence (EI) is the best predictor of who will emerge as a leader. Consider what aspects of emotional intelligence make this so as you think about leadership in the workplace.

---

F. Emotions and Emotional Intelligence.

   1. Emotions.

      a. Object specific.

      b. Six universal emotions.

         (i)        Anger.

         (ii)       Fear.

         (iii)     Sadness.

         (iv)     Happiness.

         (v)       Disgust.

         (vi)     Surprise.

      c. People respond differently to identical emotion-provoking stimuli.

   2. Emotional Intelligence (EI).

      a. Five dimensions.

         (i)        Self-awareness.

         (ii)       Self-management.

         (iii)     Self-motivation.

         (iv)     Empathy.

         (v)       Social skills.

      b. EI is positively related to job performance.

G. Implications for Managers.

   1. Major value in understanding personality lies in employee selection.

   2. Holland's Typology. (See Exhibit 14-4)

      a. Personality and occupation should be compatible to produce high satisfaction and low turnover.

H. Learning Review.

- Contrast the MBTI and the Big Five Model of personality.
- Describe the five personality traits that have proved to be the most powerful in explaining individual behavior in organizations.

- Tell how emotions and emotional intelligence impact behavior.
  I. Key Terms.
    1. Personality – The unique combination of emotional, thought, and behavioral patterns that affect how a person reacts and interacts with others.
    2. Big Five Model – Five-factor model of personality.
    3. Locus of control – The degree to which people believe they are masters of their own fate.
    4. Machiavellianism – The degree to which people are pragmatic, maintain emotional distance, and believe that ends justify means.
    5. Self-esteem – An individual's degree of like or dislike for himself or herself.
    6. Self-monitoring – An individual's ability to adjust his or her behavior to external situational factors.
    7. Impression management – When individuals attempt to control the impressions others form of them.
    8. Emotions – Intense feelings that are directed at someone or something.
    9. Emotional intelligence (EI) – The ability to notice and manage emotional cues and information.

IV. Perception.
   A. Individuals may look at the same thing yet perceive it differently.
   B. Factors That Influence Perception.
      1. The Perceiver.
      2. The Target. (Refer to Exhibit 14-5)
      3. The Situation.
   C. Attribution Theory.
      1. Three Factors. (Refer to Exhibit 14-6)
         a. Distinctiveness – refers to whether an individual displays different behaviors in different situations.
         b. Consensus – when everyone who's faced with a similar situation responds in the same way.
         c. Consistency – refers to whether a person engages in behaviors regularly and consistently.
      2. Fundamental attribution error.
      3. Self-serving bias.
   D. Shortcuts Frequently Used in Judging Others.
      1. Assumed similarity.
      2. Stereotyping.
      3. Halo effect.
   E. Implications for Managers.
      1. Employees react to perceptions, not to reality.
      2. Employees organize and interpret what they see, so there is always potential for perceptual distortion.
   F. Learning Review.
      - Explain how an understanding of perception can help managers better understand individual bchavior.
      - Describe the key elements of attribution theory.

199

- Discuss how the fundamental attribution error and self-serving bias can distort attributions.
- Name three shortcuts used in judging others.
G. Key Terms.
  1. Perception – The process of organizing and interpreting sensory impressions in order to give meaning to the environment.
  2. Attribution theory – A theory used to explain how we judge people differently depending on the meaning we attribute to a given behavior.
  3. Fundamental attribution error – The tendency to underestimate the influence of external factors and overestimate the influence of internal factors when making judgments about the behavior of others.
  4. Self-serving bias – The tendency for individuals to attribute their own successes to internal factors while putting the blame for failures on external factors.
  5. Assumed similarity – The belief that others are like oneself.
  6. Stereotyping – Judging a person on the basis of one's perception of a group to which he or she belongs.
  7. Halo effect – A general impression of an individual based on a single characteristic.

V. Learning.
  A. If we want to explain, predict, and influence behavior, we need to understand how people learn.
  B. Operant Conditioning.
    1. Behavior is a function of its consequences.
    2. Research by B.F. Skinner.
    3. Positive reinforcement increases desired behaviors.
    4. Rewards are most effective immediately following desired response.
  C. Social Learning.
    1. Influence of others is central to social learning.
    2. Four processes that determine the influence of a model.
       a. Attentional processes.
       b. Retention processes.
       c. Motor reproduction processes.
       d. Reinforcement processes.
  D. Shaping: A Managerial Tool.
    1. Shaping Behavior.
    2. Four ways to shape behavior.
       a. Positive reinforcement – when a behavior is followed by something pleasant.
       b. Negative reinforcement – rewarding a response with the elimination or withdrawal of something unpleasant.
       c. Punishment – penalizes undesirable behavior.
       d. Extinction – eliminating any reinforcement that's maintaining a behavior.

    E. Implications for Managers.
       1. Managers should reward desired behaviors.
       2. Employees look to managers as role models.
    F. Learning Review.
- Explain how operant conditioning helps managers understand, predict, and influence behavior.
- Describe the implications of social learning theory for managing people at work.
- Discuss how managers can shape behavior.

    G. Key Terms.
       1. Learning – Any relatively permanent change in behavior that occurs as a result of experience.
       2. Operant conditioning – A type of learning in which desired voluntary behavior leads to a reward or prevents a punishment.
       3. Social learning theory – A learning theory that says people can learn through observation and direct experience.
       4. Shaping behavior – Systematically reinforcing each successive step to move an individual closer to the desired behavior.

VI. Contemporary Issues in OB.
    A. Managing Generational Differences in the Workplace.
       1. Just Who Is Gen Y?
          a. Individuals born after 1978.
          b. Want work life to provide wide array of experiences. (Refer to Exhibit 14-7)
       2. Dealing with the Managerial Challenges.
          a. Conflicts can arise over issues including appearance, technology, and management style.
    B. Managing Negative Behavior in the Workplace.
       1. Managers must recognize the existence of negative behavior.
       2. Preventative and responsive actions are needed.
    C. Learning Review.
- Describe the challenges managers face in managing Gen Y workers.
- Explain what managers can do to deal with workplace misbehavior.

## Multiple-Choice Questions

1. The focus of organizational behavior is _____.
   a) individual and group behavior
   b) to predict behavior
   c) to understand behavior
   d) manipulating employee behavior
   (pp. 388-389)

2. High _____ can be a problem because of increased recruiting, selection, and training costs.
   a) employee satisfaction
   b) workplace misbehavior
   c) turnover
   d) productivity
   (p. 389)

3. _____ is discretionary behavior that's not part of an employee's formal job requirements, but which promotes the effective functioning of the organization.
   a) Employee productivity
   b) Organizational citizenship behavior
   c) Community service
   d) Job commitment
   (p. 389)

4. Evaluative statements concerning people, objects, or events are called _____.
   a) perceptions
   b) attitudes
   c) personality traits
   d) dissonance
   (p. 390)

5. The beliefs, opinions, knowledge, or information held by a person is _____.
   a) the behavioral component of an attitude
   b) the cognitive component of an attitude
   c) the affective component of an attitude
   d) cognitive dissonance
   (p. 391)

6. Which is true about the satisfaction-production controversy?
   a) The positive relationship between satisfaction and productivity is strong.
   b) The satisfaction-productivity relationship is stronger when the employee behavior is constrained by outside forces.
   c) Satisfaction-productivity correlations are only important at the individual level.
   d) Satisfaction leads to productivity rather than the other way around.
   (p. 391)

7. Which of the following best describes the relationship between job satisfaction and customer satisfaction?
   a) Satisfied employees increase customer satisfaction and loyalty.
   b) Dissatisfied employees increase customer satisfaction and loyalty.
   c) Dissatisfied customers increase employee satisfaction.
   d) Satisfied customers increase employee dissatisfaction.
   (p. 392)

8. _____ is the degree to which an employee identifies with a particular organization and its goals and wishes to maintain membership in the organization.
   a) Job satisfaction
   b) Job involvement
   c) Organizational commitment
   d) Cognitive dissonance
   (p. 393)

9. Cognitive dissonance _____.
   a) is raising people's awareness of an issue by appealing to their cognitive minds
   b) is primarily an irrational process, which drives people wild until they resolve the contradiction involved
   c) is how people perceive the world and seek to work within it
   d) is any incompatibility between two or more attitudes or between behavior and attitudes
   (p. 394)

10. _____ is the unique combination of psychological characteristics that affect how a person reacts and interacts with others. It is most often described in terms of measurable traits that a person exhibits.
   a) Attitude
   b) Emotional intelligence
   c) IQ
   d) Personality
   (p. 397)

11. Which of the following is NOT one of the dimensions of the MBTI?
   a) Extrovert or Introvert
   b) Sensing or Intuitive
   c) Feeling or Thinking
   d) Masculine or Feminine
   (p. 398)

12. In terms of the MBTI, if two managers were discussing an employee's problem-solving patterns, such as dealing with new problems, etc., the managers would be discussing their _____ dimension.
   a) social interaction
   b) preference for gathering data
   c) preference for decision making
   d) style of making decisions
   (p. 398)

13. The Big Five Model of personality includes the personality dimension of _____, which describes the degree to which someone is responsible, dependable, and achievement oriented.
   a) extroversion
   b) agreeableness
   c) conscientiousness
   d) emotional stability
   (p. 399)

14. Research evidence indicates that employees who rate high on _____ are less satisfied with their jobs, more alienated from the work setting, and less involved in their jobs.
   a) external locus of control
   b) Machiavellianism
   c) internal locus of control
   d) self-esteem
   (p. 400)

15. A worker who has an attitude that "the ends justify the means" is high in _____.
   a) locus of control
   b) self-monitoring
   c) risk taking
   d) Machiavellianism
   (p. 400)

16. It is generally true that in other countries _____.
   a) there is a common personality in each country
   b) national culture can and does influence a dominant personality type
   c) there is no correlation between personality and job satisfaction
   d) there is less willingness to take risks than in the United States
   (p. 402)

17. Self-motivation and empathy are two of the five dimensions of _____.
   a) emotional intelligence
   b) Machiavellianism
   c) positive reinforcement
   d) locus of control
   (p. 404)

18. In Holland's Typology of Personality, the personality type that would do well as a small business manager or lawyer is the _____ personality.
   a) realistic
   b) investigative
   c) conventional
   d) enterprising
   (p. 404, Exhibit 14-4)

19. If we explain why people perceive things differently because of their attitudes, motives, interests, etc., we are basing our understanding of perception on the nature of the _____.
   a) perceiver
   b) target
   c) process
   d) situation
   (p. 406)

20. Tom believes that Jane's recent difficult behavior is the result of the current tension she's experiencing with a poorly performing employee she will probably have to terminate. Tom's attribution of Jane's behavior is based on the factor of _____.
   a) distinctiveness
   b) consensus
   c) stereotyping
   d) consistency
   (p. 407)

21. There are various biases that distort our attributions. If a manager underestimates the influence of internal factors and overestimates the influence of external factors on an employee's behavior, the manager is _____.
   a) demonstrating a self-serving bias
   b) making a fundamental attribution error
   c) misinterpreting the employee's locus of control
   d) assuming similarity
   (pp. 407-408)

22. When a manager judges a potential employee to be just like him, the manager is making the attribution error of _____.
   a) the halo effect
   b) stereotyping
   c) assuming similarity
   d) fundamental attribution
   (p. 408)

23. "Union people expect something for nothing" and "Married people are more stable employees" are examples of _____.
   a) assumed similarity
   b) halo effect
   c) sexual harassment
   d) stereotyping
   (p. 408)

24. _____ says people can learn through observation and direct experience.
   a) Operant conditioning
   b) Selectivity
   c) Shaping
   d) Social learning theory
   (p. 411)

25. _____ is molding workers by guiding their learning in graduated steps.
   a) Operant conditioning
   b) Selectivity
   c) Shaping behavior
   d) Social learning theory
   (p. 411)

## True/False Questions

1. T  F  Characteristics of individual behavior include norms, roles, team building, leadership, and conflict.
   (p. 389)

2. T  F  The behavioral component of an attitude refers to an intention to behave in a certain way toward someone or something.
   (p. 390)

3. T  F  Research shows that satisfied employees have lower levels of absenteeism than do dissatisfied employees, and the correlation is strong.
   (pp. 391-392)

4. T  F  There is little if any relationship between satisfaction and productivity among employees.
   (p. 391)

5. T  F  Job involvement is identifying with your job, and organizational commitment is identifying with your employing organization.
   (p. 393)

6. T   F   When there is inconsistency between an individual's attitudes and behavior, she will take steps to make it consistent either by altering the attitudes or the behavior or by developing a rationalization for the inconsistency.
(pp. 393-394)

7. T   F   High or valued rewards can act to make dissonance less important to the individual.
(p. 395)

8. T   F   Attitude surveys rarely provide managers with valuable insights.
(p. 395)

9. T   F   Personality is most often described in terms of measurable traits that a person exhibits.
(p. 397)

10. T   F   If managers are discussing an employee's ability to socially interact, preference for gathering data, preference in making decisions, etc., they are clearly using a Big Five Model of personality.
(p. 398)

11. T   F   In recent years, research has supported the Myers-Briggs Type Indicator as a means of classifying personality.
(p. 398)

12. T   F   Unlike the MBTI, the Big Five Model of personality has evidence to support its validity.
(pp. 398-399)

13. T   F   People with an internal locus of control believe that others control their lives.
(p. 400)

14. T   F   Individuals who are high in self-esteem (high SEs) will take more risks in job selection and are more likely to choose unconventional jobs than are people who are low SEs.
(pp. 400-401)

15. T   F   Individuals who are high in self-monitoring are capable of presenting striking contradictions between their public persona and their private selves.
(p. 401)

16. T   F   Countries have personality tendencies in that certain nationalities have many more of certain types of personalities.
(p. 402)

17. T   F   Emotional Intelligence (EI) has been shown to be positively related to job
performance at all levels.
(p. 404)

18. T   F   If a manager can match a personality to a job, the employee will be more
likely to be high performing and satisfied.
(p. 404)

19. T   F   Attribution is the process by which individuals give meaning to their
environments by organizing and interpreting their sensory impressions.
(p. 407)

20. T   F   John sees two people frowning in two different meetings.  In the first case he
believes the person to be unhappy with the contents of the conversation and in
the second case he believes that the bright lights in the room are causing the
person to frown.  This is an example of attribution theory.
(p. 407)

21. T   F   "Union people expect something for nothing" is an example of self-serving
bias.
(p. 408)

22. T   F   Operant conditioning argues that behavior is a function of its consequences.
(p. 409)

23. T   F   The use of punishment and extinction do not result in learning by the
employee.
(p. 411)

24. T   F   Generally speaking, both positive and negative reinforcement result in
learning by the employee.
(p. 412)

25. T   F   Pretending that negative behavior in the workplace doesn't exist is an
effective use of extinction to eliminate the misbehavior.
(p. 413)

## Match Terms with Definitions

a. Shaping behavior
b. Social learning theory
c. Operant conditioning
d. Self-serving bias
e. Perception
f. Cognitive component
g. Affective component

h. Cognitive dissonance
i. Attitudes
j. Stereotyping
k. Fundamental attribution error
l. Organizational commitment
m. Machiavellianism
n. Halo effect

o. Self-monitoring
p. Attribution theory
q. Learning
r. Organizational behavior
s. Employee productivity
t. Job satisfaction

_____ 1. A performance measure of both efficiency and effectiveness.
_____ 2. An employee's general attitude toward his or her job.
_____ 3. The part of an attitude made up of beliefs, opinions, knowledge, or information held by a person.
_____ 4. The tendency for individuals to attribute their own successes to internal factors while putting the blame for failures on external factors.
_____ 5. The process of organizing and interpreting sensory impressions in order to give meaning to the environment.
_____ 6. Any incompatibility between two or more attitudes or between behavior and attitudes.
_____ 7. An employee's orientation toward his firm in terms of loyalty to, identification with, and involvement in the organization.
_____ 8. A measure of the degree to which people are pragmatic, maintain emotional distance, and believe that ends can justify means.
_____ 9. The emotional or feeling segment of an attitude.
_____ 10. A general impression of an individual based on a single characteristic.
_____ 11. The tendency to underestimate the influence of external factors and overestimate the influence of internal factors when making judgments about the behavior of others.
_____ 12. The study of the actions of people at work.
_____ 13. A personality trait that measures an individual's ability to adjust his or her behavior to external situational factors.
_____ 14. Any relatively permanent change in behavior that occurs as a result of experience.
_____ 15. A theory used to develop explanations of how we judge people differently depending on the meaning we attribute to a given behavior.
_____ 16. Evaluative statements concerning objects, people, or events.
_____ 17. Judging a person on the basis of one's perception of a group to which he or she belongs.
_____ 18. A type of conditioning in which desired voluntary behavior leads to a reward or prevents a punishment.
_____ 19. People can learn through observation and direct experience.
_____ 20. Systematically reinforcing each successive step that moves an individual closer to the desired response.

**Essay Questions**

1.  The goals of organizational behavior are to explain, predict, and influence behavior. Describe the six employee behaviors that organizational behavior has identified as the most important for managers to explain, predict, and influence.
    (pp. 389-390)

2.  Explain the four dimensions of the MBTI (Myers-Briggs Type Indicator).
    (p. 398)

3.  What are the five dimensions of emotional intelligence? Why is EI important for managers?
    (pp. 402-405)

4.  What is attribution theory, what are its implications for managers, and what shortcuts do managers use in making judgments regarding people?
    (pp. 407-409)

5.  How do operant conditioning and social learning help us or hinder us in our learning? What are the implications for managers?
    (pp. 409-411)

# Chapter 15  Understanding Groups and Teams

## Learning Outline

**Understanding Groups**
- Define the different types of groups.
- Describe the five stages of group development.

**Explaining Work Group Behavior**
- Explain the major components that determine group performance and satisfaction.
- Discuss how roles, norms, conformity, status systems, group size, and group cohesiveness influence group behavior.
- Explain how group norms can both help and hurt an organization.
- Define groupthink and social loafing.
- Describe the relationships between group cohesiveness and productivity.
- Discuss how conflict management influences group behavior.
- Describe the advantages and disadvantages of group decision making.

**Creating Effective Teams**
- Compare groups and teams.
- Explain why teams have become so popular in organizations.
- Describe the four most common types of teams.
- List the characteristics of effective teams.

**Current Challenges in Managing Teams**
- Discuss the challenges of managing global teams.
- Explain the role of informal (social) networks in managing teams.

---

**A Manager's Dilemma**

Dadi Perlmutter leads the Intel chip design group in Haifa, Israel, that was responsible for developing the highly successful Centrino chip.  Consider the following questions and compare your answers to **Managers Respond** at the end of the chapter.

1. What are some of the advantages and disadvantages of maintaining a team so far away from the home office?
2. What can Mr. Perlmutter do to maintain his team's effectiveness at challenging the status quo when new designers join his group?

---

## Lecture Outline

I.  Understanding Groups.
    A.  Individuals act differently in groups than they do when they are alone.
    B.  What Is a Group?
        1.  Formal groups.  (Refer to Exhibit 15-1)
            a.  Defined by the organization's structure.
            b.  Have designated work assignments and specific tasks.

    c.  Appropriate behaviors are established by and directed toward organizational goals.

  2.  Informal groups.

    a.  Occur naturally in the workplace in response to the need for social contact.

    b.  Tend to form around friendships and common interests.

C.  Stages of Group Development.  (Refer to Exhibit 15-2)

  1.  Forming.

    a.  People join the group either because of a work assignment (formal group) or for some other benefit desired (informal group).

    b.  Includes the task of defining the group's purpose, structure, and leadership.

    c.  This stage is characterized by a great deal of uncertainty.

  2.  Storming.

    a.  Stage of intragroup conflict.

    b.  Conflict over who will control the group.

  3.  Norming.

    a.  Close relationships develop and the group demonstrates cohesiveness.

    b.  This stage is complete when group structure solidifies and there is a common set of expectations about correct member behavior.

  4.  Performing.

    a.  Group structure is fully functional and accepted.

    b.  Group energy has moved to performing the task at hand.

    c.  The last stage in the development of permanent work groups.

  5.  Adjourning.

    a.  Temporary groups prepare to disband.

D.  Learning Review.

- Define the different types of groups.
- Describe the five stages of group development.

E.  Key Terms.

  1.  Group – Two or more interacting and interdependent individuals who come together to achieve particular goals.

  2.  Forming – The first stage of group development in which people join the group and then define the group's purpose, structure, and leadership.

  3.  Storming – The second stage of group development which is characterized by intragroup conflict.

  4.  Norming – The third stage of group development which is characterized by close relationships and cohesiveness.

  5.  Performing – The fourth stage of group development when the group is fully functional.

  6.  Adjourning – The final stage of group development for temporary groups during which group members are concerned with wrapping up activities rather than task performance.

II.  Explaining Work Group Behavior.

A.  Major components that determine group performance and satisfaction. (Refer to Exhibit 15-3)

B.  External Conditions Imposed on the Group.

1. Workgroup is a subset of a larger organization.
2. External conditions include overall strategy, authority structures, formal regulations, availability or absence of resources, employee selection criteria, performance management system, organizational culture, and physical layout of the work space.

C. Group Member Resources.
1. Includes members' knowledge, abilities, and skills; and personality characteristics.
2. Group members' knowledge and abilities set parameters on what members can do and how effectively they will perform in a group.
3. Interpersonal skills consistently emerge as important for high performance by work groups.

---

**Managing Workforce Diversity:  The Challenge of Managing Diverse Teams**
The benefits to be gained from the diverse work team far outweigh the effort required to manage and understand them.  After reading the scenario presented to you, respond to the following questions.
1. What are four interpersonal behaviors that are critical to managing diverse work teams?
2. Explain the importance of each of these interpersonal behaviors.

---

D. Group Structure.
1. Roles.
    a. Individuals play multiple roles.
    b. Role conflict.
2. Norms.
    a. Norms dictate factors such as work output levels, absenteeism, promptness, and the amount of socializing allowed on the job.
3. Conformity.
    a. Because individuals want to be accepted by the group to which they belong, they are susceptible to conformity pressures.
    b. Research by Solomon Asch.
        (i)        Current research suggests that levels of conformity have declined.  (Refer to Exhibit 15-4)
    c. Groupthink.

---

**Thinking Critically About Ethics**
Every group has its own unique set of norms.  After reading the scenario presented, respond to the following questions.
1. What are the norms of this group?
2. Should the same rules apply to all group members?
3. If you were the manager of this group, what could you do to alter or change the present habits within the group?

---

4. Status Systems.
    a. Status.
        (i)        Informally conferred.
        (ii)       Formally conferred.
    b. Congruency between status and rewards.
5. Group Size.
    a. Small groups are faster at completing tasks.
    b. Large groups are better at problem solving.
    c. Social loafing.
6. Group Cohesiveness.
    a. Related to group productivity.
    b. Highly cohesive groups are more effective.
    c. Conclusions about cohesiveness and productivity.  (Refer to Exhibit 15-5)

---

**Managing IT: IT and Groups**

Technology has enabled greater online communication and collaboration within groups of all types.  Consider the role of technology-aided collaboration in the increasing mobile and global work environment as you think about IT in the workplace.

---

E. Group Processes.
    1. Group Decision Making.
        a. Managers spend up to 30 hours a week in group meetings.
        b. Advantages of group decisions.
            (i)        Generate more complete information and knowledge.
            (ii)       Generate more diverse alternatives.
            (iii)      Increase acceptance of a solution.
            (iv)       Increase legitimacy.
        c. Disadvantages of group decisions.
            (i)        Time consuming.
            (ii)       Minority domination.
            (iii)      Pressures to conform.
            (iv)       Ambiguous responsibility.
        d. Groups versus individual decision making.  (Refer to Exhibit 15-6)
        e. Techniques for making more creative group decisions.  (Refer to Exhibit 15-7)
    2. Conflict Management.
        a. Conflict refers to perceived incompatible differences resulting in some form of interference or opposition.
        b. Traditional view of conflict.
        c. Human relations view of conflict.
        d. Interactionist view of conflict.
        e. Functional vs. dysfunctional conflicts.

  f. Three types of conflict.
   (i)   Task conflict.
   (ii)   Relationship conflict.
   (iii)   Process conflict.
  g. Conflict Management Techniques. (Refer to Exhibit 15-9)
   (i)   Avoidance.
   (ii)   Accommodation.
   (iii)   Forcing.
   (iv)   Compromise.
   (v)   Collaboration.

F. Group Tasks.
 1. Complexity and interdependence of tasks influence the group's effectiveness.
  a. Simple tasks are routine and standardized.
  b. Complex tasks are novel or nonroutine.
  c. Interdependence increases the need for members to interact.

G. Learning Review.
- Explain the major components that determine group performance and satisfaction.
- Discuss how roles, norms, conformity, status systems, group size, and group cohesiveness influence group behavior.
- Tell how group norms can both help and hurt an organization.
- Define groupthink and social loafing.
- Describe the relationship between group cohesiveness and productivity.
- Discuss how conflict management influences group behavior.

H. Key Terms.
 1. Role –Behavior patterns expected of someone occupying a given position in a social unit.
 2. Norms –Standards or expectations that are accepted and shared by a group's members.
 3. Groupthink – When a group exerts extensive pressure on an individual to align his or her opinions with others' opinions.
 4. Status – A prestige grading, position, or rank within a group.
 5. Social loafing – The tendency for individuals to expend less effort when working collectively than when working individually.
 6. Group cohesiveness – The degree to which group members are attracted to one another and share the group's goals.
 7. Conflict – Perceived incompatible differences that result in interference or opposition.
 8. Traditional view of conflict – The view that all conflict is bad and must be avoided.
 9. Human relations view of conflict – The view that conflict is a natural and inevitable outcome in any group.
 10. Interactionist view of conflict – The view that some conflict is necessary for a group to perform effectively.
 11. Functional conflicts – Conflicts that support a group's goals and improve its performance.

12. Dysfunctional conflicts – Conflicts that prevent a group from achieving its goals.
13. Task conflict – Conflicts over content and goals of the work.
14. Relationship conflict – Conflict based on interpersonal relationships.
15. Process conflict – Conflict over how work gets done.

III. Turning Groups into Effective Teams.
  A. Teams typically outperform individuals when the tasks being done require multiple skills, judgment, and experience.
  B. What Is a Team?
    1. Work teams vs. work groups. (Refer to Exhibit 15-10)
  C. Types of Teams.
    1. Problem-solving teams.
    2. Self-managed work teams.
    3. Cross-functional teams.
    4. Virtual teams.
  D. Creating Effective Teams.
    1. Characteristics of effective teams. (Refer to Exhibit 15-11)
        a. Clear Goals.
        b. Relevant Skills.
        c. Mutual Trust.
        d. Unified Commitment.
        e. Good Communication.
        f. Negotiating Skills.
        g. Appropriate Leadership.
        h. Internal and External Support.
  E. Learning Review.
    • Compare groups and teams.
    • Explain why teams have become so popular in organizations.
    • Describe the four most common types of teams.
    • List the characteristics of effective teams.
  F. Key Terms.
    1. Work teams – Groups whose members work intensely on a specific, common goal using their positive synergy, individual and mutual accountability, and complementary skills.
    2. Problem-solving teams – A team of employees from the same department or functional area who are involved in efforts to improve work activities or to solve specific problems.
    3. Self-managed work team – A type of work team that operates without a manager and is responsible for a complete work process or segment.
    4. Cross-functional team – A type of work team that's composed of individuals from various specialties.
    5. Virtual team – A type of work team that uses computer technology to link physically dispersed members in order to achieve a common goal.

IV. Current Challenges in Managing Teams.
  A. Managing Global Teams.
    1. Drawbacks and benefits of using global teams. (Refer to Exhibit 15-12)
    2. Group member resources in global teams.
    3. Group Structure.
        a. Asch's findings are culture-bound.
        b. Importance of status and status criteria vary between cultures.
        c. Social loafing in individualistic vs. collectivistic societies.
    4. Group Processes.
        a. Language-based communication problems.
        b. Conflict management.
    5. Manager's Role.
        a. Develop group communication skills.
        b. Consider cultural differences.
  B. Understanding Social Networks.
    1. Social network structure.
  C. Learning Review.
    • Discuss the challenges of managing global teams.
    • Explain the role of informal (social) networks in managing teams.
  D. Key Term.
    1. Social network structure – The patterns of informal connections among individuals within a group.

## Multiple-Choice Questions

1. _____ are work groups defined by the organization's structure that have designated work assignments and specific tasks.
   a) Formal groups
   b) Social groups
   c) Cohort groups
   d) Informal groups
   (p. 424)

2. Group energy, in the _____ stage of the group development process, moves from getting to know and understand each other to executing the task at hand.
   a) performing
   b) norming
   c) storming
   d) forming
   (p. 425)

3. The _____ stage of group development is the stage in which close relationships develop and the group demonstrates cohesiveness.
   a) forming
   b) storming
   c) norming
   d) performing
   (p. 425)

4. The last stage in the development of *permanent* work groups is _____.
   a) forming
   b) norming
   c) performing
   d) adjourning
   (p. 426)

5. Gabriella and Garth are evaluating the task-relevant and intellectual abilities of their problem-solving group. These two managers are reviewing the group behavior variable _____.
   a) group processes
   b) group member resources
   c) group tasks
   d) external conditions imposed on the group
   (p. 427)

6. _____ dictate(s) output levels, absenteeism rates, and promptness or tardiness.
   a) Status systems
   b) Norms
   c) Group cohesiveness
   d) Roles
   (p. 429)

7. When a group member withholds ideas that are different or unpopular, the individual is conforming to _____.
   a) the nominal group technique
   b) groupthink
   c) the Delphi technique
   d) electronic meetings
   (p. 431)

8. When a group exerts extensive pressure on the individual to align his or her opinions to conform to others' opinions, this is known as _____.
   a) the Delphi technique
   b) groupthink
   c) status
   d) norming
   (p. 431)

9. _____ can be informally conferred on individuals because of their education, age, skill, or experience.
   a) Status
   b) Norms
   c) Group cohesiveness
   d) Roles
   (p. 431)

10. What impact does group size have on group processes?
   a) The larger the group, the poorer the quality of decisions.
   b) Small groups create the free rider effect.
   c) Large groups gather more information and evaluate more alternatives.
   d) It has no impact on the group processes.
   (p. 432)

11. _____ directly challenges the logic that the group's productivity should at least equal the sum of the productivity of each group member.
   a) Group cohesiveness
   b) Social loafing
   c) Groupthink
   d) Status
   (p. 432)

12. The degree to which members are attracted to a group and share the group's goals is referred to as _____.
   a) social loafing
   b) social facilitation
   c) groupthink
   d) group cohesiveness
   (p. 432)

13. The research on the relationship between group cohesiveness and productivity shows that there will be a strong increase in productivity when cohesiveness is _____ and alignment of group and organizational goals is _____.
   a) high; high
   b) high; low
   c) low; high
   d) low; low
   (p. 433, Exhibit 15-5)

14. Group decision making has a number of advantages, including _____.
   a) it creates esprit de corps
   b) it allows management to think strategically
   c) it facilitates workforce diversity
   d) it provides more complete information
   (p. 434)

15. A company should use teams when it wants _____.
    a) to decrease the costs of decision making
    b) to control the content of decisions
    c) to take advantage of workforce diversity
    d) to create individual responsibility
    (p. 434)

16. Which of the following is an advantage of group decisions over individual decisions?
    a) Saves time
    b) Assigns responsibility
    c) Increases acceptance of a solution
    d) Reduces conflict
    (p. 435, Exhibit 15-6)

17. If a manager believes that group conflict is inevitable and a natural part of group work, he/she has a(n) _____ view of group conflict.
    a) traditional
    b) human relations
    c) interactionist
    d) functional
    (p. 436)

18. Conflicts over content and goals of the work are _____ conflict.
    a) process
    b) task
    c) relationship
    d) traditional
    (p. 436)

19. Bethany is in conflict with other members of her team. She decides to withdraw and let them do whatever they wish. Bethany has chosen a(n) _____ strategy of conflict management.
    a) avoidance
    b) compromising
    c) accommodating
    d) collaborating
    (p. 437, Exhibit 15-9)

20. When all parties to a team conflict decide to give up some part of their needs and concerns in order to come to an agreement, they have chosen a(n) _____ conflict management strategy.
    a) avoidance
    b) compromising
    c) accommodating
    d) collaborating
    (p. 437, Exhibit 15-9)

21. _____ are groups whose members work intensely on a specific common goal using their positive synergy, individual and mutual accountability, and complementary skills.
    a) Work teams
    b) Problem-solving teams
    c) Virtual teams
    d) Cross-functional teams
    (p. 439)

22. _____ bring together the knowledge and skills of individuals from various work areas in order to come up with solutions to operational problems.
    a) Command groups
    b) Cross-functional teams
    c) Self-managed teams
    d) Task forces
    (p. 440)

23. _____ teams operate without a manager and are responsible for a complete work process or segment.
    a) Problem-solving
    b) Self-managed
    c) Cross-functional
    d) Virtual
    (p. 440)

24. In a _____ team, members collaborate online with tools such as wide-area networks, videoconferencing, fax, e-mail, or even Web sites where the team can hold online conferences.
    a) problem-solving
    b) self-managed
    c) cross-functional
    d) virtual
    (p. 440)

25. Which of the following is NOT a characteristic of effective teams?
   a) Mutual trust
   b) Commitment to individual goals
   c) Negotiating skills
   d) Appropriate leadership
   (pp. 440-442)

## True/False Questions

1. T  F  In informal groups, appropriate behaviors are established by and directed toward organizational goals.
   (p. 424)

2. T  F  The five stages of group development are forming, storming, norming, performing, and adjourning.
   (p. 425)

3. T  F  Storming is the first stage of group development characterized by tension but full functioning.
   (p. 425)

4. T  F  The external conditions imposed on a work group may consist of the organization's strategy, authority, structures, formal regulations, etc.
   (p. 427)

5. T  F  A norm is a set of behavior patterns expected of someone occupying a given position in a social unit.
   (p. 427)

6. T  F  Individuals play multiple roles and when confronted by different role expectations, they may experience role conflict.
   (p. 429)

7. T  F  Norms dictate factors such as work output levels, absenteeism, promptness, and the amount of socializing allowed on the job.
   (p. 429)

8. T  F  Solomon Asch's experiment in group conformity showed that individuals can be pressured to conform to group norms even when they know that conformity is wrong.
   (p. 430)

9. T  F  Groupthink is a form of conformity in which group members withhold different or unpopular views in order to give the appearance of agreement.
   (p. 431)

10. T   F   The importance of status varies between cultures.
(p. 431)

11. T   F   When groups are engaged in problem solving, large groups consistently get better results than smaller ones.
(p. 432)

12. T   F   Social loafing results in an individual exerting more energy when working as part of a team than when working alone.
(p. 432)

13. T   F   Research has generally shown that highly cohesive groups are less effective than less cohesive ones.
(p. 432)

14. T   F   If cohesiveness is low and goals are supported, productivity increases, but not as much as when both cohesiveness and goal support are high.
(p. 433, Exhibit 15-5)

15. T   F   Group decisions tend to be faster and bring clearer responsibility for outcomes than nongroup decisions do.
(pp. 434-435)

16. T   F   In the human relations view of conflict, conflict is seen as necessary for a group to perform effectively.
(p. 436)

17. T   F   The traditional view of conflict indicates that all conflict is bad and must be avoided.
(p. 435)

18. T   F   Conflict over how work gets done is referred to as process conflict.
(p. 436)

19. T   F   When group members manage conflict by placing other's needs above their own, they are using accommodation as a conflict management strategy.
(p. 437, Exhibit 15-9)

20. T   F   Compromising is a conflict-resolution technique in which each party gives up something of value.
(p. 437, Exhibit 15-9)

21. T   F   Teams typically outperform individuals when the tasks being done require multiple skills, judgment, and expertise.
(p. 438)

22. T  F  A virtual team is a type of work team that is a hybrid grouping of individuals who are experts in various specialties and who work together on various tasks. (p. 440)

23. T  F  In a work team, the combined individual efforts of team members result in a level of performance that is greater than the sum of those individual inputs. (p. 439)

24. T  F  A team of employees from the same department or functional area who are involved in efforts to improve work activities or to solve specific problems is a self-managed work team. (p. 440)

25. T  F  Effective teams are characterized by high mutual trust among members. That is, members believe in each other's ability, character, and integrity. (p. 440)

# Match Terms with Definitions

a. Group cohesiveness
b. Collaborating
c. Forming
d. Norming
e. Storming
f. Functional conflicts
g. Cross-functional teams

h. Self-managed teams
i. Process Conflict
j. Compromising
k. Adjourning
l. Status
m. Task Conflict
n. Norms

o. Performing
p. Role
q. Group
r. Virtual team
s. Social loafing
t. Conflict

_____ 1. The tendency for individuals to expend less effort when working collectively than when working individually.

_____ 2. The degree to which members are attracted to one another and share the group's goals.

_____ 3. Conflict over content and goals of the work.

_____ 4. The second stage of group development which is characterized by intragroup conflict.

_____ 5. A set of behavior patterns expected of someone occupying a given position in a social unit.

_____ 6. The fourth stage in group development when the group is fully functional.

_____ 7. The final stage in group development for temporary groups, characterized by concern with wrapping up activities rather than task performance.

_____ 8. A prestige grading, position, or rank within a group.

_____ 9. Perceived incompatible differences that result in interference or opposition.

_____ 10. A type of work team that uses computer technology to link physically dispersed members in order to achieve a common goal.

_____ 11. Conflict over how work gets done.

_____ 12. Two or more interacting and interdependent individuals who come together to achieve particular objectives.

_____ 13. Acceptable standards shared by a group's members.

_____ 14. Resolving conflicts by each party giving up something of value.

_____ 15. The first stage in group development during which people join the group and then define the group's purpose, structure, and leadership; characterized by uncertainty.

_____ 16. The third stage of group development, characterized by close relationships and cohesiveness.

_____ 17. A type of work team that operates without a manager and is responsible for a complete work process or segment that delivers a product or service to an external or internal customer.

_____ 18. A type of work team in which a hybrid grouping of individuals who are experts in various specialties (or functions) work together on various organizational tasks.

_____ 19. Resolving conflicts by seeking an advantageous solution for all parties.

_____ 20. Conflict that support a group's goals and improve its performance.

## Essay Questions

1. Discuss the stages of group formation.
   (pp. 425-426, Exhibit 15-2)

2. Discuss the basic group concepts of roles, norms, conformity, and status systems.
   (pp. 429-431)

3. Identify and describe the advantages and disadvantages of group versus individual decision making.
   (pp. 434-435)

4. Explain the traditional, human relations, and interactionist views of conflict.
   (pp. 435-437)

5. What are the characteristics associated with effective teams?
   (pp. 440-442)

# Chapter 16  Motivating Employees

## Learning Outline

**What Is Motivation?**
- Define motivation.
- Explain the energy, direction, and persistence aspects of motivation.

**Early Theories of Motivation**
- Describe Maslow's hierarchy of needs and how it can be used to motivate.
- Discuss how Theory X and Theory Y managers approach motivation.
- Describe Herzberg's motivation-hygiene theory.
- Explain Herzberg's views of satisfaction and dissatisfaction.

**Contemporary Theories of Motivation**
- Describe the three needs McClelland proposed as being present in work settings.
- Explain how goal-setting and reinforcement theories explain employee motivation.
- Describe the job characteristics model as a way to design motivating jobs.
- Discuss the motivation implications of equity theory.
- Contrast distributive justice and procedural justice.
- Explain the three key linkages in expectancy theory and their role in motivation.

**Current Issues in Motivation**
- Describe the cross-cultural challenges of motivation.
- Discuss the challenges managers face in motivating unique groups of workers.
- Describe open-book management and employee recognition, pay-for-performance, and stock option programs.

---

**A Manager's Dilemma**

Tom Depres, president and director of StorageTek's Puerto Rican plant, manages one of *Industry Week's* Best Plants for 2005. His employees are motivated and passionate about their work and have been able to control costs to such an extent that StorageTek's CEO decided not to close the plant and move production to China. What should Mr. Depres do to ensure that his employees continue to put forth their best efforts when giving them more money isn't really an option if they're going to keep costs down?  Compare your thoughts to **Managers Respond** at the end of the chapter.

---

## Lecture Outline

I.  What Is Motivation?
    A.  Motivation is the result of an interaction between a person and a situation.

B.  Three key elements of motivation.
    1.  Energy.
    2.  Direction.
    3.  Persistence.
C.  Learning Review.
    • Define motivation.
    • Explain motivation as a need-satisfying process.
D.  Key Term.
    1.  Motivation – The process by which a person's efforts are energized, directed, and sustained toward attaining a goal.

II. Early Theories of Motivation.
    A.  Maslow's Hierarchy of Needs Theory.  (Exhibit 16-1)
        1.  Proposed that within every person is a hierarchy of five needs.
            a.  Physiological needs.
            b.  Safety needs.
            c.  Social needs.
            d.  Esteem needs.
            e.  Self-actualization needs.
        2.  Each level of need must be substantially satisfied before the next is activated.
        3.  Lower order needs are satisfied externally.
            a.  Physiological needs.
            b.  Safety needs.
        4.  Higher order needs are satisfied internally.
            a.  Social needs.
            b.  Esteem needs.
            c.  Self-actualization needs.
    B.  McGregor's Theory X and Theory Y.
        1.  Theory X presents an essentially negative view of people.
            a.  Assumes workers have little ambition, dislike work, want to avoid responsibility, and need to be closely controlled.
        2.  Theory Y offers a positive view of people.
            a.  Assumes workers can exercise self-direction, accept and actually seek out responsibility, and consider work to be a natural activity.
    C.  Herzberg's Two-Factor Theory.
        1.  Intrinsic factors (motivators) are related to job satisfaction and motivation.
        2.  Extrinsic factors (hygiene factors) are associated with job dissatisfaction.
        3.  Examples of motivators and hygiene factors.  (Refer to Exhibit 16-2)
        4.  View of a dual continuum.  (Refer to Exhibit 16-3)
    D.  Learning Review.
        • Describe Maslow's hierarchy of needs and how it can be used to motivate.
        • Discuss how Theory X and Theory Y managers approach motivation.
        • Describe Herzberg's motivation-hygiene theory.
        • Explain Herzberg's views of satisfaction and dissatisfaction.

E. Key Terms.
  1. Hierarchy of needs theory – Maslow's theory that there is a hierarchy of five human needs: physiological, safety, social, esteem, and self-actualization.
  2. Physiological needs – A person's need for food, drink, shelter, sexual satisfaction, and other physical needs.
  3. Safety needs – A person's need for security and protection from physical and emotional harm.
  4. Social needs – A person's need for affection, belongingness, acceptance, and friendship.
  5. Esteem needs – A person's need for internal factors such as self-respect, autonomy, and achievement, and external factors such as status, recognition, and attention.
  6. Self-actualization needs – A person's need to become what he or she is capable of becoming.
  7. Theory X – The assumption that employees dislike work, are lazy, avoid responsibility, and must be coerced to perform.
  8. Theory Y – The assumption that employees are creative, enjoy work, seek responsibility, and can exercise self-direction.
  9. Motivation-hygiene theory – The motivation theory that intrinsic factors are related to job satisfaction and motivation, whereas extrinsic factors are associated with job dissatisfaction.
  10. Hygiene factors – Factors that eliminate job dissatisfaction, but don't motivate.
  11. Motivators – Factors that increase job satisfaction and motivation.

III. Contemporary Theories of Motivation.
  A. Three-Needs Theory.
    1. David McClelland proposed that there are three acquired (not innate) needs that are major motives for work.
       a. Need for achievement (nAch).
       b. Need for power (nPow).
       c. Need for affiliation (nAff).
    2. Need for achievement has been researched the most.
    3. Needs for affiliation and power are closely related to managerial success.
    4. The Thematic Apperception Test (TAT) measures the level of each need. (Refer to Exhibit 16-4)
  B. Goal-Setting Theory. (Refer to Exhibit 16-5)
    1. Specific goals increase performance and difficult goals, when accepted, result in higher performance than do easy goals.
    2. People do better when they get feedback.
    3. Three other factors that influence the goals-performance relationship.
       a. Goal commitment.
       b. Adequate self-efficacy.
       c. National culture.
    4. Argues that an individual's purpose directs his behavior.

C. Reinforcement Theory.
   1. Argues that behavior is externally caused.
   2. Reinforcers increase the probability that behavior will be repeated.
   3. Ignores goals, expectations, and needs and focuses on what happens to a person when he takes some action.
   4. B.F. Skinner's explanation.
D. Designing Motivating Jobs.
   1. Job Design.
   2. Job Enlargement.
      a. Job scope.
      b. Knowledge enlargement activities.
   3. Job Enrichment.
      a. Increases job depth.
      b. Feedback.
E. Job Characteristics Model (JCM).  (Refer to Exhibit 16-6)
   1. Five core dimensions of any job.
      a. Skill variety.
      b. Task identity.
      c. Task significance.
      d. Autonomy.
      e. Feedback.
   2. Employees are likely to be motivated when they learn that they personally performed well on tasks that they care about.
   3. JCM provides guidance to managers for job design.  (Refer to Exhibit 16-7)
      a. Combine tasks.
      b. Create natural work units.
      c. Establish client relationships.
      d. Expand jobs vertically.
      e. Open feedback channels.
F. Equity Theory.  (Refer to Exhibit 16-8)
   1. Related to the concept of fairness and equal treatment compared with others who behave in similar ways.
   2. How employees act when they perceive inequity.
   3. The referent.
      a. Persons.
      b. System.
      c. Self.
   4. Distributive justice.
   5. Procedural justice.
G. Expectancy Theory.  (Refer to Exhibit 16-9)
   1. Three variables or relationships.
      a. Expectancy or effort-performance linkage.
      b. Instrumentality or performance-reward linkage.
      c. Valence or attractiveness of reward.

2. Key to expectancy theory is understanding an individual's goal and the linkage between effort and performance, between performance and rewards, and between rewards and individual goal satisfaction.
H. Integrating Contemporary Theories of Motivation. (Refer to Exhibit 16-10)
   1. Theories should not be viewed independently.
   2. Examination and explanation of how the theories fit together.
I. Learning Review.
   - Describe the three needs McClelland proposed were present in work settings.
   - Explain how goal-setting and reinforcement theories explain employee motivation.
   - Describe the job characteristics model as a way to design motivating jobs.
   - Discuss the motivation implications of equity theory.
   - Contrast distributive justice and procedural justice.
   - Explain the three key linkages in expectancy theory and their role in motivation.
J. Key Terms.
   1. Three-needs theory – The motivation theory that says three acquired (not innate) needs—achievement, power, and affiliation—are major motives in work
   2. Need for achievement (nAch) – The drive to excel, to achieve in relation to a set of standards, and to strive to succeed.
   3. Need for power (nPow) – The need to make others behave in a way that they would not have behaved otherwise.
   4. Need for affiliation (nAff) – The desire for friendly and close interpersonal relationships.
   5. Goal-setting theory – The proposition that specific goals increase performance and that difficult goals, when accepted, result in higher performance than do easy goals.
   6. Self-efficacy – An individual's belief that he or she is capable of performing a task.
   7. Reinforcement theory – The theory that behavior is a function of its consequences.
   8. Reinforcers – Consequences immediately following a behavior that increases the probability that the behavior will be repeated.
   9. Job design – The way tasks are combined to form complete jobs.
   10. Job scope – The number of different tasks required in a job and the frequency with which those tasks are repeated.
   11. Job enlargement – The horizontal expansion of a job by increasing job scope.
   12. Job enrichment – The vertical expansion of a job by adding planning and evaluating responsibilities.
   13. Job depth – The degree of control employees have over their work.
   14. Job characteristics model (JCM) – A framework for analyzing and designing jobs that identifies five primary job characteristics, their interrelationships, and their impact on outcomes.
   15. Skill variety – The degree to which a job requires a variety of activities so that an employee can use a number of different skills and talents.

16. Task identity – The degree to which a job requires completion of a whole and identifiable piece of work.
17. Task significance – The degree to which a job has a substantial impact on the lives or work of other people.
18. Autonomy – The degree to which a job provides substantial freedom, independence, and discretion to the individual in scheduling work and determining the procedures to be used in carrying it out.
19. Feedback – The degree to which carrying out work activities required by a job results in the individual's obtaining direct and clear information about his or her performance effectiveness.
20. Equity theory – The theory that an employee compares his or her job's input-outcomes ratio with that of relevant others and then corrects any inequity.
21. Referents – The persons, systems, or selves against which individuals compare themselves to assess equity.
22. Distributive justice – Perceived fairness of the amount and allocation of rewards among individuals.
23. Procedural justice – Perceived fairness of the process used to determine the distribution of rewards.
24. Expectancy theory – The theory that an individual tends to act in a certain way based on the expectation that the act will be followed by a given outcome and on the attractiveness of that outcome to the individual.

IV. Current Issues in Motivation.
   A. Cross-Cultural Challenges.
      1. Most current motivation theories were developed in the U.S. by Americans and about Americans.
      2. Examples of American bias.
   B. Motivating Unique Groups of Workers.
      1. Motivating a Diverse Workforce.
         a. Flexibility needed.
         b. Flexible working schedules.
            (i) Compressed workweek.
            (ii) Flexible work hours (flextime).
            (iii) Job sharing.
            (iv) Telecommuting.

---

**Managing Workforce Diversity: Developing Employee Potential**

An important goal for all managers is helping employees develop their full potential. A diverse workforce can present unique problems to managers. After reading the scenario presented, respond to the following questions.
1. Identify ways managers can develop employee potential in a diverse workplace.
2. Why is it so important that managers attempt to accomplish this goal?

---

2. Motivating Professionals.
   a. Professionals have a strong and long-term commitment to their field of expertise.
   b. Job challenge and support motivate professionals, not money and promotions.
3. Motivating Contingent Workers.
   a. Most temporary workers are not temporary by choice.
   b. Involuntarily temporary employees are motivated by the opportunity to become a permanent employee and by opportunities for training.
4. Motivating Low-Skilled, Minimum-Wage Employees.
C. Designing Appropriate Rewards Programs.
   1. Open-Book Management.
      a. Goal is to get employees to think like an owner by seeing the impact their decisions and actions have on financial results.
   2. Employee Recognition Programs.
   3. Pay-for-Performance.
      a. Most compatible with expectancy theory.
      b. Studies indicate pay-for-performance programs work.

---

**Thinking Critically About Ethics**

Performance incentive programs can present an ethical dilemma for employees and managers. After reading the scenario presented to you, respond to the following questions.

1. What ethical issues do you see for (a) the employee, (b) the organization, and (c) the customer.
2. How could an organization design performance incentive programs that encourage high levels of performance without compromising ethics?

---

   4. Stock Option Programs.
      a. Stock options.
      b. Recommendations for designing stock options. (Refer to Exhibit 16-11)
D. Learning Review.
   - Describe the cross-cultural challenges of motivation.
   - Discuss the challenges managers face in motivating today's workforce.
   - Describe open-book management and employee recognition, pay-for-performance, and stock option programs.

E. Key Terms.
1. Compressed workweek – A workweek where employees work longer hours per day but fewer days per week.
2. Flexible work hours (flextime) – A scheduling system in which employees are required to work a certain number of hours per week, but are free, within limits, to vary the hours of work.
3. Job sharing – The practice of having two or more people split a full-time job.
4. Telecommuting – A job approach where employees work at home and are linked to the workplace by computer and modem.
5. Open-book management – A motivational approach in which an organization's financial statements (the "books") are shared with all employees.
6. Employee recognition programs – Personal attention and expressing interest, approval, and appreciation for a job well done.
7. Pay-for-performance programs – Variable compensation plans that pay employees on the basis of some performance measure.
8. Stock options – Financial instruments that give employees the right to purchase shares of stock at a set price.

V. From Theory to Practice:  Suggestions for Motivating Employees.
   A. Recognize Individual Differences.
   B. Match People to Jobs.
   C. Use Goals.
   D. Ensure That Goals Are Perceived as Attainable.
   E. Individualize Rewards.
   F. Link Rewards to Performance.
   G. Check the System for Equity.
   H. Use Recognition.
   I. Show Care and Concern for Your Employees.
   J. Don't Ignore Money.


## Multiple-Choice Questions

1. _____ is the result of an interaction between a person and a situation.
   a) Motivation
   b) Need
   c) Effort
   d) Tension
   (p. 452)

2. Which of the following is NOT one of the three key elements of motivation?
   a) Energy
   b) Organization
   c) Direction
   d) Persistence
   (p. 452)

3. Which of the following is one of Maslow's lower-order needs?
   a) Safety needs
   b) Social needs
   c) Esteem needs
   d) Self-actualization needs
   (p. 454)

4.  Who developed Theory X and Theory Y?
    a) Abraham Maslow
    b) Douglas McGregor
    c) Frederick Herzberg
    d) Victor Vroom
    (p. 454)

5.  Which of the following is an example of Herzberg's hygiene factors?
    a) Achievement
    b) Responsibility
    c) Salary
    d) Growth
    (p. 455, Exhibit 16-2)

6.  Which of the following is NOT one of David McClelland's three needs?
    a) Achievement
    b) Affiliation
    c) Power
    d) Safety
    (p. 456)

7.  If an individual is characterized by a high need for power (nPow), he _____.
    a) desires to make others behave in a way that they would not have behaved otherwise
    b) strives for friendships, prefers cooperative situations, etc
    c) dislikes gambling, accepts personal responsibility, and avoids tasks that are too easy or hard
    d) has a compelling drive to succeed, desires to do something better than others, etc
    (p. 456)

8.  Goal-setting theory ____.
    a) contradicts achievement theory
    b) is not a contingency theory of motivation
    c) deals with people in general and refers to goals that are accepted
    d) is in conflict with expectancy theory
    (p. 458)

9.  _____ is different than other motivational theories in that it suggests individuals are externally rather than internally motivated.
    a) Maslow's needs theory
    b) Goal-setting theory
    c) Achievement theory
    d) Reinforcement theory
    (p. 460)

10. _____ refers to the way tasks are combined to form complete jobs.
   a) Job design
   b) Job scope
   c) Job enlargement
   d) Job enrichment
   (p. 461)

11. In the job characteristics model, if a manager wants to increase the task identity of a job, she should _____.
   a) provide timely and honest feedback to the employee at regular intervals
   b) consolidate the various tasks involved into one job
   c) provide the employee with more freedom and independence
   d) increase the number of skills and talents needed to complete the job
   (p. 461)

12. If a manager vertically loads a job, he/she is increasing the _____ of the job.
   a) boredom
   b) duplication
   c) task identity
   d) autonomy
   (p. 461)

13. Which theory proposes that employees perceive what they get from a job situation in relation to what they put into it and then compare their inputs-outcomes ratio with the inputs-outcomes ratios of relevant others?
   a) Goal setting theory
   b) Equity theory
   c) Expectancy theory
   d) Job characteristics model
   (p. 464)

14. Perceived fairness of the process used to determine the distribution of rewards is _____.
   a) distributive justice
   b) procedural justice
   c) interpersonal justice
   d) referent justice
   (p. 465)

15. The attractiveness of a reward in expectancy theory is the _____ of the reward.
   a) valence
   b) instrumentality
   c) attainability
   d) expectancy
   (p. 466)

16. Central to expectancy theory is _____.
    a) the linkage between effort and performance
    b) the linkage between performance and rewards
    c) the linkage between rewards and individual goal satisfaction
    d) All of the above
    (p. 466)

17. In expectancy theory, _____ is the degree to which the individual believes that performing at a particular level is vital to achieving the desired outcomes.
    a) valence
    b) goal satisfaction
    c) instrumentality
    d) effort-performance linkage
    (p. 466)

18. In the integration of the various theories of motivation, it is evident to see that reinforcement theory _____.
    a) works only with the high achieving, internally motivated person
    b) plays a key role in equity theory and will help good performance to continue
    c) increases the motivation that comes from job satisfaction
    d) does none of the above
    (p. 467, Exhibit 16-10)

19. An effective tool for motivating employees who want to work but can't take a full-time job is _____.
    a) contingency work
    b) flexible work hours
    c) job sharing
    d) compressed workweek
    (p. 470)

20. A full-time employee must work in the office from 9:00 a.m. to 11:00 a.m. each day, but can schedule the rest of her work time to match her needs.  This is an example of _____.
    a) telecommuting
    b) flexible work hours
    c) job sharing
    d) the compressed workweek
    (p. 470)

21. When motivating professionals, it is important to remember that their primary motivator is _____.
    a) money
    b) recognition
    c) power
    d) job challenge
    (pp. 471-472)

22. Contingent workers can be motivated by _____.
    a) the offer of more money
    b) jobs that develop marketable skills
    c) recognition and nonfinancial reward programs
    d) working alongside of permanent employees
    (p. 472)

23. Open-book management is when managers _____.
    a) show respect for all ethnic backgrounds of employees
    b) let the employees set their own goals and compensation
    c) let employees see the firm's financial statements
    d) do all of the above
    (p. 473)

24. Which of the following is an example of a pay-for-performance program?
    a) Piece-rate pay plan
    b) Profit-sharing
    c) Lump-sum bonus
    d) All of the above
    (pp. 474-475)

25. Which of the following is true about matching people with jobs?
    a) There is no direct motivational link in matching people to jobs.
    b) It is very difficult to do, so most managers don't try.
    c) Research shows that this is a powerful motivator.
    d) None of the above is true.
    (p. 477)

## True/False Questions

1. T  F  Level of motivation varies both between individuals and within an individual at different times and in different situations.
       (p. 452)

2. T  F  In general terms, motivation refers to effort exerted toward a goal.
       (p. 452)

3. T  F  In terms of motivation, Maslow argued that needs become dominant in different orders for different people and that several needs could motivate an individual at the same time.
(p. 454)

4. T  F  McGregor believed that Theory X assumptions best captured the true nature of workers and should guide management practice.
(p. 454)

5. T  F  Frederick Herzberg's two-factor theory proposes that intrinsic factors are related to job satisfaction and motivation, whereas extrinsic factors are associated with job dissatisfaction.
(p. 455)

6. T  F  Herzberg's two-factor theory views job satisfaction and job dissatisfaction as being on a continuum where job satisfaction and job dissatisfaction were opposites.
(p. 455)

7. T  F  McClelland's three-needs theory says there are three acquired needs that are major motives in work: the need for achievement, the need for power, and the need for affiliation.
(p. 456)

8. T  F  McClelland's three-needs theory holds that high achievers avoid what they perceive to be very difficult or very easy tasks.
(p. 456)

9. T  F  Goal-setting theory proposes that specific goals increase performance.
(p. 458)

10. T  F  The key to reinforcement theory is its focus on goals and expectations.
(p. 460)

11. T  F  Knowledge enlargement in job design leads to greater employee satisfaction.
(p. 461)

12. T  F  When a manager increases the degree of control an employee has over his/her job by empowering the employee to take over some of the tasks typically done by the supervisor, the manager is using job enlargement to motivate behavior.
(p. 461)

13. T  F  In the job characteristics model, task significance refers to the degree to which a job has a substantial impact on the lives or work of other people.
(p. 461)

14. T    F    Managers can increase employee motivation by creating natural work units and giving the employee "ownership" of the work.
(p. 463)

15. T    F    In equity theory, individuals are concerned only with the absolute rewards they receive for their efforts.
(p. 464)

16. T    F    Interpersonal justice refers to perceived fairness in the amount and allocation of rewards among individuals.
(p. 465)

17. T    F    Key to understanding expectancy theory is understanding an individual's goals.
(p. 466)

18. T    F    The expectancy theory is concerned with perceptions and reality is irrelevant.
(p. 466)

19. T    F    Most current motivation theories have an American bias. The most blatant pro-American characteristic in these theories is the strong emphasis on individualism and quantity-of-life cultural characteristics.
(p. 469)

20. T    F    Central to motivating a diverse workforce is compensation; everyone is motivated by money.
(p. 469)

21. T    F    Flextime is one of the most desired benefits among employees.
(p. 470)

22. T    F    The loyalty of most professionals is to their employing organization, not to their profession.
(p. 472)

23. T    F    The goal of open-book management is to get the employees to think like an owner by seeing the impact their decisions and actions can have on the financial results of the organization.
(p. 473)

24. T    F    Pay-for-performance programs tend to conflict with expectancy theory.
(pp. 474-475)

25. T    F    Stock options are financial instruments that give employees the right to purchase shares of stock at a set price.
(pp. 475-476)

# Match Terms with Definitions

a. Reinforcers
b. Equity theory
c. Task identity
d. Reinforcement theory
e. Task significance
f. Job characteristics model
g. Job depth
h. Self-efficacy
i. Pay-for-performance
j. Goal-setting theory
k. Skill variety
l. Job scope
m. Need for power
n. Need for achievement
o. Stock option program
p. Job enrichment
q. Hygiene factors
r. Motivation
s. Expectancy theory

_____ 1. Behavior is a function of its consequences.

_____ 2. Specific goals increase performance and difficult goals, when accepted, result in higher performance than easy goals.

_____ 3. An individual's belief that he or she is capable of performing a task.

_____ 4. Compensation plans that pay employees on the basis of some performance measures.

_____ 5. The theory that an individual tends to act in a certain way based on the expectation that the act will be followed by a given outcome and on the attractiveness of that outcome to the individual.

_____ 6. The drive to excel, to achieve in relation to a set of standards, to strive to succeed.

_____ 7. The willingness to exert high levels of effort to reach organizational goals, conditioned by the effort's ability to satisfy some individual need.

_____ 8. A compensation program in which employees become part owners of the organization by receiving stock as a performance incentive.

_____ 9. Vertical expansion of a job by adding planning and evaluating responsibilities.

_____ 10. The need to make others behave in a way that they wouldn't have behaved otherwise.

_____ 11. The number of different tasks required in a job and the frequency with which these tasks are repeated.

_____ 12. The degree to which a job requires a variety of activities so that an employee can use a number of different skills and talents.

_____ 13. The degree of control employees have over their work.

_____ 14. A framework for analyzing and designing jobs; identifies five primary job characteristics, their interrelationships, and impact on outcome variables.

_____ 15. Factors that eliminate dissatisfaction.

_____ 16. The degree to which a job has a substantial impact on the lives or work of other people.

_____ 17. The theory that an employee compares his or her job's inputs-outputs ratio to that of relevant others and then corrects any inequity.

_____ 18. Any consequence immediately following a response that increases the probability that the behaviors will be repeated.

_____ 19. The degree to which a job requires completion of a whole and identifiable piece of work.

## Essay Questions

1. Explain McGregor's Theory X and Theory Y.  Which did he believe was true? (pp. 454-455)

2. Describe McClelland's three-needs theory and its implications for managers. (pp. 456-457)

3. Explain the five core dimensions of the job characteristics model (JCM). (pp. 461-464)

4. List and discuss the various flexible working schedules available to organizations. (p. 470)

5. What are the guidelines for motivating employees discussed in your text? (pp. 476-478)

# Chapter 17  Leadership

## Learning Outline

**Who Are Leaders and What Is Leadership**
- Define leaders and leadership.
- Explain why managers should be leaders.

**Early Leadership Theories**
- Discuss what research has shown about leadership traits
- Contrast the findings of the four behavioral leadership theories.
- Explain the dual nature of a leader's behavior.

**Contingency Theories of Leadership**
- Explain how Fiedler's model of leadership is a contingency model.
- Contrast situational leadership theory and the leader participation model.
- Discuss how path-goal theory explains leadership.

**Contemporary Views on Leadership**
- Differentiate between transactional and transformational leaders.
- Describe charismatic and visionary leadership.
- Discuss what team leadership involves.

**Leadership Issues in the Twenty-First Century**
- Tell the five sources of a leader's power.
- Discuss the issues today's leaders face.
- Explain why leadership is sometimes irrelevant.

---

**A Manager's Dilemma**

From the start, MTV was considered hip and cutting edge.  MTV is now over 25 years old and CEO and chairman Judy McGrath's challenge is to keep her employees focused on making sure that MTV stays bold and experimental.  Consider the following questions and compare your answers to **Managers Respond** at the end of the chapter.

1. What skills has Ms. McGrath shown that make her a good leader?
2. What else can she do to be a good team leader, especially with her global employees?

---

## Lecture Outline

I. Who Are Leaders and What Is Leadership?
   A. Ideally, all managers should be leaders.
   B. Groups often have informal leaders who emerge.
   C. Learning Review.
- Define leaders and leadership.
- Explain why managers should be leaders.

D. Key Terms.
   1. Leader – Someone who can influence others and who has managerial authority.
   2. Leadership – The process of influencing a group to achieve goals.

II. Early Leadership Theories.
  A. Trait Theories.
    1. Focus on characteristics that might be used to differentiate leaders from nonleaders.
    2. It proved impossible to identify one set of traits that would always differentiate leaders from nonleaders.
    3. Seven Traits Associated with Leadership. (Refer to Exhibit 17-1)
      a. Drive.
      b. Desire to lead.
      c. Honesty and integrity.
      d. Self-confidence.
      e. Intelligence.
      f. Job-relevant knowledge.
      g. Extraversion.
    4. Traits alone were not sufficient for explaining effective leadership.
  B. Behavioral Theories. (Refer to Exhibit 17-2)
    1. University of Iowa Studies.
      a. Explored three leadership styles.
        (i) Autocratic.
        (ii) Democratic.
        (iii) Laissez-faire.
      b. Group members' satisfaction levels were higher under democratic versus autocratic leaders.
    2. The Ohio State Studies.
      a. Two dimensions of leader behavior.
        (i) Initiating Structure.
        (ii) Consideration.
      b. High-high leaders achieved high group task performance and satisfaction more frequently than others.
    3. University of Michigan Studies.
      a. Two dimensions of leadership behavior.
        (i) Employee-oriented emphasized interpersonal relationships.
        (ii) Production-oriented emphasized accomplishing group's tasks.
      b. Conclusions favored leaders who were employee oriented.
    4. The Managerial Grid. (Refer to Exhibit 17-3)
      a. Two behavioral dimensions.
        (i) Concern for people.
        (ii) Concern for production.
      b. Researchers concluded 9,9 style was best.
      c. No evidence supports conclusion of researchers.

C. Learning Review.
- Discuss what research has shown about leadership traits.
- Contrast the findings of the four behavioral leadership theories.
- Explain the dual nature of a leader's behavior.

D. Key Terms.
1. Behavioral theories – Leadership theories that identified behaviors that differentiated effective leaders from ineffective leaders.
2. Autocratic style – A leader who tended to centralize authority, dictate work methods, make unilateral decisions, and limit employee participation.
3. Democratic style – A leader who tended to involve employees in decision making, delegate authority, encourage participation in deciding work methods and goals, and use feedback as an opportunity for coaching employees.
4. Laissez-faire style – A leader who generally gave the group complete freedom to make decisions and complete the work in whatever way it saw fit.
5. Initiating structure – The extent to which a leader defined and structured his or her role and the roles of group members.
6. Consideration – The extent to which a leader had job relationships characterized by mutual trust and respect for group members' ideas and feelings.
7. High-high leader – A leader high in both initiating structure and consideration behaviors.
8. Managerial grid – A grid of two leadership behaviors—concern for people and concern for production—which resulted in five different leadership styles.

III. Contingency Theories of Leadership.
A. Contingency theories attempt to answer the *if-then* contingencies.
B. The Fiedler Model.
1. Proposed that effective group performance depended on the proper match between the leader's style and the situation. (Refer to Exhibit 17-4)
2. Least-preferred coworker (LPC) questionnaire developed to measure a leader's style.
   a. High LPC leaders were relationship oriented.
   b. Low LPC leaders labeled as task oriented.
3. Three key situational factors.
   a. Leader-member relations.
   b. Task structure.
   c. Position power.
4. Leadership style considered to be fixed.
C. Hersey and Blanchard's Situational Leadership Theory.
1. Focuses on followers' readiness.
2. Two leadership dimensions.
   a. Task.
   b. Relationship.

3. Four leadership styles.
    a. Telling.
    b. Selling.
    c. Participating.
    d. Delegating.
4. Four stages of follower readiness.
    a. R1 – unable and unwilling.
    b. R2 – unable but willing.
    c. R3 – able but unwilling.
    d. R4 – able and willing.
D. Leader Participation Model. (Refer to Exhibits 17-5 and 17-6)
    1. Leader behavior must adjust to reflect the task structure.
    2. Normative model that provides a set of rules.
E. Path-Goal Model.
    1. It's the leader's job to assist followers in attaining goals.
    2. Takes key elements from the expectancy theory of motivation.
    3. Four leadership behaviors.
        a. Directive leader.
        b. Supportive leader.
        c. Participative leader.
        d. Achievement-oriented leader
    4. Assumed leadership style is flexible.
    5. Two situational variables moderate the leadership behavior-outcome relationship. (Refer to Exhibit 17-7)
        a. Environment.
        b. Follower.
    6. Examples of predictions from path-goal theory.
F. Learning Review.
    • Explain how Fiedler's model of leadership is a contingency model.
    • Contrast situational leadership theory and the leadership participation model.
    • Discuss how path-goal theory explains leadership.
G. Key Terms.
    1. Fiedler contingency model – A contingency theory that proposed that effective group performance depended upon the proper match between a leader's style of interacting with his or her followers and the degree to which the situation allows the leader to control and influence.
    2. Least-preferred coworker (LPC) questionnaire – A questionnaire that measured whether a leader was task or relationship oriented.
    3. Leader-member relations – One of Fiedler's situational contingencies that described the degree of confidence, trust, and respect employees had for their leader.
    4. Task structure – One of Fiedler's situational contingencies that described the degree to which job assignments were formalized and procedurized.
    5. Position power – One of Fiedler's situational contingencies that described the degree of influence a leader had over power-based activities such as hiring, firing, discipline, promotions, and salary increases.

6. Situational leadership theory (SLT) – A leadership contingency theory that focuses on followers' readiness.
7. Readiness – The extent to which people have the ability and willingness to accomplish a specific task.
8. Leader participation model – A leadership contingency model that related leadership behavior and participation in decision making.
9. Path-goal theory – A leadership theory that says it's the leader's job to assist his or her followers in attaining their goals and to provide the direction or support needed to ensure that their goals are compatible with the overall objectives of the group or organization.

IV. Contemporary Views on Leadership
   A. Transformational-Transactional Leadership.
      1. Transactional leaders.
      2. Transformational leaders.
      3. Transformational leadership is built on top of transactional leadership.
      4. Evidence supports that transformational leadership is superior.
   B. Charismatic-Visionary Leadership.
      1. Charismatic leaders.
      2. Characteristics of charismatic leaders.
          (i)      Have a vision.
          (ii)     Able to articulate the vision.
          (iii)    Willing to take risks.
          (iv)   Sensitive to both environmental constraints and follower needs.
          (v)      Exhibit behaviors that are out of the ordinary.
        b. Correlated to high performance and follower satisfaction.
      3. Visionary leadership goes beyond charisma.
        a. Qualities of visionary leaders.
          (i)      Ability to explain the vision to others.
          (ii)     Ability to express the vision not just verbally but through behavior.
          (iii)    Ability to extend or apply the vision to different leadership contexts.
   C. Team Leadership.
      1. Role of team leader is different from the traditional leadership role.
      2. Managers must learn new skills to be team leaders.
      3. Common roles. (Refer to Exhibit 17-8)
        a. Liaison with external constituencies.
        b. Troubleshooter.
        c. Conflict manager.
        d. Coach.
   D. Learning Review.
      • Differentiate between transactional and transformational leaders.
      • Describe charismatic and visionary leadership.
      • Discuss what team leadership involves.
   E. Key Terms.

1. Transactional leaders – Leaders who lead primarily by using social exchange (or transactions).
2. Transformational leaders – Leaders who stimulate and inspire (transform) followers to achieve extraordinary outcomes.
3. Charismatic leader – An enthusiastic, self-confident leader whose personality and actions influence people to behave in certain ways.
4. Visionary leadership – The ability to create and articulate a realistic, credible, and attractive vision of the future that improves upon the present situation.

V. Leadership Issues in the Twenty-First Century.
   A. Managing Power.
      1. Five sources of leader power.
         a. Legitimate power.
         b. Coercive power.
         c. Reward power.
         d. Expert power.
         e. Referent power.

---

**Thinking Critically About Ethics**
Read this scenario about an ethical dilemma and respond to the following questions.
1. Identify the type of power being displayed by the colleague.
2. What can be done to effectively handle this situation?

---

   B. Developing Trust.
      1. Leaders must build trust and credibility.
      2. Honesty is the number-one characteristic of admired leaders.
      3. Credibility involves honesty, competence, and ability to inspire.
      4. Five dimensions of trust.
         a. Integrity.
         b. Competence.
         c. Consistency.
         d. Loyalty.
         e. Openness.
      5. Integrity is the most important dimension of trust.
      6. Suggestions for building trust. (Refer to Exhibit 17-9)
   C. Providing Ethical Leadership.
      1. Ethics are part of leadership.
      2. Providing moral leadership involves addressing the *means* that a leader uses to achieve goals.

---

**Focus on Leadership: Developing Effective Leaders**
While it may be a bit optimistic to think that "vision-creation" can be taught, people can and do learn implementation skills. Consider what aspects of leadership can and cannot be taught as you think about the role of the leader in the workplace.

---

   D. Empowering Employees.

     1.  Increased decision-making discretion of workers.

     2.  Reasons to empower employees.

        a.  Need for quick decisions.

        b.  Organizational downsizing increases spans of control.

E.  Cross-Cultural Leadership.

     1.  National culture is an important situational variable in determining which leadership style will be most effective.

     2.  National culture influences how followers will respond.

     3.  Selected Cross-Cultural Leadership Findings.  (Refer to Exhibit 17-10)

     4.  GLOBE research project found some universal aspects to leadership.

F.  Gender Differences and Leadership.

     1.  Women tend to adopt a more democratic or participative style.

     2.  Women tend to use transformational leadership.

     3.  Comparison of effectiveness of male and female leaders.  (Refer to Exhibit 17-11).

G.  The Demise of Celebrity Leadership.

     1.  Trust in business executives has decreased.

     2.  Publicity from ongoing ethical and financial scandals.

     3.  Controversy surrounding executive pay.

     4.  Reasons for demise of the "celebrity leader" view.

     5.  Suggestions for CEOs.

H.  Substitutes for Leadership.

     1.  In some situations, any behaviors a leader exhibits are irrelevant.

     2.  Follower characteristics can neutralize the effect of leadership.

     3.  Some structural characteristics of both jobs and organizations can substitute for formal leadership.

I.  Learning Review.

- Tell the five sources of a leader's power.
- Discuss the issues today's leaders face.
- Explain why leadership is sometimes irrelevant.

J.  Key Terms.

     1.  Legitimate power – The power a leader has as a result of his or her position in the organization.

     2.  Coercive power – The power a leader has because of his or her ability to punish or control.

     3.  Reward power – The power a leader has because of his or her ability to give positive benefits or rewards.

     4.  Expert power – Influence that's based on expertise, special skills, or knowledge.

     5.  Referent power – Power that arises because of a person's desirable resources or personal traits.

     6.  Credibility – The degree to which followers perceive someone as honest, competent, and able to inspire.

     7.  Trust – The belief in the integrity, character, and ability of a leader.

     8.  Empowerment – Increasing the decision-making discretion of workers.

## Multiple-Choice Questions

1. Theories isolating characteristics that differentiate leaders from nonleaders are _____.
   a) behavioral theories
   b) trait theories
   c) contingency theories
   d) path-goal theories
   (pp. 488-489)

2. Which of the following traits is associated with effective leadership?
   a) Drive
   b) Honesty
   c) Intelligence
   d) All of the above
   (p. 489)

3. The _____ style leader generally gives the group complete freedom to make decisions and complete the work in whatever way it sees fit.
   a) autocratic
   b) democratic
   c) laissez-faire
   d) command and control
   (p. 490)

4. What two behavioral dimensions were identified by the Ohio State studies?
   a) Consideration and initiating structure
   b) Employee oriented and production oriented
   c) Concern for people and concern for production
   d) Trustworthiness and autocratic nature
   (p. 490, Exhibit 17-2)

5. The researchers associated with the _____ concluded that 9,9 leadership was the best style.
   a) Ohio State studies
   b) University of Michigan studies
   c) University of Iowa studies
   d) managerial grid
   (p. 493)

6. The LPC (least preferred coworker) questionnaire was used to develop situational aspects important to leaders in which theory?
   a) Path-goal theory
   b) Leader-participation theory
   c) Fiedler's contingency model
   d) Hersey-Blanchard situational leadership theory
   (p. 493)

251

7. In Fiedler's contingency model, _____.
   a) leader behavior is flexible and can be changed to meet the situation
   b) you can only improve leadership effectiveness by changing the leader or the situation
   c) anyone can learn to lead in any situation
   d) leadership traits ultimately choose the form of power used by the leader
   (p. 495)

8. Hersey and Blanchard's situational leadership model describes the _____ leadership style as one in which the leader and followers share in decision making.
   a) telling
   b) selling
   c) participating
   d) delegating
   (p. 496)

9. This theory provides a sequential set of rules that should be followed in determining the form and amount of participation needed in decision making.
   a) Charismatic leadership theory
   b) Leader-participation model
   c) Fiedler contingency model
   d) Path-goal theory
   (p. 497)

10. Path-goal theory is different from Fiedler's contingency model in that path-goal _____.
    a) assumes that a leader can be flexible in his/her style and can display any or all of the leadership styles
    b) is a trait-based theory rather than a contingency theory
    c) uses styles based on task rather than employee needs
    d) is based on all of the above, whereas Fiedler's contingency model is not
    (p. 499)

11. In path-goal theory, the subordinate contingency factors that determine the best leadership style are _____.
    a) performance and level of satisfaction
    b) task structure, the authority system used, and if they are in a work group
    c) locus of control, experience, and perceived ability
    d) the rules previously set between leader and member regarding the amount of participation
    (p. 499, Exhibit 17-7)

12. A _____ is enthusiastic and self-confident with the ability to influence people to behave in a certain way.
    a) charismatic leader
    b) visionary leader
    c) team leader
    d) conflict manager
    (p. 501)

13. A leader who guides or motivates followers in the direction of established goals by clarifying role and task requirements _____.
    a) is a transactional leader
    b) leads on the basis of authority
    c) is a transformational leader
    d) leads on the basis of his/her referent power
    (p. 504)

14. A type of leadership that focuses on the ability to create and articulate a realistic, credible, and attractive vision of the future is the _____.
    a) charismatic leadership
    b) leader-participant
    c) visionary leadership
    d) attributional leader
    (p. 502)

15. The greatest challenge in implementing team leadership is _____.
    a) training employees in effective team processes
    b) identifying the traits of effective team leaders
    c) training managers how to be effective team leaders
    d) setting the rules and procedures
    (p. 503)

16. Coach, conflict manager, liaison with external constituencies, and troubleshooter are examples of _____ leadership roles.
    a) team
    b) democratic
    c) autocratic
    d) laissez-faire
    (p. 503)

17. The power a person has due to his/her ability to threaten and deliver sanctions or punishment is _____.
    a) coercive power
    b) reward power
    c) expert power
    d) referent power
    (p. 504)

18. A manager exercises _____ power when he/she allows workers to have a day off from work after completing an especially difficult project.
    a) coercive
    b) reward
    c) expert
    d) referent
    (p. 504)

19. Trust is built on five concepts, which include _____.
    a) integrity
    b) competence
    c) consistency
    d) All of the above
    (p. 507)

20. If managers practice openness, strive to be fair, speak their feelings, etc., they will be able to build _____.
    a) their referent power
    b) credibility with their employees
    c) trust in their leadership
    d) their contingency leadership skills
    (p. 507, Exhibit 17-9)

21. Empowerment is a growing movement because of _____.
    a) the general failure in training managers to lead groups
    b) the downsizing of organizations
    c) the growth of the acceptance of the attribution theory of leadership
    d) increased unionization of employees
    (p. 509)

22. In other countries, the national culture will affect leadership style because of _____.
    a) the demand for leaders to be highly directive
    b) the gender biases
    c) the need for a strong charismatic style leader
    d) how the followers will respond
    (p. 510)

23. Which of the following is true about leadership in other countries?
    a) Men and women are largely free to choose their leadership style.
    b) Arab cultures prefer leaders who do not show kindness or generosity without being asked to do so.
    c) Asian cultures prefer directive, low-communication leadership styles.
    d) Direction is preferred over participation in Denmark and Finland.
    (p. 510, Exhibit 17-10)

24. Women are more likely to lead using a _____ leadership style.
    a) command and control
    b) transactional
    c) transformational
    d) autocratic
    (p. 511)

25. Leadership may be irrelevant if _____.
    a) followers are not well trained
    b) the leader lacks expertise
    c) the organization has explicit goals and there is a cohesive work group
    d) training is not offered
    (p. 514)

## True/False Questions

1.  T   F   Ideally, all managers should be leaders.
            (p. 488)

2.  T   F   Early leadership theories focused on the leader and how the leader interacted
            with his or her group members.
            (p. 488)

3.  T   F   The University of Iowa studies on leadership focused on two dimensions of
            leadership: consideration and initiating structure.
            (p. 490)

4.  T   F   The managerial grid provided a framework for conceptualizing leadership
            style and the conclusion that the 9,9 leadership style is the best has been well-
            supported by research evidence.
            (pp. 492-493)

5.  T   F   Fiedler's contingency model proposes that effective group performance
            depends on the proper match between the leader's style of interacting with
            his/her subordinates and the degree to which the situation gives control and
            influence to the leader.
            (p. 493)

6.  T   F   The degree to which the job assignments were formalized and procedurized is
            called leader-member relations.
            (p. 494)

7.  T   F   Situational leadership theory focuses on followers' readiness.
            (p. 496)

8. T  F   Vroom and Yetton's leader participation model is a contingency model of leadership.
(p. 497)

9. T  F   The essence of path-goal leadership theory is the leader helping subordinates achieve their goals.
(p. 498)

10. T  F   Developed by Robert House, the path-goal theory is a contingency model of leadership that takes key elements from the expectancy theory of motivation.
(p. 498)

11. T  F   One of the predictions from the path-goal theory is that subordinates with an external locus of control will be more satisfied with a participative leadership style.
(p. 500)

12. T  F   Transformational leaders guide or motivate their followers in the direction of established goals by clarifying role and task requirements.
(p. 500)

13. T  F   The evidence supporting the superiority of transformational leadership over transactional leadership is overwhelmingly impressive.
(p. 500)

14. T  F   Charismatic leadership is positively correlated with high performance and satisfaction among followers.
(p. 501)

15. T  F   Most managers are naturally effective team leaders as they have already been trained in how to accomplish tasks through others.
(p. 503)

16. T  F   The power people have because of their positions in the formal organization is known as position power.
(p. 504)

17. T  F   Expert power arises because of a person's desirable resources or personal traits.
(p. 504)

18. T  F   Trust is the degree to which followers perceive someone as honest, competent, and able to inspire.
(pp. 506-507)

19. T    F    Surveys show that honesty is consistently singled out as the number-one characteristic of admired leaders.
(p. 506)

20. T    F    Of the five dimensions that make up the concept of trust, loyalty seems to be the most critical when someone assesses another's trustworthiness.
(p. 506)

21. T    F    Providing moral leadership involves addressing the means that leaders use in trying to achieve goals.
(p. 508)

22. T    F    Efforts to lead through empowering employees are in decline as more and more employees refuse to accept responsibility without more pay.
(p. 509)

23. T    F    National culture has little impact on leadership style as leadership transcends national boundaries.
(pp. 510-511)

24. T    F    The tendency for female leaders to be more democratic than males declines when women are in male-dominated jobs.
(p. 511)

25. T    F    Certain individual, job, and organizational variables can act as substitutes for leadership, resulting in negating the influence of the leader.
(p. 514)

# Match Terms with Definitions

a.  Autocratic style
b.  Transformational leaders
c.  Consideration
d.  Leader participation model
e.  Initiating structure
f.  Task structure
g.  Least-preferred coworker questionnaire
h.  Legitimate power
i.  Leader-member relations
j.  Position power
k.  Transactional leaders
l.  Path-goal theory
m.  Fiedler contingency model
n.  Charismatic leader
o.  Leaders
p.  Managerial grid
q.  Visionary leader
r.  Coercive power
s.  Trust
t.  Integrity

_____ 1.  A leadership theory that provides a set of rules to determine the form and amount of participative decision making in different situations.

_____ 2.  Shows two dimensions of leader behaviors: concern for people and concern for production.

_____ 3.  The degree to which the job assignments are procedurized.

_____ 4.  The extent to which a leader defines and structures his or her role and those of subordinates to attain goals.

_____ 5.  When power and authority come out of a person's position in the formal organization.

_____ 6.  Ability to create and articulate a realistic, credible, and attractive vision of the future that improves upon the present situation.

_____ 7.  An instrument that measures whether a person is task or relationship oriented.

_____ 8.  Those who are able to influence others and who possess managerial authority.

_____ 9.  The degree of confidence, trust, and respect subordinates have in their leader.

_____ 10. The power a leader has because of his or her ability to punish or control.

_____ 11. The extent to which a leader had job relationships characterized by mutual trust and respect for group members' ideas and feelings.

_____ 12. The degree of influence a leader has over power variables such as hiring, firing, discipline, promotions, and salary increases.

_____ 13. A leader who tended to centralize authority, dictate work methods, make unilateral decisions, and limit employee participation.

_____ 14. The belief in the integrity, character, and ability of a leader.

_____ 15. Honesty and truthfulness.

_____ 16. Leaders who provide individualized consideration, intellectual stimulation, and possess charisma.

_____ 17. An enthusiastic, self-confident leader whose personality and actions influence people to behave in certain ways.

_____ 18. Leaders who guide or motivate their followers in the direction of established goals by clarifying role and task requirements.

_____ 19. Contingency model of leadership that takes key elements from the expectancy theory of motivation.

_____ 20. The effectiveness of leadership depends on the fit between the style of the leader and the degree to which the leader can influence and control.

## Essay Questions

1. Compare and contrast the behavioral leadership theories described in your text (University of Iowa, Ohio State, University of Michigan, and managerial grid). (p. 490, Exhibit 17-2)

2. Discuss path-goal leadership. Include a description of the different styles and the assumptions of the model. (pp. 498-500)

3. How is charismatic leadership different from visionary leadership? (pp. 501-502)

4. Why do managers have difficulty being team leaders, and what can be done to improve their effectiveness? (pp. 502-504)

5. List and describe the five sources of leader power. (p. 504)

# Chapter 18  Foundations of Control

## Learning Outline

### What Is Control and Why Is It Important?
- Define control.
- Contrast the three approaches to designing control systems.
- Discuss the reasons why control is important.
- Explain the planning-controlling link.

### The Control Process
- Describe the three steps in the control process.
- Explain why what is measured is more critical than how it's measured.
- Explain the three courses of action managers can take in controlling.

### Controlling for Organizational Performance
- Define organizational performance.
- Describe the most frequently used measures of organizational performance.

### Tools for Controlling Organizational Performance
- Contrast feedforward, concurrent, and feedback controls.
- Explain the types of financial and information controls managers can use.
- Describe how balanced scorecards and benchmarking are used in controlling.

### Contemporary Issues in Control
- Describe how managers may have to adjust controls for cross-cultural differences.
- Discuss the types of workplace concerns managers face and how they can address those concerns.
- Explain why control is important in customer interactions.
- Explain what corporate governance is and how it's changing.

---

**A Manager's Dilemma**

When Russell Chew joined the FFA as chief operating officer in 2003, he faced the significant challenge of bringing "business principles and discipline to a sprawling operation dogged by cost overruns and outdated technology." Consider the following questions and compare your answers to **Managers Respond** at the end of the chapter.
1. What approaches did Mr. Chew take to improving the operations of the FAA?
2. What management control tools might he use to help continue improving his agency's performance.

---

## Lecture Outline

I.  What Is Control?
    A.  Three approaches to designing control systems. (Refer to Exhibit 18-1)
        1.  Market control.
            a.  Emphasizes use of external market mechanisms such as price competition and relative market share.

2. Bureaucratic control.
   a. Emphasizes organizational authority and relies on administrative rules, regulations, procedures, and policies.
3. Clan control.
   a. Behaviors are regulated by the shared values, norms, traditions, rituals, beliefs, and other aspects of the organization's culture.

B. Why Is Control Important?
1. Control is the only way managers know whether organizational goals are being met and if not, the reasons why.
2. Controlling provides a critical link back to planning. (Refer to Exhibit 18-2)
3. Control facilitates employee empowerment.
4. Control is important to protect the organization and its assets.

C. Learning Review.
   • Define control.
   • Contrast the three approaches to designing control systems.
   • Discuss the reasons control is important.
   • Explain the planning-controlling link.

D. Key Terms.
1. Control – The process of monitoring, comparing, and correcting work performance.
2. Market control – An approach to control that emphasizes the use of external market mechanisms to establish the control standards.
3. Bureaucratic control – An approach to control that emphasizes organizational authority and relies on administrative rules, regulations, procedures, and policies.
4. Clan control – An approach to control in which employee behavior is regulated by the shared values, norms, traditions, rituals, beliefs, and other aspects of the organization's culture.

II. The Control Process.
A. The control process is a three-step process. (Refer to Exhibit 18-3)
1. Measuring actual performance
2. Comparing actual performance against a standard
3. Taking managerial action to correct deviations or inadequate standards.

B. Measuring.
1. How We Measure.
   a. Four sources of information. (Refer to Exhibit 18-4)
      (i)     Personal observation.
      (ii)    Statistical reports.
      (iii)   Oral reports.
      (iv)    Written reports.
2. What We Measure.
   a. What we measure is more critical than how we measure.
   b. Performance indicators can be stated in either quantitative terms or in subjective measures.

C. Comparing.
   1. Range of variation.
   2. Defining the Acceptable Range of Variation. **(Refer to Exhibit 18-5)**
D. Taking Managerial Action.
   1. Correct Actual Performance.
      a. Immediate corrective action.
      b. Basic corrective action.
   2. Revise the Standard.
      a. If employees or managers don't meet the standard, the first thing they're likely to do is attack the standard.
E. Summary of Managerial Decisions. **(Refer to Exhibit 18-7)**
F. Learning Review.
- Describe the three steps in the control process.
- Explain why what is measured is more critical than how it's measured.
- Explain the three courses of action managers can take in controlling.
G. Key Terms.
   1. Control process – A three-step process including measuring actual performance, comparing actual performance against a standard, and taking managerial action.
   2. Range of variation – The acceptable parameters of variance between actual performance and the standard.
   3. Immediate corrective action – Corrective action that corrects problems at once to get performance back on track.
   4. Basic corrective action – Corrective action that looks at how and why performance deviated and then proceeds to correct the source of deviation.

III. Controlling for Organizational Performance.
  A. What Is Organizational Performance?
    1. Performance.
    2. Organizational performance.
  B. Measures of Organizational Performance.
    1. Managers must know what measures will give them the information they need.
    2. Organizational Productivity.
       a. Productivity.
       b. Management's job is to increase the ratio between output and input.
    3. Organizational Effectiveness.
       a. Systems resource model proposes that effectiveness is measured by the organization's ability to exploit its environment in acquiring scarce and valued resources.
       b. Process model emphasizes the transformation processes of the organization and how well the organization converts inputs into desired outputs.
       c. Multiple constituencies model says several different effectiveness measures should be used, reflecting the different criteria of the organization's constituencies.

       4. Industry Rankings.
         a. Popular Industry and Company Rankings. (Refer to Exhibit 18-8)
         b. American Customer Satisfaction Index (ACSI).
   C. Learning Review.
     • Define organizational performance.
     • Describe the most frequently used measures of organizational performance.
   D. Key Terms.
       1. Performance – The end result of an activity.
       2. Organizational performance – The accumulated end results of all the organization's work activities.
       3. Productivity – The overall output of goods or services produced divided by the inputs needed to generate the output.
       4. Organizational effectiveness – A measure of how appropriate organizational goals are and how well an organization is achieving the goals.

IV. Tools for Controlling Organizational Performance.
   A. Feedforward/Concurrent/Feedback Controls. (Refer to Exhibit 18-9)
       1. Feedforward Control.
         a. Takes place before an activity begins.
         b. Most desirable type of control.
         c. The key is to take managerial action before a problem occurs.
       2. Concurrent Control.
         a. Takes place while an activity is in progress.
         b. Management by walking around.
         c. Technical equipment can be programmed for concurrent controls.
       3. Feedback Control.
         a. Takes place after the activity is done.
         b. Most popular type of control.
         c. Advantages.
           (i) Meaningful information on how effective planning efforts were.
           (ii) Enhance employee motivation.
   B. Financial Controls.
       1. Traditional Financial Control Measures. (Refer to Exhibit 18-10)
         a. Liquidity ratios measure ability to meet current debt obligations.
         b. Leverage ratios examine use of debt to finance assets.
         c. Activity ratios measure how efficiently assets are used.
         d. Profitability ratios measure how efficiently and effectively the firm is using its assets to generate profits.

      e. Budgets provide managers with quantitative standards against which to measure and compare resource consumption.

  2. Other Financial Control Measures.

      a. Economic value added (EVA).

      b. Market value added (MVA).

      c. Companies are supposed to take capital from investors and make it worth more.

  3. The Practice of Managing Earnings.

      a. "Time" income and expenses to enhance current financial performance.

      b. Sarbanes-Oxley Act.

C. Balanced Scorecard.

  1. Looks at four areas.

      a. Financial.

      b. Customer.

      c. Internal processes.

      d. People/innovation/growth assets.

  2. Scorecards reflect strategies.

D. Information Controls.

  1. Two ways to view information.

      a. A tool to help managers control.

      b. An organizational area managers need to control.

  2. How Are Information Systems Used in Controlling?

      a. Most of the information tools that managers use arise out of the organization's management information system.

      b. Data vs. Information.

---

**Thinking Critically About Ethics**

Duplicating software is a widespread practice that is in violation of copyright laws. After reading the short scenario, respond to the following questions.

1. Is reproducing copyrighted software ever an acceptable practice?
2. What types of ethical guidelines could a manager establish for software use?
3. What would you do if you were a manager in another country where software piracy was an accepted practice?

---

  3. Controlling information.

E. Benchmarking of Best Practices.

  1. Benchmarking means learning from others.

  2. Steps to Benchmarking. (Refer to Exhibit 18-11)

F. Learning Review.

- Contrast feedforward, concurrent, and feedback controls.
- Explain the types of financial and information controls managers can use.
- Describe how balanced scorecards and benchmarking are used in controlling.

G. Key Terms.
   1. Feedforward control – A type of control that takes place in advance of the actual work activity.
   2. Concurrent control – A type of control that takes place while a work activity is in progress.
   3. Management by walking around – A term used to describe when a manager is out in the work area, interacting directly with employees.
   4. Feedback control – A type of control that takes place after a work activity is done.
   5. Economic value added (EVA) – A financial tool for measuring corporate and divisional performance, calculated by taking after-tax operating profit minus the total annual cost of capital.
   6. Market value added (MVA) – A financial tool that measures the stock market's estimate of the value of a firm's past and expected investment projects.
   7. Balanced scorecard – A performance measurement tool that looks at four areas—financial, customer, internal processes, and people/innovation/growth assets—that contribute to a company's performance.
   8. Management information system (MIS) – A system used to provide management with needed information on a regular basis.
   9. Data – Raw, unanalyzed facts.
   10. Information – Processed and analyzed data.
   11. Benchmarking – The search for the best practices among competitors or noncompetitors that lead to their superior performance.
   12. Benchmark – The standard of excellence against which to measure and compare.

V. Contemporary Issues in Control.
   A. Adjusting Controls for Cross-Cultural Differences.
      1. Methods of control in global organizations.
      2. Technology's impact on control.
      3. Legal constraints.
      4. Comparability between countries.
   B. Workplace Concerns.
      1. Workplace Privacy.
         a. Types of Workplace Monitoring by Employers.  (Refer to Exhibit 18-12)
         b. Reasons for employee monitoring.
         c. How to maintain control without demeaning employees.
      2. Employee Theft.
         a. Types of employee theft.
         b. Why do employees steal?
         c. Control Measures.  (Refer to Exhibit 18-13)
   C. Workplace Violence.
      1. Survey of employees.  (Refer to Exhibit 18-14)
      2. Contributing factors.
      3. Control Measures.  (Refer to Exhibit 18-15)

D. Controlling Customer Interactions.
  1. Customer service.
  2. Service profit chain.  (Refer to Exhibit 18-16)
E. Corporate Governance.
  1. Protection of corporate owners.
  2. Reform of corporate governance.
    a. The Role of Boards of Directors.  (Refer to Exhibit 18-17)
    b. Financial Reporting.  (Refer to Exhibit 18-18)
F. Learning Review.
  • Tell how managers may have to adjust controls for cross-cultural differences.
  • Discuss the types of workplace concerns managers face and how they can address those issues.
  • Explain why control is important to customer interactions.
  • Discuss what corporate governance is and how it's changing.
G. Key Terms.
  1. Employee theft – Any unauthorized taking of company property by employees for their personal use.
  2. Service profit chain – The service sequence from employees to customers to profit.
  3. Corporate governance – The system used to govern a corporation so that the interests of corporate owners are protected.

## Multiple-Choice Questions

1. If an organization has products or services that are clearly specified and distinct in a marketplace with strong competition, then _____ control would be an effective control system.
   a) clan
   b) bureaucratic
   c) product
   d) market
   (p. 527, Exhibit 18-1)

2. _____ control is dependent on the individual and the group identifying appropriate and expected behaviors and performance measures.
   a) Clan
   b) Bureaucratic
   c) Product
   d) Market
   (p. 527, Exhibit 18-1)

3. In the planning-control link, organizational structure and human resource management are elements of the _____ step.
   a) planning
   b) organizing
   c) leading
   d) controlling
   (p. 529, Exhibit 18-2)

4. The control process begins with _____.
   a) setting objectives and planning
   b) comparing actual performance to standards
   c) measuring actual performance
   d) taking managerial action
   (p. 529)

5. The range of variation _____.
   a) involves choosing the most appropriate unit of measurement for assessing performance
   b) involves concurrent feedback and taking corrective action before problems occur
   c) is the acceptable parameters between actual performance and the standard
   d) explains the maximum possible deviation from the budget
   (p. 531)

6. _____ looks at how and why performance deviated and then proceeds to correct the source of deviation.
   a) Feedforward control
   b) Revising the standard
   c) Basic corrective action
   d) Immediate corrective action
   (p. 532)

7. The overall output of goods or services produced divided by the inputs needed to generate that output is termed _____.
   a) performance
   b) productivity
   c) liquidity
   d) effectiveness
   (p. 535)

8. _____ control takes place while an activity is in process.
   a) Budgetary
   b) Feedforward
   c) Concurrent
   d) Feedback
   (p. 538)

9. The best-known form of _____ is direct supervision.
   a) feedforward control
   b) basic control
   c) concurrent control
   d) feedback control
   (p. 538)

10. An entrepreneur or manager who controls processes by being out in the work area, interacting with his/her employees, and engaging in direct information exchange about what is going on is practicing _____.
    a) feedforward control
    b) delegating
    c) feedback control
    d) managing by walking around
    (p. 538)

11. James is using financial information which compares last quarter's actual performance with budgeted performance. James is using _____ control.
    a) feedforward
    b) concurrent
    c) feedback
    d) proactive
    (p. 539)

12. A ratio that is used to assess how efficiently inventory assets are being used is the _____.
    a) current ratio
    b) acid test ratio
    c) return-on-investment ratio
    d) inventory turnover ratio
    (p. 540, Exhibit 18-10)

13. Which financial ratio measures how far profits can decline before the organization is unable to meet its interest expense?
    a) Total asset turnover
    b) Times-interest-earned
    c) Profit-margin-on-sales
    d) Current ratio
    (p. 540, Exhibit 18-10)

14. A management tool for measuring corporate and divisional performance is _____.
    a) economic value added
    b) the economic order quantity
    c) the acid test
    d) market value added
    (p. 541)

15. When _____ is used as a performance measure, employees learn that they can improve performance by either using less capital or by investing capital in high-return projects.
   a) market value added (MVA)
   b) economic value added (EVA)
   c) budgetary controls
   d) risk analysis
   (p. 541)

16. A management tool that measures the stock market's estimate of the value of a firm's past and expected capital investment projects is _____.
   a) market value added
   b) the acid test
   c) a control chart
   d) a behavioral control technique
   (p. 541)

17. The _____ approach to performance measurement was introduced as a way to evaluate organizational performance from more than just the financial perspective.
   a) critical incidents technique
   b) graphic bars scale
   c) multiperson comparison
   d) balanced scorecard
   (p. 542)

18. The balanced scorecard approach to performance measurement looks at all of the following areas EXCEPT _____.
   a) financial
   b) customer
   c) internal processes
   d) corporate governance
   (p. 542)

19. Analyzed and processed data is known as _____.
   a) a management information system
   b) information
   c) an operations control chart
   d) a sales ratio
   (p. 544)

20. _____ is the search for the best practices among competitors or noncompetitors that lead to their superior performance.
   a) Use of MBO-type objectives
   b) The appraisal interview
   c) Multiperson comparison
   d) Benchmarking
   (p. 545)

21. Employers have several ethical issues in terms of control over employee behavior, which include _____.
   a) workplace privacy
   b) workplace violence
   c) computer monitoring
   d) All of the above
   (pp. 547-551)

22. In terms of privacy in the workplace, which of the following is true?
   a) Employees have privacy rights whenever their personal comments are included in company communication.
   b) Employers have the right to monitor any communication systems they provide and pay for.
   c) Although employees' e-mail may be read, employers may not monitor their voice mail.
   d) Employers are prohibited from tapping an employee's telephone without a court order.
   (p. 547)

23. _____ is defined as any unauthorized taking of company property by employees for their personal use.
   a) Employee theft
   b) Feedback control
   c) MVA
   d) The service profit chain
   (p. 549)

24. Which of the following is described by experts as a primary contributor to workplace violence?
   a) Explicit policies and procedures
   b) Authoritarian leadership
   c) Challenging work
   d) Feedback
   (p. 551)

25. According to _____, a company's strategy and service delivery system influence how employees service customers.
    a) feedforward control theory
    b) the service profit chain
    c) MIS theory
    d) economic value added (EVA) theory
    (p. 552)

## True/False Questions

1. T  F  A bureaucratic approach to control systems emphasizes the use of elements external to the organization to control processes.
   (p. 527)

2. T  F  When managers use organizational norms, traditions, and shared values to control processes and employees, they are taking a clan approach to control systems.
   (p. 527)

3. T  F  Effective control systems ensure that activities are completed in ways that lead to the attainment of goals.
   (p. 526)

4. T  F  Although an effective measurement tool, personal observation often relies too heavily on quantifiable elements, ignoring important but more subjective elements.
   (p. 530, Exhibit 18-4)

5. T  F  With the many ways to measure performance, all jobs and activities can be expressed in tangible, measurable terms.
   (p. 531)

6. T  F  Any deviation from the plan needs corrective action.
   (p. 531)

7. T  F  A manager takes basic corrective action by determining how and why the performance deviation occurred and correcting the source of the deviation.
   (p. 532)

8. T  F  Productivity is the end result of an activity.
   (p. 535)

9. T  F  The systems resource model of organizational effectiveness proposes that effectiveness is measured by the organization's ability to exploit its environment in acquiring scarce and valuable resources.
   (p. 536)

10. T  F  Feedforward control corrects problems as they occur.
(p. 538; Exhibit 18-9)

11. T  F  The activity ratio is used to test an organization's ability to meet short-term obligations.
(p. 538)

12. T  F  In considering financial ratios, one activity test is the current ratio.  Current ratio is obtained by dividing current assets by current liabilities.
(p. 540, Exhibit 18-10)

13. T  F  The profit margin on sales identifies the profits that various products of the organization are generating.
(p. 540, Exhibit 18-10)

14. T  F  A tool for measuring corporate and divisional performance is economic value added, which focuses managers' attention on earning a rate of return over and above the cost of capital.
(p. 541)

15. T  F  A positive MVA is achieved when the company's market value is greater than all the capital invested in it.
(p. 541)

16. T  F  The balanced scorecard approach to performance measurement was introduced as a way to evaluate organizational performance from a financial perspective.
(p. 542)

17. T  F  When information is analyzed and processed, data is the result.
(p. 544)

18. T  F  At its most fundamental level, benchmarking means learning from others.
(p. 545)

19. T  F  When using systems across national boundaries, companies usually have little problem in measuring performance and applying corrective actions.
(pp. 546-547)

20. T  F  The courts have held that e-mail is the property of the employer so the employer can read your e-mail.
(p. 548)

21. T  F  The federal Electronic Communications Privacy Act prohibits unauthorized interception of electronic communication.
(p. 548)

22. T　F　Nearly 85 percent of organizational theft in the United States is committed by employees.
(p. 549)

23. T　F　A dysfunctional work environment is a primary contributor to workplace violence.
(p. 551)

24. T　F　Customer loyalty improves organizational revenue growth and profitability.
(p. 552)

25. T　F　Reform of corporate governance is a U.S. phenomenon and is not currently a global concern.
(p. 553)

## Match Terms with Definitions

a. Benchmarking
b. Economic value added
c. Clan control
d. Performance
e. Management by walking around
f. Productivity
g. Balanced scorecard

h. Range of variation
i. Organizational effectiveness
j. Market value added
k. Employee theft
l. Basic corrective action
m. Concurrent control
n. Control process

o. Immediate corrective action
p. Feedforward control
q. Feedback control
r. Control
s. Market control
t. Bureaucratic control

_____ 1. A performance measurement tool that looks at financial, customer, internal processes, and people/innovation/growth assets to assess performance.

_____ 2. The overall output of goods and services produced divided by the inputs needed to generate that output.

_____ 3. A financial tool for measuring performance calculated by taking after-tax operating profit minus the total annual cost of capital.

_____ 4. An approach to control that emphasizes organizational authority and relies on administrative rules, regulations, procedures, and policies.

_____ 5. Control that prevents anticipated problems.

_____ 6. The search for the best practices among competitors or noncompetitors that leads to their superior performance.

_____ 7. A financial tool that measures the stock market's estimate of the value of a firm's past and expected investment projects.

_____ 8. The end result of an activity.

_____ 9. The acceptable parameters of variance between actual performance and the standard.

_____ 10. A measure of how appropriate organizational goals are and how well an organization is achieving those goals.

_____ 11. Correcting an activity at once in order to get performance back on track.

_____ 12. An approach to designing control systems that emphasizes the use of external market mechanisms to establish the standards used in the control system.

_____ 13. A controlling technique in which the manager is out in the work area, interacting directly with employees.

_____ 14. A control system in which employee behaviors are regulated by the shared values, norms, and other aspects of the organization's culture.

_____ 15. Control that occurs while an activity is in process.

_____ 16. The process of measuring actual performance, comparing it against a standard, and taking managerial action to correct deviations or inadequate standards.

_____ 17. Any unauthorized taking of company property by employees for their personal use.

_____ 18. The process of monitoring, comparing, and correcting work performance.

_____ 19. Determining how and why performance has deviated and correcting the source of deviation.

_____ 20. Control imposed after an action has occurred.

## Essay Questions

1. Identify and describe the three different approaches to designing a control system.
   (p. 527, Exhibit 18-1)

2. The control process is a three-step process. What are the three steps and what are the assumptions that this process makes?
   (p. 530, Exhibit 18-3)

3. Explain feedforward, concurrent, and feedback controls.
   (pp. 538-539)

4. Traditional financial measures include ratio analysis. Give two ratios that measure each of the following: liquidity, leverage, activity, and profitability.
   (p. 540, Exhibit 18-10)

5. Explain benchmarking and how it can be used as a tool for monitoring and measuring organizational performance.
   (pp. 544-546)

# Chapter 19  Operations and Value Chain Management

## Learning Outline

### What Is Operations Management and Why Is It Important?
- Explain what operations management is.
- Contrast manufacturing and service organizations.
- Describe managers' roles in improving productivity.
- Discuss the strategic role of operations management.

### Value Chain Management
- Define value chain and value chain management.
- Describe the goal of value chain management.
- Discuss the requirements for successful value chain management.
- Describe the benefits that result from value chain management.
- Explain the obstacles to value chain management.

### Current Issues in Operations Management
- Discuss technology's role in manufacturing.
- Describe some of the various quality dimensions.
- Explain ISO 9000 and Six Sigma.
- Describe mass customization and how operations management contributes to it.

---

**A Manager's Dilemma**

Carlos Rodarte, head of regional operations for Sepomex, Mexico's state postal system, is dedicated to improving the efficiency and effectiveness of his organization in order to combat widespread skepticism of Sepomex by the public. Consider the following questions and compare your answer with **Managers Respond** at the end of the chapter.

1. What measures has Mr. Rodarte taken to improve the quality of this organization's service?
2. What else could he do to successfully implement a quality program?

---

## Lecture Outline

I.  What Is Operations Management and Why Is It Important?
   A. Operations management. (Refer to Exhibit 19-1)
   B. Importance of operations management.
      1. Encompasses both services and manufacturing.
      2. Important in effectively and efficiently managing productivity.
      3. Plays a strategic role in the organization's competitive success.
   C. Services and Manufacturing.
      1. Manufacturing organizations produce physical goods.
      2. Service organizations produce nonphysical goods in the form of services.
      3. Most of the world's industrialized nations are predominantly service economies.

D. Managing Productivity.
   1. Improving productivity is a major goal in virtually every organization.
   2. High productivity can lead to economic growth.
   3. Productivity is a composite of people and operations variables.
   4. W. Edwards Deming believed managers, not workers, were the primary source of increased productivity.
      a. Deming's 14 points for improving management's productivity. (Refer to Exhibit 19-2)
E. Strategic Role of Operations Management.
   1. Historical overview.
   2. Modern view.
F. Learning Review.
   - Explain what operations management is.
   - Contrast manufacturing and service organizations.
   - Describe managers' roles in improving productivity.
   - Discuss the strategic role of operations management.
G. Key Terms.
   1. Operations management – The design, operation, and control of the transformation process that converts resources into finished goods or services.
   2. Manufacturing organizations – Organizations that produce physical goods.
   3. Service organizations – Organizations that produce nonphysical outputs in the form of services.
   4. Productivity – The overall output of goods or services produced divided by the inputs needed to generate the output.

II. Value Chain Management.
   A. What Is Value Chain Management?
      1. Value.
      2. How is value provided to customers?
      3. The value chain.
      4. Value chain management.
   B. Goal of Value Chain Management.
      1. Customers are the ones who have the power to define what value is and how it's created and provided.
      2. Goal of value chain management is to create a value chain strategy that meets and exceeds customers' needs and desires and allows for full and seamless integration among all members of the chain.
   C. Requirements for Value Chain Management.
      1. Six Requirements for Successful Value Chain Management. (Refer to Exhibit 19-3)
         a. Coordination and Collaboration.
            (i) Sharing of information and analysis requires more open communication.
         b. Technology Investment.
            (i) Information technology can be used to restructure the value chain.

c. Organizational Processes.
   (i) Value chain management radically changes organizational processes.
   (ii) Three important conclusions.
      a) Better demand forecasting is necessary and possible because of closer ties with customers and suppliers.
      b) Selected functions may need to be done collaboratively.
      c) New measures are needed for evaluating performance of various activities along the value chain.

---

**Thinking Critically About Ethics**
Sometimes one partner in the value chain is a bully and "suggests" that a smaller partner alter its way of doing business.
1. What are your feelings about the behavior described in the scenario?
2. How can this type of behavior affect the value chain?
3. Do you believe this type of behavior is ethical? Why or why not?

---

d. Leadership.
   (i) Successful value chain management isn't possible without strong and committed leadership.
   (ii) Managers must outline expectations and clarify each employee's role.
e. Employees/Human Resources.
   (i) Employees are the organization's most important resource.
   (ii) Flexibility is the key to job design in value chain management.
   (iii) Employees must be flexible.
   (iv) There must be significant investment in continual and ongoing employee training.
f. Organizational Culture and Attitudes.
   (i) Supportive organizational culture and attitudes are important.
D. Benefits of Value Chain Management.
   1. Four primary benefits of value chain management.
      a. Improved procurement.
      b. Improved logistics.
      c. Improved product development.
      d. Enhanced customer order management.
E. Obstacles to Value Chain Management. (Refer to Exhibit 19-4)
   1. Organizational Barriers.
      a. Among the most difficult to handle.
      b. Include refusal or reluctance to share information, reluctance to shake up the status quo, and security issues.
   2. Cultural Attitudes.
      a. Trust issue is critical, either lack of trust or too much trust.
      b. Theft of intellectual property.
      c. Collaboration.
   3. Required Capabilities.

4. People.
  a. Flexibility is key.
  b. Managers must motivate employees to give high levels of effort.
  c. Lack of managers who are experienced in leading value chain management.

F. Learning Review.
  - Define value chain and value chain management.
  - Describe the goal of value chain management.
  - Discuss the requirements for successful value chain management.
  - Describe the benefits that result from value chain management.
  - Explain the obstacles to value chain management.

G. Key Terms.
  1. Value – The performance characteristics, features, and attributes, and any other aspects of goods and services for which customers are willing to give up resources.
  2. Value chain – The entire series of organizational work activities that add value at each step beginning with the processing of raw materials and ending with finished product in the hands of end users.
  3. Value chain management – The process of managing the sequence of activities and information along the entire value chain.
  4. Organizational processes – The ways that organizational work is done.
  5. Intellectual property – Proprietary company information that's critical to an organization's efficient and effective functioning and competitiveness.

III. Current Issues in Operations Management.
  A. Technology's Role in Operations Management.
    1. Competition puts pressure on organizations.
    2. Management must be more responsive.
    3. Technology allows greater collaboration and cost control in manufacturing.
  B. Quality Initiatives.
    1. Quality problems are expensive.
    2. Quality Dimensions of Goods and Services. (Refer to Exhibit 19-5)
    3. Planning for Quality.
      a. Quality improvement goals.
      b. Strategies and plans to achieve goals.
    4. Organizing and Leading for Quality.
      a. Reliance on two important people approaches.
        (i)      Cross-functional work teams.
        (ii)     Self-directed or empowered work teams.
      b. Reliance on well-trained, flexible, and empowered employees.
    5. Controlling for Quality.
  C. Quality Goals.
    1. ISO 9000.
      a. A series of international quality management standards.
      b. Established by the International Organization for Standardization.
      c. Becoming a prerequisite for doing business globally.

279

2. Six Sigma.
   a. Popularized by Motorola.
   b. Quality standard that establishes a goal of no more than 3.4 defects per million units or procedures.
   c. Six Sigma is close to defect-free.
3. Summary.
   a. The goal of quality certification should be having work processes and an operations system in place that enable organizations to meet customers' needs and employees to perform their jobs in a consistently high-quality way.
D. Mass Customization.
   1. Requires flexible manufacturing techniques and continual dialogue with customers.
E. Learning Review.
   - Discuss technology's role in manufacturing.
   - Describe some of the various quality dimensions.
   - Explain ISO 9000 and Six Sigma.
   - Describe mass customization and how operations management contributes to it.
F. Key Terms.
   1. Quality – The ability of a product or service to reliably do what it's supposed to do and to satisfy customer expectations.
   2. ISO 9000 – A series of international quality management standards that set uniform guidelines for processes to ensure that products conform to customer requirements.
   3. Six Sigma – A quality standard that establishes a goal of no more than 3.4 defects per million parts or procedures.
   4. Mass customization – Providing consumers with a product when, where, and how they want it.
   5. Cellular manufacturing – An approach to manufacturing that uses work cells or groups of workstations to process products progressively.
   6. RFID – An automatic identification method in which information can be stored and remotely retrieved.

## Multiple-Choice Questions

1. The design, operation, and control of the transformation process is the focus of
   _____.
   a) quality control
   b) operations management
   c) project management
   d) re-engineering efforts
   (p. 564)

2. In an operations management system, people, technology, capital, and information are considered to be _____.
   a) outputs
   b) inputs
   c) goods
   d) services
   (p. 564, Exhibit 19-1)

3. _____ organizations produce nonphysical outputs.
   a) Service
   b) Merchandising
   c) Retailing
   d) Manufacturing
   (p. 565)

4. Most of the world's industrialized nations are predominantly _____ economies.
   a) command
   b) manufacturing
   c) service
   d) retail
   (p. 565)

5. _____ is considered to be a key to global competition.
   a) Increasing productivity
   b) Understanding ISO 9000
   c) Value chain management
   d) Strategic planning
   (p. 566)

6. _____ is a composite of people and operations variables.
   a) Productivity
   b) Six Sigma
   c) Operations management
   d) A value chain
   (p. 566)

7. The view that managers, not workers, were the primary source of increased productivity was proposed by _____.
   a) Abraham Maslow
   b) W. Edwards Deming
   c) Frederick W. Taylor
   d) Michael Hammer
   (p. 566)

8. _____ is(are) the performance characteristics, features and attributes, and any other aspects of goods and services for which customers are willing to give up resources.
   a) Attributes
   b) A warranty
   c) Value
   d) Productivity
   (p. 568)

9. The entire series of organizational work activities that add value at each step beginning with the processing of raw materials and ending with finished product in the hands of end users is the _____.
   a) value chain
   b) business model
   c) job description
   d) organization's strategy
   (p. 569)

10. The goal of _____ is to create a value chain strategy that meets and exceeds customers' needs and desires.
    a) total quality management
    b) value chain management
    c) reengineering
    d) differential management
    (p. 569)

11. Successful value chain management has six main requirements including _____.
    a) customer service centers
    b) coordination and collaboration
    c) accelerated delivery times
    d) ISO 9000 certification
    (p. 570, Exhibit 19-3)

12. Value chain management radically changes _____ – that is, the ways that organizational work is done.
    a) organizational processes
    b) production
    c) human resource policies
    d) the organizational structure
    (p. 570)

13. What is the key to job design in a value chain management organization?
    a) Job descriptions
    b) Chain of command
    c) Flexibility
    d) Predictability
    (p. 573)

14. One of the major benefits of value chain management is _____.
    a) improved procurement
    b) improved logistics
    c) improved product development
    d) All of the above
    (p. 574)

15. People, required capabilities, and _____ are all considered obstacles to value chain management.
    a) organizational barriers
    b) logistics management
    c) decreased sales
    d) foreign market shares
    (p. 574)

16. Proprietary company information that is critical to its efficient and effective functioning and competitiveness is _____.
    a) organizational culture
    b) intellectual property
    c) organizational attitude
    d) value chain
    (p. 574)

17. The ability of a product or service to reliably do what it is supposed to do and to satisfy customer expectation is called _____
    a) value
    b) dependability
    c) serviceability
    d) quality
    (p. 577)

18. _____ refers to how a product looks and feels.
    a) Completeness
    b) Durability
    c) Perceived quality
    d) Aesthetics
    (p. 578, Exhibit 19-5)

19. The service quality dimension of _____ refers to accessibility to customers.
    a) courtesy
    b) completely
    c) consistency
    d) convenience
    (p. 578, Exhibit 19-5)

20. Organizations that possess extensive and successful quality improvement programs tend to rely on _____.
    a) cross-functional work teams and self-directed work teams
    b) quality circles and value chain management
    c) ISO 9000 and Six Sigma requirements
    d) re-engineering and matrix organizations
    (p. 578)

21. Which of these sets uniform guidelines for processes to ensure that products conform to customer requirements?
    a) Pay-for-performance compensation systems
    b) ISO 9000
    c) Value chain management
    d) Six Sigma
    (p. 579)

22. _____ was popularized by Motorola's stringent quality standards more than 30 years ago.
    a) Total quality management
    b) Six Sigma
    c) Flexible manufacturing systems
    d) Information management systems
    (p. 579)

23. ISO 9000 is a _____.
    a) set of manufacturing standards established by the European Union
    b) form of TQM
    c) flexible manufacturing system
    d) series of quality standards that cover manufacturing processes from contract review to product delivery
    (p. 579)

24. Companies now provide consumers with design-to-order products when, where, and how they want it through _____.
    a) 360 degree feedback
    b) mass customization
    c) increased reliance on just-in-time methods
    d) standardization
    (p. 580)

25. Mass customization requires _____ and continual dialogue with customers.
    a) ISO 9000 certification
    b) standardization
    c) flexible manufacturing
    d) an increase in employees
    (p. 580)

## True/False Questions

1. T   F   Every organization has an operations system that creates value by
            transforming inputs into outputs.
            (p. 564)

2. T   F   For countries, high productivity can lead to economic growth and
            development.
            (pp. 565-566)

3. T   F   Service organizations produce goods such as cars and cell phones.
            (p. 565)

4. T   F   Military forces, hospitals, and cruise lines are examples of service
            organizations.
            (p. 565)

5. T   F   Improving quality has become a major goal of virtually every organization.
            (p. 565)

6. T   F   For W. Edwards Deming, the key to quality and increases in productivity was
            the workers.
            (p. 566)

7. T   F   High employee productivity will come solely from managers utilizing
            "effective people management" skills.
            (p. 566)

8. T   F   Operations management plays a strategic role in successful organizational
            performance as organizations move toward managing their operations from a
            value chain perspective.
            (p. 567)

9. T   F   Supply chain management is externally oriented and focuses on both
            incoming materials and outgoing products and services, whereas value chain
            management is internally oriented and focused on efficient flows of incoming
            materials.
            (p. 569)

10. T   F   Supply chain management is efficiency oriented whereas value chain management is effectiveness oriented.
(p. 569)

11. T   F   The value chain is a strategic design for how a company intends to profit from its broad array of strategies, processes, and activities.
(p. 569)

12. T   F   In value chain management, ultimately customers are the ones who define value.
(p. 569)

13. T   F   Value chain management usually is possible without a significant investment in information technology, since it is mostly about relationships.
(p. 569)

14. T   F   In value chain management, managers should avoid laying out explicit expectations for employees in order to encourage creativity.
(p. 571)

15. T   F   The three main human resource requirements for value chain management are flexible approaches to job design, an effective hiring process, and ongoing training.
(p. 573)

16. T   F   An organization's culture and attitude does not impact the success of its value chain management.
(p. 573)

17. T   F   A major human resource problem in value chain management is the lack of experienced managers.
(p. 574)

18. T   F   Value chain management takes an incredible amount of time and energy by an organization's employees.
(p. 575)

19. T   F   The service quality dimension "convenience" refers to the accessibility of the service provider to customers.
(p. 578, Exhibit 19-5)

20. T   F   The product quality dimension "flexibility" refers to amount of use before performance deteriorates.
(p. 578, Exhibit 19-5)

21. T  F  The service quality dimension "completion" is described as fully serviced, as required.
(p. 578, Exhibit 19-5)

22. T  F  Quality improvement initiatives aren't possible without having some way to monitor and evaluate their progress.
(p. 578)

23. T  F  ISO 9000 certification is becoming a prerequisite for doing business globally.
(p. 579)

24. T  F  Six Sigma is a quality standard that establishes a goal of no more than 3.4 defects per thousand units or procedure.
(p. 579)

25. T  F  Mass customization requires flexible manufacturing techniques and continual dialogue with customers.
(p. 580)

# Match Terms with Definitions

a. Organizational processes
b. Operations management
c. Value chain
d. Productivity
e. Value

f. Quality
g. Intellectual property
h. Value chain management
i. Manufacturing organizations
j. Six Sigma

k. Service organizations
l. ISO 9000
m. Mass customization
n. Cellular manufacturing
o. RFID

_____ 1. The design, operation, and control of the transformation process that converts resources into finished goods or services.

_____ 2. The ways that organizational work is done.

_____ 3. Providing customers with a product when, where, and how they want it.

_____ 4. A series of international quality management standards that set uniform guidelines for processes to ensure that products conform to customer requirements.

_____ 5. An approach to manufacturing that uses work cells or groups of workstations to process products progressively.

_____ 6. The ability of a product or service to reliably do what it's supposed to do and to satisfy customer expectations.

_____ 7. The overall output of goods or services produced divided by the inputs needed to generate the output.

_____ 8. An automatic identification method in which information can be stored and remotely retrieved.

_____ 9. A quality standard that establishes a goal of no more than 3.4 defects per million parts or procedures.

_____ 10. Organizations that produce nonphysical outputs in the form or services.

_____ 11. The entire series of organizational work activities that add value at each step beginning with the processing of raw materials and ending with finished product in the hands of end users.

_____ 12. Organizations that produce physical goods.

_____ 13. Proprietary company information that's critical to its efficient and effective functioning and competitiveness.

_____ 14. The process of managing the entire sequence of integrated activities and information about product flows along the entire value chain.

_____ 15. The performance characteristics, features and attributes, and any other aspects of goods and services for which customers are willing to give up resources.

## Essay Questions

1. Discuss operations management and explain why it is important.
   (p. 564)

2. List and describe the six requirements for successful value chain management.
   (pp. 569-573, Exhibit 19-3)

3. Describe the benefits and the obstacles associated with value chain management.
   (pp. 574-575)

4. Compare and contrast ISO 9000 and Six Sigma.
   (p. 579)

5. Explain mass customization and how it can help organizations stay competitive.
   (pp. 580-581)

# Appendix A  Managing Entrepreneurial Ventures

## Learning Outline

**The Context of Entrepreneurship**
- Differentiate between entrepreneurial ventures and small businesses.
- Explain why entrepreneurship is important in the United States and globally.
- Describe the four key steps in the entrepreneurial process.
- Explain what entrepreneurs do.
- Discuss why social responsibility and ethics are important considerations for entrepreneurs.

**Start-Up and Planning Issues**
- Discuss how opportunities are important to entrepreneurial ventures.
- Describe each of the seven sources of potential opportunity.
- Explain why it's important for entrepreneurs to understand competitive advantage.
- List possible financing options for entrepreneurs.
- Describe the six major sections of a business plan.

**Organizing Issues**
- Contrast the six different forms of legal organization.
- Describe the organizational design issues that entrepreneurs face.
- Discuss the unique human resource management issues entrepreneurs face.
- Describe what an innovation-supportive culture looks like.

**Leading Issues**
- Explain what personality research shows about entrepreneurs.
- Discuss how entrepreneurs can empower employees.
- Explain how entrepreneurs can be effective at leading employee work teams.

**Controlling Issues**
- Describe how entrepreneurs should plan, organize, and control growth.
- Describe the boiled frog phenomenon and why it's useful for entrepreneurs.
- Discuss the issues an entrepreneur needs to consider when deciding whether to exit the entrepreneurial venture.

## Lecture Outline

I.  The Context of Entrepreneurship.
    A. What is Entrepreneurship?
        1. Define entrepreneurship.
        2. Differences between entrepreneurial ventures and small businesses.
    B. Why is Entrepreneurship Important?
        1. Innovation.
        2. Number of new start-ups.
        3. Job creation.
        4. Global entrepreneurship. (Refer to Exhibit A-1)

C. The Entrepreneurial Process.
  1. Four key steps of the entrepreneurial process.
     a. Exploring the entrepreneurial context.
     b. Identifying opportunities and possible competitive advantages.
     c. Starting the venture.
     d. Managing the venture.
D. What do Entrepreneurs Do?
  1. Explore the context
     a. Gather information.
     b. Identify potential opportunities.
     c. Pinpoint possible competitive advantages.
  2. Plan the venture.
     a. Develop a viable organizational mission.
     b. Explore organizational culture issues.
     c. Create a well-thought-out business plan.
  3. Organize the venture.
     a. Choose a legal form of business organization.
     b. Address other legal issues such as patent or copyright searches.
     c. Come up with an appropriate organizational design for structuring how work is going to be done.
  4. Launch the venture.
     a. Set goals and strategies.
     b. Establish the technology-operations methods.
     c. Establish marketing plans.
     d. Establish information systems.
     e. Establish financial-accounting systems.
     f. Establish cash flow management systems.
  5. Manage the venture.
     a. Make decisions.
     b. Establish action plans.
     c. Analyze external and internal environments.
     d. Measure and evaluate performance.
     e. Make needed changes.
     f. Manage human resources.
     g. Manage the venture's growth.
E. Social Responsibility and Ethics Issues Facing Entrepreneurs.
  1. Wide prevalence of belief that community relations are important for achieving business goals.
  2. Majority of businesses lack formal programs for connecting with their communities.
F. Learning Review.
  • Differentiate between entrepreneurial ventures and small businesses.
  • Explain why entrepreneurship is important in the United States.
  • Discuss the importance of entrepreneurship globally.
  • Describe the four key steps in the entrepreneurial process.
  • Explain what entrepreneurs do.

- Discuss why social responsibility and ethics are important considerations for entrepreneurs.
  G. Key Terms.
    1. Entrepreneurship – The process of starting new businesses, generally in response to opportunities.
    2. Entrepreneurial ventures – Organizations that are pursuing opportunities, are characterized by innovative practices, and have growth and profitability as their main goals.
    3. Small business – An organization that is independently owned, operated, and financed; has fewer than 100 employees; doesn't necessarily engage in any new or innovative practices, and has relatively little impact on its industry.


II. Start-up and Planning Issues
  A. Identifying Environmental Opportunities and Competitive Advantage.
    1. Define opportunities. (Refer to Chapter 8)
    2. Entrepreneurs need to be able to pinpoint pockets of opportunities that a changing context provides.
    3. Peter Drucker's seven potential sources of opportunities for entrepreneurs.
       a. The unexpected.
       b. The incongruous.
       c. The process need.
       d. Industry and market structures.
       e. Demographics.
       f. Changes in perception.
       g. New knowledge.
  B. Researching the Venture's Feasibility – Generating and Evaluating Ideas.
    1. Generating ideas.
       a. Sources of ideas are unique and varied.
       b. Look for limitations of what's currently available, new and different approaches, advances and breakthroughs, unfilled niches, or trends and changes.
    2. Evaluating ideas. (Refer to Exhibit A-2)
       a. Feasibility study. (Refer to Exhibit A-3)
       b. Relationship between feasibility study and business plan.
  C. Researching the Venture's Feasibility – Researching Competitors.
    1. Competitor analysis.
  D. Researching the Venture's Feasibility – Researching Financing.
    1. Possible financing options. (Refer to Exhibit A-4)
  E. Planning the Venture – Developing a Business Plan.
    1. Define business plan.
    2. Six major areas covered by a good business plan.
       a. Executive summary.
       b. Analysis of opportunity.
       c. Analysis of the context.
       d. Description of the business.

     e.  Financial data and projections.

     f.  Supporting documentation.

F.  Learning Review.
- Discuss how opportunities are important to entrepreneurial ventures.
- Describe each of the seven sources of potential opportunity.
- Explain why it's important for entrepreneurs to understand competitive advantage.
- List possible financing options for entrepreneurs.
- Describe the six major sections of a business plan.

G.  Key Terms.
1. Feasibility study – An analysis of the various aspects of a proposed entrepreneurial venture designed to determine its feasibility.
2. Venture capitalists – External equity financing provided by professionally-managed pools of investor money.
3. Angel investors – A private investor (or group of private investors) who offers financial backing to an entrepreneurial venture in return for equity in the venture.
4. Initial public offering (IPO) – The first public registration and sale of a company's stock.
5. Business plan – A written document that summarizes a business opportunity and defines and articulates ho the identified opportunity is to be seized and exploited.

III. Organizing Issues

A.  Legal Forms of Organization.
1. Entrepreneurs want to minimize the impact of both taxes and legal liability.
2. Three ways to organize an entrepreneurial venture. (Refer to Exhibit A-5)
    a.  Sole proprietorship.
    b.  Partnership.
        (i)        General partnership.
        (ii)       Limited liability partnership (LLP).
            a.  Limited partners.
            b.  General partners.
    c.  Corporation.
        (i)        C corporation.
            a.  Closely held corporation.
            b.  S corporation.
            c.  Limited liability company (LLC).
            d.  Operating agreement.

B.  Organizational Design and Structure.
1. Changes in organizational structure as entrepreneurial ventures grow.
2. Elements of organizational structure. (Refer to Chapter 10)

C.  Human Resource Management Issues in Entrepreneurial Ventures.
1. Employee recruitment.
    a.  One of the biggest challenges that entrepreneurs face.
    b.  Entrepreneurs focus on matching the person to the organization.

2. Employee retention.
    a. Entrepreneurial firms are more likely to view compensation from a total rewards perspective.
D. Stimulating and Making Changes.
    1. Entrepreneurs face a context of dynamic change.
    2. Entrepreneurs should act as change agents.
    3. Entrepreneurs may have to guide the actual change process.
E. The Continuing Important of Innovation.
    1. Innovation is a key characteristic of entrepreneurial ventures.
    2. Innovation-supportive culture is crucial.
F. Learning Review.
    • Contrast the six different forms of legal organization.
    • Describe the organizational design issues entrepreneurs face as the venture grows.
    • Explain when a more mechanistic or a more organic structure would be most desirable.
    • Discuss the unique HRM issues entrepreneurs face.
    • Describe what an innovation-supportive culture looks like.
G. Key Terms.
    1. Sole proprietorship – a form of legal organization in which the owner maintains sole and complete control over the business and is personally liable for business debts.
    2. General partnership – a form of legal organization in which two or more business owners share the management and risk of the business.
    3. Limited liability partnership (LLP) – a form of legal organization in which there are general partner(s) and limited liability partner(s).
    4. Corporation – a legal business entity that is separate from its owners and managers.
    5. Closely held corporation – a corporation owned by a limited number of people who do not trade the stock publicly.
    6. S corporation – a specialized type of corporation that has the regular characteristics of a C corporation but is unique in that the owners are taxed as a partnership as long as certain criteria are met.
    7. Limited liability company (LLC) – a form of legal organization that's a hybrid between a partnership and a corporation.
    8. Operating agreement – the document that outlines the provisions governing the way an LLC will conduct business.

IV. Leading Issues
A. Personality Characteristics of Entrepreneurs.
    1. Proactive personality.
    2. Risk propensity moderated by primary goals.
B. Motivating Employees Through Empowerment.
    1. Empowered employees often display stronger work motivation, better work quality, higher job satisfaction, and lower turnover.
    2. Many entrepreneurs resist empowering employees.

3. Participative decision making and delegation are intermediate steps.
C. The Entrepreneur as Leader.
1. Leading the venture.
a. Importance of visionary leadership.
2. Leading employee work teams.
a. Work teams tend to be popular in entrepreneurial ventures.
b. Empowered teams facilitate adaptable and change-ready ventures.
D. Learning Review.
- Explain what personality research shows about entrepreneurs.
- Discuss how entrepreneurs can empower employees.
- Explain how entrepreneurs can be effective at leading employee work teams.
E. Key Terms
1. Proactive personality – A personality trait that describes individuals who are more prone to take actions that influence their environments.
V. Controlling Issues

---

**Managing IT: IT for Entrepreneurs**
IT presents a number of challenges – and opportunities – for entrepreneurs. Identify a few of those challenges and opportunities facing entrepreneurs.

---

A. Managing Growth.
1. Growth is what distinguishes an entrepreneurial venture.
2. Planning for growth.
a. The best growth strategy is a well-planned one.
b. Flexibility.
3. Organizing for growth.
a. Key challenges.
(i)      Finding capital.
(ii)     Finding people.
(iii)    Strengthening the organizational culture. (Refer to Exhibit A-6).
4. Controlling for growth.
a. Reinforce already established organizational controls.
B. Managing Downturns.
1. Recognizing crisis situations.
a. "Boiled frog" phenomenon.
2. Dealing with downturns, declines, and crises.
a. Important to have an up-to-date plan for covering crises.
(i)      Plan should provide specific details for controlling the fundamental and critical aspects of running the venture.
C. Exiting the Venture.
1. Harvesting.
2. Business valuation methods.
a. Asset valuations.
b. Earnings valuations.
c. Cash flow valuations.
3. Other important considerations in exiting the venture. (Refer to Exhibit A-7)

D. Managing Personal Life Choices and Challenges.
   1. Become a good time manager.
   2. Delegate.
   3. Seek professional advice.
   4. Deal with conflicts.
   5. Develop a network of trusted friends and peers.
   6. Recognize when your stress levels are too high.
E. Learning Review.
   - Describe how entrepreneurs should plan, organize, and control growth.
   - Describe the boiled frog phenomenon and how it's useful for entrepreneurs.
   - Discuss the issues an entrepreneur needs to consider when deciding to exit the entrepreneurial venture.
F. Key Terms.
   1. "Boiled frog" phenomenon – a perspective on recognizing performance declines that suggests watching out for subtly declining situations.
   2. Harvesting – exiting a venture when an entrepreneur hopes to capitalize financially on the investment in the venture.

**Multiple-Choice Questions**

1. Entrepreneurial ventures differ from small businesses in that they _____.
   a) are independently owned, operated, and financed
   b) are innovative and seek out new opportunities
   c) have relatively little impact on their industries
   d) All of the above.
   (p. 591)

2. _____ is process of changing, experimenting, transforming and revolutionizing, and is a key aspect of entrepreneurial activity.
   a) Business development
   b) Job creation
   c) Globalization
   d) Innovation
   (p. 591)

3. Globally, the highest levels of entrepreneurial activity tend to be found in _____.
   a) middle-income countries
   b) high-income countries
   c) low-income countries
   d) countries with younger populations, regardless of income level
   (p. 592)

4. In which of the following steps of the entrepreneurial process does the entrepreneur explore the realities of the economic, political/legal, social, and work environment?
   a) Identifying opportunities and possible competitive advantages.
   b) Managing the venture.
   c) Exploring the entrepreneurial context.
   d) Starting the venture.
   (p. 593)

5. Which of the following steps of the entrepreneurial process involves setting goals and strategies, and establishing the technology-operations methods, marketing plans, information systems, financial-accounting systems, and cash flow management systems of the venture?
   a) Identifying opportunities and possible competitive advantages.
   b) Managing the venture.
   c) Exploring the entrepreneurial context.
   d) Starting the venture.
   (p. 593)

6. When something is _____, there are inconsistencies and incompatibilities in the way it appears. This characteristic is often a fruitful source of entrepreneurial opportunity.
   a) unexpected
   b) incongruous
   c) unique
   d) significant
   (p. 595)

7. Of Peter Drucker's seven potential sources of opportunity for entrepreneurs, _____ involves the existence of opportunities for entrepreneurs in making the small steps along the way to big, industry-changing discoveries.
   a) the process need
   b) industry and market structure
   c) perceptual change
   d) shifting demographics
   (p. 596)

8. A _____ should give descriptions of the most important elements of the entrepreneurial venture and the entrepreneur's analysis of the viability of those elements.
   a) financial evaluation
   b) feasibility study
   c) competitor analysis
   d) value chain
   (p. 598)

9. In a good business plan, the _____ involves a description of the demographics of the target market, an evaluation of industry trends, and an analysis of the competitive environment.
   a) description of the business
   b) executive summary
   c) financial projection
   d) analysis of opportunity
   (p. 601)

10. In deciding on the legal form of an organization, the entrepreneur seeks to _____.
    a) minimize the impact of both taxes and legal liability
    b) maximize the impact of both taxes and legal liability
    c) minimize the impact of taxes, while maximizing legal liability
    d) maximize the impact of taxes, while minimizing legal liability
    (p. 602)

11. One of the drawbacks of a sole proprietorship is _____.
    a) the high cost and complexity of formation
    b) the high potential for conflict among owners
    c) agency issues between shareholders and managers
    d) the unlimited personal liability for the owner
    (p. 603, Exhibit A-5)

12. Which of the following is NOT true of human resources issues that entrepreneurs face?
    a) Entrepreneurs are most likely to view compensation from the perspective of monetary rewards.
    b) Entrepreneurs are concerned with matching characteristics of the person to the values and culture of the organization.
    c) Entrepreneurs are looking for high-potential people who can perform multiple roles during various stages of venture growth.
    d) All of the above are false.
    (p. 606)

13. Which of the following is true of planning for growth?
    a) Planning for growth is rarely effective in the face of intense competitive pressures and high failure rates for entrepreneurial ventures.
    b) Effectively flexible growth plans avoid estimating future numbers and types of employees needed by the organization, but rather let the increasing workload dictate human resources requirements as they go along.
    c) Planning for growth involves fostering a positive, growth-oriented culture that enhances the opportunities to achieve success, both organizationally and individually.
    d) Entrepreneurs should develop very rigid growth strategies as part of their business planning.
    (pp. 611-612)

14. Which of the following is NOT a business valuation method presented in the text?
    a) Asset valuation.
    b) Cash flow valuation.
    c) Opportunity valuation.
    d) Earnings valuation.
    (p. 614)

15. Which of the following is an important thing an entrepreneur can do to balance his or her work and personal lives?
    a) Recognize when stress levels are too high.
    b) Develop a network of trusted friends and peers.
    c) Deal with conflicts.
    d) All of the above.
    (p. 614)

## True/False Questions

1. T  F  To be entrepreneurial means that the business must be innovative, seeking out new opportunities.
   (p. 591)

2. T  F  Over the last decade, small businesses were responsible for the majority of new job creation.
   (p. 592)

3. T  F  Opportunities are negative trends in external environmental factors which open up niches in the market upon which entrepreneurs can capitalize.
   (p. 595)

4. T  F  Unexpected successes, but not unexpected failures, create potential opportunities for entrepreneurs.
   (p. 595)

5. T  F  When changes in technology or shifts in social values and consumer tastes shift the structure of an industry or market, existing firms can become obsolete if they are not attuned to the changes or are unwilling to change in response.
   (p. 596)

6. T  F  When changes in perception take place, the facts vary, but their meanings do not.
   (p. 597)

7. T  F  The sources of an entrepreneur's ideas are unique and varied.
   (p. 597)

8.  T   F   Effective business plans should focus on the opportunity and the context. Financial plans should be left to be developed as the entrepreneurial venture grows and its needs change.
(p. 601)

9.  T   F   An S corporation differs from a C corporation in the flexibility of the way profits are taxed.
(p. 603, Exhibit A-5)

10. T   F   One of the advantages of a general partnership is that partnering with others makes it somewhat easier to access financing than is the case for a sole proprietorship.
(p. 603, Exhibit A-5)

11. T   F   In a limited liability partnership, no one partner retains unlimited liability.
(p. 603, Exhibit A-5)

12. T   F   For entrepreneurial ventures, compensation is likely to encompass psychological rewards, learning opportunities, and recognition in addition to monetary rewards.
(p. 606)

13. T   F   Entrepreneurs are always willing to empower employees, because employee empowerment represents one of the best ways to foster an innovative culture.
(p. 607)

14. T   F   Visionary companies tend to outperform nonvisionary ones on standard financial criteria, and their stocks tend to outperform the general market.
(p. 610)

15. T   F   Companies experiencing rapid growth do not need to reinforce their controls while the venture is expanding. Such reinforcement would increase the rigidity of the organization and hamper potential further growth.
(p. 612)

## Match Terms with Definitions

a. Sole proprietorship
b. Small business
c. Entrepreneurship
d. "Boiled frog" phenomenon

e. Limited liability company
f. Operating agreement
g. Feasibility study
h. Business plan

i. General partnership
j. Harvesting
k. Corporation
l. Venture capitalists

_____ 1. Exiting a venture when an entrepreneur hopes to capitalize financially on the investment in the venture.

_____ 2. A written document that summarizes a business opportunity and defines and articulates how the identified opportunity is to be seized and exploited.

_____ 3. The process of starting new businesses, generally in response to opportunities.

_____ 4. An organization that is independently owned, operated, and financed; has fewer than 100 employees; doesn't necessarily engage in any new or innovative practices, and has relatively little impact on its industry.

_____ 5. An analysis of the various aspects of a proposed entrepreneurial venture designed to determine its feasibility.

_____ 6. External equity financing provided by professionally-managed pools of investor money.

_____ 7. A legal business entity that is separate from its owners and managers.

_____ 8. A form of legal organization in which two or more business owners share the management and risk of the business.

_____ 9. The document that outlines the provisions governing the way an LLC will conduct business.

_____ 10. A form of legal organization that's a hybrid between a partnership and a corporation.

_____ 11. A form of legal organization in which the owner maintains sole and complete control over the business and is personally liable for business debts.

_____ 12. A perspective on recognizing performance declines that suggests watching out for subtly declining situations.


## Essay Questions

1. Identify and discuss the four key steps that entrepreneurs must address as they start and manage their entrepreneurial ventures.
(pp. 593-594)

2. List and discuss the seven potential sources of opportunity that entrepreneurs might look for in the external context, as identified by Peter Drucker.
(pp. 595-597)

3. Describe the six major areas covered by a good business plan.
(pp. 601-602)

# Answers to the Objective Questions

## Chapter 1

| Multiple Choice | | True/False | | Matching | |
|---|---|---|---|---|---|
| 1. b | 14. a | 1. T | 14. F | 1. j | |
| 2. c | 15. d | 2. F | 15. F | 2. h | |
| 3. b | 16. a | 3. F | 16. F | 3. c | |
| 4 a | 17. c | 4. T | 17. F | 4. b | |
| 5. b | 18. a | 5. T | 18. T | 5. g | |
| 6. a | 19. a | 6. T | 19. F | 6. l | |
| 7. a | 20. d | 7. F | 20. F | 7. k | |
| 8. c | 21. c | 8. T | 21. T | 8. i | |
| 9. d | 22. b | 9. T | 22. F | 9. f | |
| 10. b | 23. c | 10. T | 23. F | 10. e | |
| 11. d | 24. a | 11. F | 24. F | 11. a | |
| 12. d | 25. c | 12. F | 25. T | 12. d | |
| 13. c | | 13. T | | | |

### Essay
1. p. 8
2. p. 9, Exhibit 1-3
3. p. 11, Exhibit 1-4
4. pp. 12-13, Exhibit 1-5, Exhibit 1-6
5. pp. 15-17, Exhibit 1-8

## Chapter 2

| Multiple Choice | | True/False | | Matching | |
|---|---|---|---|---|---|
| 1. a | 14. a | 1. T | 14. F | 1. j | 14. b |
| 2. c | 15. a | 2. T | 15. F | 2. h | 15. m |
| 3. d | 16. b | 3. F | 16. F | 3. i | |
| 4 a | 17. b | 4. T | 17. T | 4. c | |
| 5. c | 18. a | 5. F | 18. F | 5. k | |
| 6. d | 19. c | 6. F | 19. T | 6. g | |
| 7. a | 20. d | 7. F | 20. T | 7. d | |
| 8. a | 21. b | 8. T | 21. T | 8. a | |
| 9. c | 22. c | 9. T | 22. T | 9. l | |
| 10. c | 23. a | 10. F | 23. F | 10. e | |
| 11. b | 24. c | 11. F | 24. T | 11. f | |
| 12. a | 25. d | 12. T | 25. F | 12. n | |
| 13. a | | 13. T | | 13. o | |

### Essay
1. p. 28
2. p. 36, Exhibit 2-5
3. p. 40, Exhibit 2-7
4. p. 42, Exhibit 2-8
5. pp. 40-49

**Chapter 3**

**Multiple Choice**

| | | | |
|---|---|---|---|
| 1. | b | 14. | b |
| 2. | d | 15. | b |
| 3. | b | 16. | a |
| 4 | c | 17. | c |
| 5. | a | 18. | a |
| 6. | d | 19. | c |
| 7. | d | 20. | d |
| 8. | a | 21. | b |
| 9. | d | 22. | c |
| 10. | a | 23. | a |
| 11. | b | 24. | d |
| 12. | d | 25. | a |
| 13. | c | | |

**True/False**

| | | | |
|---|---|---|---|
| 1. | T | 14. | F |
| 2. | T | 15. | F |
| 3. | F | 16. | F |
| 4. | T | 17. | T |
| 5. | T | 18. | T |
| 6. | T | 19. | F |
| 7. | F | 20. | T |
| 8. | T | 21. | T |
| 9. | T | 22. | F |
| 10. | T | 23. | T |
| 11. | T | 24. | T |
| 12. | T | 25. | T |
| 13. | T | | |

**Matching**

| | | | |
|---|---|---|---|
| 1. | o | 14. | a |
| 2. | d | 15. | k |
| 3. | f | | |
| 4. | n | | |
| 5. | m | | |
| 6. | l | | |
| 7. | c | | |
| 8. | i | | |
| 9. | e | | |
| 10. | h | | |
| 11. | g | | |
| 12. | j | | |
| 13. | b | | |

**Essay**
1. pp. 58-59
2. p. 61, Exhibit 3-2
3. pp. 64-66
4. pp. 69-70
5. pp. 73-78

**Chapter 4**

**Multiple Choice**

| | | | |
|---|---|---|---|
| 1. | a | 14. | c |
| 2. | c | 15. | a |
| 3. | d | 16. | d |
| 4 | c | 17. | c |
| 5. | a | 18. | a |
| 6. | b | 19. | a |
| 7. | c | 20. | b |
| 8. | d | 21. | c |
| 9. | a | 22. | d |
| 10. | d | 23. | b |
| 11. | b | 24. | b |
| 12. | b | 25. | a |
| 13. | b | | |

**True/False**

| | | | |
|---|---|---|---|
| 1. | F | 14. | T |
| 2. | T | 15. | F |
| 3. | T | 16. | T |
| 4. | F | 17. | F |
| 5. | T | 18. | T |
| 6. | T | 19. | T |
| 7. | T | 20. | T |
| 8. | F | 21. | F |
| 9. | F | 22. | F |
| 10. | T | 23. | T |
| 11. | T | 24. | T |
| 12. | T | 25. | T |
| 13. | F | | |

**Matching**

| | | | |
|---|---|---|---|
| 1. | f | 14. | m |
| 2. | c | 15. | e |
| 3. | h | | |
| 4. | j | | |
| 5. | d | | |
| 6. | i | | |
| 7. | k | | |
| 8. | n | | |
| 9. | o | | |
| 10. | l | | |
| 11. | g | | |
| 12. | b | | |
| 13. | a | | |

**Essay**
1. p. 92, Exhibit 4-1
2. pp. 94-95
3. pp. 98-100
4. pp. 101-104
5. pp. 104-105

## Chapter 5

### Multiple Choice

| | | | |
|---|---|---|---|
| 1. | a | 14. | c |
| 2. | b | 15. | b |
| 3. | b | 16. | a |
| 4 | b | 17. | a |
| 5. | a | 18. | c |
| 6. | c | 19. | a |
| 7. | a | 20. | d |
| 8. | c | 21. | c |
| 9. | b | 22. | d |
| 10. | b | 23. | d |
| 11. | a | 24. | a |
| 12. | b | 25. | b |
| 13. | d | | |

### True/False

| | | | |
|---|---|---|---|
| 1. | F | 14. | T |
| 2. | F | 15. | T |
| 3. | F | 16. | F |
| 4. | T | 17. | T |
| 5. | T | 18. | F |
| 6. | F | 19. | T |
| 7. | T | 20. | T |
| 8. | F | 21. | T |
| 9. | T | 22. | F |
| 10. | T | 23. | F |
| 11. | T | 24. | T |
| 12. | F | 25. | F |
| 13. | T | | |

### Matching

| | | | |
|---|---|---|---|
| 1. | f | 14. | d |
| 2. | e | 15. | l |
| 3. | h | | |
| 4. | k | | |
| 5. | g | | |
| 6. | j | | |
| 7. | m | | |
| 8. | i | | |
| 9. | n | | |
| 10. | b | | |
| 11. | a | | |
| 12. | c | | |
| 13. | o | | |

### Essay
1. pp. 116-117
2. pp. 120-122
3. pp. 130-132, Exhibit 5-8
4. pp. 130, Exhibit 5-9
5. pp. 140-142

## Chapter 6

### Multiple Choice

| | | | |
|---|---|---|---|
| 1. | c | 14. | c |
| 2. | c | 15. | d |
| 3. | a | 16. | b |
| 4 | d | 17. | a |
| 5. | b | 18. | c |
| 6. | b | 19. | c |
| 7. | a | 20. | a |
| 8. | c | 21. | c |
| 9. | a | 22. | a |
| 10. | c | 23. | b |
| 11. | b | 24. | d |
| 12. | c | 25. | a |
| 13. | d | | |

### True/False

| | | | |
|---|---|---|---|
| 1. | T | 14. | F |
| 2. | F | 15. | F |
| 3. | T | 16. | F |
| 4. | F | 17. | T |
| 5. | T | 18. | F |
| 6. | T | 19. | F |
| 7. | T | 20. | T |
| 8. | T | 21. | T |
| 9. | F | 22. | T |
| 10. | T | 23. | F |
| 11. | F | 24. | T |
| 12. | F | 25. | T |
| 13. | T | | |

### Matching

| | | | |
|---|---|---|---|
| 1. | j | 14. | c |
| 2. | f | 15. | d |
| 3. | i | | |
| 4. | e | | |
| 5. | n | | |
| 6. | g | | |
| 7. | m | | |
| 8. | h | | |
| 9. | l | | |
| 10. | k | | |
| 11. | a | | |
| 12. | o | | |
| 13. | b | | |

### Essay
1. pp. 156-161, Exhibit 6-1
2. pp. 162-163, Exhibit 6-6
3. p. 164, Exhibit 6-7
4. pp. 165-167
5. pp. 170-171, Exhibit 6-12

## Chapter 7

### Multiple Choice

| | |
|---|---|
| 1. c | 14. a |
| 2. b | 15. c |
| 3. b | 16. a |
| 4 b | 17. c |
| 5. d | 18. c |
| 6. a | 19. d |
| 7. d | 20. d |
| 8. a | 21. b |
| 9. d | 22. a |
| 10. b | 23. d |
| 11. b | 24. c |
| 12. b | 25. b |
| 13. a | |

### True/False

| | |
|---|---|
| 1. F | 14. F |
| 2. T | 15. T |
| 3. T | 16. F |
| 4. T | 17. F |
| 5. T | 18. T |
| 6. F | 19. T |
| 7. F | 20. T |
| 8. T | 21. F |
| 9. F | 22. F |
| 10. F | 23. T |
| 11. F | 24. F |
| 12. T | 25. F |
| 13. T | |

### Matching

| | |
|---|---|
| 1. c | 14. m |
| 2. f | 15. i |
| 3. g | |
| 4. d | |
| 5. h | |
| 6. j | |
| 7. o | |
| 8. k | |
| 9. e | |
| 10. b | |
| 11. n | |
| 12. l | |
| 13. a | |

### Essay
1. p. 195
2. pp. 189-191, Exhibit 7-2
3. pp. 192-193, Exhibit 7-5
4. p. 195
5. pp. 195-196, Exhibit 7-7

## Chapter 8

### Multiple Choice

| | |
|---|---|
| 1. c | 14. c |
| 2. a | 15. a |
| 3. d | 16. a |
| 4 a | 17. c |
| 5. c | 18. a |
| 6. b | 19. c |
| 7. d | 20. d |
| 8. c | 21. b |
| 9. a | 22. d |
| 10. b | 23. a |
| 11. a | 24. c |
| 12. a | 25. d |
| 13. d | |

### True/False

| | |
|---|---|
| 1. T | 14. T |
| 2. T | 15. F |
| 3. T | 16. F |
| 4. F | 17. T |
| 5. F | 18. T |
| 6. F | 19. F |
| 7. F | 20. T |
| 8. T | 21. T |
| 9. F | 22. T |
| 10. T | 23. T |
| 11. T | 24. F |
| 12. F | 25. T |
| 13. T | |

### Matching

| | |
|---|---|
| 1. a | 14. c |
| 2. d | 15. b |
| 3. f | |
| 4. e | |
| 5. l | |
| 6. m | |
| 7. n | |
| 8. o | |
| 9. k | |
| 10. i | |
| 11. j | |
| 12. h | |
| 13. g | |

### Essay
1. pp. 208-210
2. pp. 210-216, Exhibit 8-1
3. pp. 217-220
4. pp. 220-221, Exhibit 8-5
5. pp. 228-230

**Chapter 9**

**Multiple Choice**

| | | | |
|---|---|---|---|
| 1. | b | 14. | a |
| 2. | a | 15. | d |
| 3. | d | 16. | b |
| 4 | d | 17. | a |
| 5. | c | 18. | c |
| 6. | b | 19. | d |
| 7. | c | 20. | a |
| 8. | a | 21. | a |
| 9. | c | 22. | c |
| 10. | b | 23. | b |
| 11. | a | 24. | c |
| 12. | a | 25. | d |
| 13. | d | | |

**True/False**

| | | | |
|---|---|---|---|
| 1. | T | 14. | F |
| 2. | F | 15. | F |
| 3. | F | 16. | F |
| 4. | T | 17. | F |
| 5. | T | 18. | T |
| 6. | T | 19. | T |
| 7. | T | 20. | T |
| 8. | F | 21. | F |
| 9. | F | 22. | T |
| 10. | T | 23. | T |
| 11. | F | 24. | F |
| 12. | F | 25. | T |
| 13. | T | | |

**Matching**

| | | | |
|---|---|---|---|
| 1. | i | 14. | d |
| 2. | k | 15. | j |
| 3. | h | | |
| 4. | n | | |
| 5. | c | | |
| 6. | e | | |
| 7. | g | | |
| 8. | b | | |
| 9. | m | | |
| 10. | a | | |
| 11. | f | | |
| 12. | l | | |
| 13. | o | | |

**Essay**
1. pp. 238-243
2. p. 243
3. pp. 244-245, Exhibit 9-3
4. pp. 247-249
5. p. 253, Exhibit 9-13

**Chapter 10**

**Multiple Choice**

| | | | |
|---|---|---|---|
| 1. | b | 14. | b |
| 2. | c | 15. | c |
| 3. | c | 16. | a |
| 4 | a | 17. | c |
| 5. | a | 18. | b |
| 6. | c | 19. | c |
| 7. | c | 20. | c |
| 8. | d | 21. | c |
| 9. | d | 22. | b |
| 10. | b | 23. | b |
| 11. | a | 24. | b |
| 12. | b | 25. | c |
| 13. | b | | |

**True/False**

| | | | |
|---|---|---|---|
| 1. | F | 14. | T |
| 2. | T | 15. | F |
| 3. | F | 16. | T |
| 4. | F | 17. | T |
| 5. | F | 18. | F |
| 6. | T | 19. | T |
| 7. | T | 20. | T |
| 8. | F | 21. | F |
| 9. | T | 22. | F |
| 10. | F | 23. | T |
| 11. | T | 24. | T |
| 12. | T | 25. | T |
| 13. | F | | |

**Matching**

| | | | |
|---|---|---|---|
| 1. | c | 14. | o |
| 2. | j | 15. | l |
| 3. | f | | |
| 4. | d | | |
| 5. | h | | |
| 6. | e | | |
| 7. | i | | |
| 8. | a | | |
| 9. | k | | |
| 10. | b | | |
| 11. | m | | |
| 12. | g | | |
| 13. | n | | |

**Essay**
1. pp. 268-270, Exhibit 10-2
2. p. 270
3. p. 272, Exhibit 10-4
4. p. 275, Exhibit 10-5
5. p. 278, Exhibit 10-7

## Chapter 11

### Multiple Choice

| | |
|---|---|
| 1. c | 14. a |
| 2. b | 15. b |
| 3. d | 16. a |
| 4 b | 17. c |
| 5. d | 18. d |
| 6. a | 19. b |
| 7. a | 20. a |
| 8. c | 21. a |
| 9. b | 22. c |
| 10. a | 23. d |
| 11. c | 24. a |
| 12. d | 25. b |
| 13. b | |

### True/False

| | |
|---|---|
| 1. T | 14. T |
| 2. T | 15. F |
| 3. F | 16. F |
| 4. F | 17. T |
| 5. T | 18. T |
| 6. F | 19. T |
| 7. T | 20. F |
| 8. F | 21. T |
| 9. T | 22. T |
| 10. T | 23. T |
| 11. T | 24. F |
| 12. T | 25. T |
| 13. T | |

### Matching

| | |
|---|---|
| 1. g | 14. l |
| 2. m | 15. a |
| 3. h | 16. n |
| 4. i | 17. p |
| 5. e | 18. r |
| 6. o | 19. s |
| 7. d | 20. t |
| 8. b | |
| 9. j | |
| 10. k | |
| 11. c | |
| 12. q | |
| 13. f | |

### Essay
1. pp. 294-295, Exhibit 11-1
2. pp. 299–301
3. p. 300, Managing Workforce Diversity
4. p. 302, Exhibit 11-3
5. p. 305, Exhibit 11-4

## Chapter 12

### Multiple Choice

| | |
|---|---|
| 1. d | 14. b |
| 2. d | 15. a |
| 3. b | 16. b |
| 4 a | 17. c |
| 5. a | 18. d |
| 6. a | 19. a |
| 7. a | 20. b |
| 8. c | 21. a |
| 9. b | 22. b |
| 10. d | 23. d |
| 11. c | 24. c |
| 12. c | 25. c |
| 13. b | |

### True/False

| | |
|---|---|
| 1. T | 14. F |
| 2. T | 15. T |
| 3. T | 16. F |
| 4. F | 17. T |
| 5. T | 18. T |
| 6. T | 19. T |
| 7. F | 20. F |
| 8. T | 21. T |
| 9. F | 22. T |
| 10. T | 23. F |
| 11. T | 24. T |
| 12. T | 25. F |
| 13. T | |

### Matching

| | |
|---|---|
| 1. g | 14. a |
| 2. l | 15. o |
| 3. h | |
| 4. i | |
| 5. e | |
| 6. m | |
| 7. d | |
| 8. b | |
| 9. j | |
| 10. c | |
| 11. n | |
| 12. e | |
| 13. k | |

### Essay
1. p. 324, Exhibit 12-2
2. p. 328, Exhibit 12-5
3. pp. 329-330
4. p. 332, Exhibit 12-9
5. p. 337, Exhibit 12-13

## Chapter 13

### Multiple Choice

| | | | |
|---|---|---|---|
| 1. | a | 14. | d |
| 2. | c | 15. | c |
| 3. | b | 16. | b |
| 4. | c | 17. | a |
| 5 | a | 18. | c |
| 6. | c | 19. | d |
| 7. | b | 20. | a |
| 8. | d | 21. | a |
| 9. | d | 22. | b |
| 10. | a | 23. | d |
| 11. | d | 24. | c |
| 12. | a | 25. | d |
| 13. | c | | |

### True/False

| | | | |
|---|---|---|---|
| 1. | T | 14. | T |
| 2. | T | 15. | F |
| 3. | F | 16. | T |
| 4. | F | 17. | T |
| 5. | T | 18. | F |
| 6. | T | 19. | T |
| 7. | F | 20. | T |
| 8. | T | 21. | F |
| 9. | T | 22. | F |
| 10. | F | 23. | T |
| 11. | T | 24. | T |
| 12. | T | 25. | T |
| 13. | T | | |

### Matching

| | |
|---|---|
| 1. | b |
| 2. | d |
| 3. | f |
| 4. | g |
| 5. | a |
| 6. | e |
| 7. | c |

### Essay
1. pp. 356-357
2. pp. 364-365
3. p. 365, Exhibit 13-4
4. pp. 367-368
5. pp. 368-370

## Chapter 14

### Multiple Choice

| | | | |
|---|---|---|---|
| 1. | a | 14. | a |
| 2. | c | 15. | d |
| 3. | b | 16. | b |
| 4 | b | 17. | a |
| 5. | b | 18. | d |
| 6. | c | 19. | a |
| 7. | a | 20. | a |
| 8. | c | 21. | b |
| 9. | d | 22. | c |
| 10. | d | 23. | d |
| 11. | d | 24. | d |
| 12. | b | 25. | c |
| 13. | c | | |

### True/False

| | | | |
|---|---|---|---|
| 1. | F | 14. | T |
| 2. | T | 15. | T |
| 3. | F | 16. | T |
| 4. | F | 17. | T |
| 5. | T | 18. | T |
| 6. | T | 19. | T |
| 7. | T | 20. | F |
| 8. | F | 21. | F |
| 9. | T | 22. | T |
| 10. | F | 23. | F |
| 11. | F | 24. | T |
| 12. | F | 25. | F |
| 13. | F | | |

### Matching

| | | | |
|---|---|---|---|
| 1. | s | 14. | q |
| 2. | t | 15. | p |
| 3. | f | 16. | i |
| 4. | d | 17. | j |
| 5. | e | 18. | c |
| 6. | h | 19. | b |
| 7. | l | 20. | a |
| 8. | m | | |
| 9. | g | | |
| 10. | n | | |
| 11. | k | | |
| 12. | r | | |
| 13. | o | | |

### Essay
1. pp. 389-390
2. p. 398
3. pp. 402-405
4. pp. 407-409
5. pp. 409-411

## Chapter 15

### Multiple Choice

| | | | |
|---|---|---|---|
| 1. | a | 14. | d |
| 2. | a | 15. | c |
| 3. | c | 16. | c |
| 4 | c | 17. | b |
| 5. | b | 18. | b |
| 6. | b | 19. | a |
| 7. | b | 20. | b |
| 8. | b | 21. | a |
| 9. | a | 22. | b |
| 10. | c | 23. | b |
| 11. | b | 24. | d |
| 12. | d | 25. | b |
| 13. | a | | |

### True/False

| | | | |
|---|---|---|---|
| 1. | F | 14. | T |
| 2. | T | 15. | F |
| 3. | F | 16. | F |
| 4. | T | 17. | T |
| 5. | F | 18. | T |
| 6. | T | 19. | T |
| 7. | T | 20. | T |
| 8. | T | 21. | T |
| 9. | T | 22. | F |
| 10. | T | 23. | T |
| 11. | T | 24. | F |
| 12. | F | 25. | T |
| 13. | F | | |

### Matching

| | | | |
|---|---|---|---|
| 1. | s | 14. | j |
| 2. | a | 15. | c |
| 3. | m | 16. | d |
| 4. | d | 17. | h |
| 5. | p | 18. | g |
| 6. | o | 19. | b |
| 7. | k | 20. | f |
| 8. | l | | |
| 9. | t | | |
| 10. | r | | |
| 11. | i | | |
| 12. | q | | |
| 13. | n | | |

### Essay
1. pp. 425-426, Exhibit 15-2
2. pp. 429-431
3. pp. 434-435
4. pp. 435-437
5. pp. 440-442

## Chapter 16

### Multiple Choice

| | | | |
|---|---|---|---|
| 1. | a | 14. | b |
| 2. | b | 15. | a |
| 3. | a | 16. | d |
| 4 | b | 17. | c |
| 5. | c | 18. | b |
| 6. | d | 19. | c |
| 7. | a | 20. | b |
| 8. | c | 21. | d |
| 9. | d | 22. | b |
| 10. | a | 23. | c |
| 11. | b | 24. | d |
| 12. | d | 25. | c |
| 13. | b | | |

### True/False

| | | | |
|---|---|---|---|
| 1. | T | 14. | T |
| 2. | T | 15. | F |
| 3. | F | 16. | F |
| 4. | F | 17. | T |
| 5. | T | 18. | T |
| 6. | F | 19. | T |
| 7. | T | 20. | F |
| 8. | T | 21. | T |
| 9. | T | 22. | F |
| 10. | F | 23. | T |
| 11. | T | 24. | F |
| 12. | F | 25. | T |
| 13. | T | | |

### Matching

| | | | |
|---|---|---|---|
| 1. | d | 14. | f |
| 2. | j | 15. | q |
| 3. | h | 16. | e |
| 4. | i | 17. | b |
| 5. | s | 18. | a |
| 6. | n | 19. | c |
| 7. | r | | |
| 8. | o | | |
| 9. | p | | |
| 10. | m | | |
| 11. | l | | |
| 12. | k | | |
| 13. | g | | |

### Essay
1. pp. 454-455
2. pp. 456-457
3. pp. 461-464
4. p. 470
5. pp. 476-478

## Chapter 17

### Multiple Choice

| | | | |
|---|---|---|---|
| 1. | b | 14. | c |
| 2. | d | 15. | c |
| 3. | c | 16. | a |
| 4 | a | 17. | a |
| 5. | d | 18. | b |
| 6. | c | 19. | d |
| 7. | b | 20. | c |
| 8. | c | 21. | b |
| 9. | b | 22. | d |
| 10. | a | 23. | b |
| 11. | c | 24. | c |
| 12. | a | 25. | c |
| 13. | a | | |

### True/False

| | | | |
|---|---|---|---|
| 1. | T | 14. | T |
| 2. | T | 15. | F |
| 3. | F | 16. | F |
| 4. | F | 17. | F |
| 5. | T | 18. | F |
| 6. | F | 19. | T |
| 7. | T | 20. | F |
| 8. | T | 21. | T |
| 9. | T | 22. | F |
| 10. | T | 23. | F |
| 11. | F | 24. | T |
| 12. | F | 25. | T |
| 13. | T | | |

### Matching

| | | | |
|---|---|---|---|
| 1. | d | 14. | s |
| 2. | p | 15. | t |
| 3. | f | 16. | b |
| 4. | e | 17. | n |
| 5. | h | 18. | k |
| 6. | q | 19. | l |
| 7. | g | 20. | m |
| 8. | o | | |
| 9. | i | | |
| 10. | r | | |
| 11. | c | | |
| 12. | j | | |
| 13. | a | | |

### Essay

1. p. 490, Exhibit 17-2
2. pp. 498-500
3. pp. 501-502
4. pp. 502-504
5. p. 504

## Chapter 18

### Multiple Choice

| | | | |
|---|---|---|---|
| 1. | d | 14. | a |
| 2. | a | 15. | b |
| 3. | b | 16. | a |
| 4 | c | 17. | d |
| 5. | c | 18. | d |
| 6. | c | 19. | b |
| 7. | b | 20. | d |
| 8. | c | 21. | d |
| 9. | c | 22. | b |
| 10. | d | 23. | a |
| 11. | c | 24. | b |
| 12. | d | 25. | b |
| 13. | b | | |

### True/False

| | | | |
|---|---|---|---|
| 1. | F | 14. | T |
| 2. | F | 15. | T |
| 3. | T | 16. | F |
| 4. | F | 17. | F |
| 5. | F | 18. | T |
| 6. | F | 19. | F |
| 7. | T | 20. | T |
| 8. | F | 21. | T |
| 9. | T | 22. | T |
| 10. | F | 23. | T |
| 11. | F | 24. | T |
| 12. | F | 25. | F |
| 13. | T | | |

### Matching

| | | | |
|---|---|---|---|
| 1. | g | 14. | c |
| 2. | f | 15. | m |
| 3. | b | 16. | n |
| 4. | t | 17. | k |
| 5. | p | 18. | r |
| 6. | a | 19. | l |
| 7. | j | 20. | q |
| 8. | d | | |
| 9. | h | | |
| 10. | i | | |
| 11. | o | | |
| 12. | s | | |
| 13. | e | | |

### Essay

1. p. 527, Exhibit 18-1
2. p. 530, Exhibit 18-3
3. pp. 538-539
4. p. 540, Exhibit 18-10
5. pp. 544-546

## Chapter 19

### Multiple Choice

| | |
|---|---|
| 1. b | 14. d |
| 2. b | 15. a |
| 3. a | 16. b |
| 4 c | 17. d |
| 5. a | 18. d |
| 6. a | 19. b |
| 7. b | 20. a |
| 8. c | 21. b |
| 9. a | 22. b |
| 10. b | 23. d |
| 11. b | 24. b |
| 12. a | 25. c |
| 13. c | |

### True/False

| | |
|---|---|
| 1. T | 14. F |
| 2. T | 15. T |
| 3. F | 16. F |
| 4. T | 17. T |
| 5. T | 18. T |
| 6. F | 19. T |
| 7. F | 20. F |
| 8. T | 21. T |
| 9. F | 22. T |
| 10. T | 23. T |
| 11. F | 24. F |
| 12. T | 25. T |
| 13. F | |

### Matching

| | |
|---|---|
| 1. b | 14.h |
| 2. a | 15.e |
| 3. m | |
| 4. l | |
| 5. n | |
| 6. f | |
| 7. d | |
| 8. o | |
| 9. j | |
| 10. k | |
| 11. c | |
| 12. i | |
| 13. g | |

### Essay
1. p. 564
2. pp. 569-573, Exhibit 19-3
3. pp. 574-575
4. p. 579
5. pp. 580-581

## Appendix A

### Multiple Choice

| | |
|---|---|
| 1. b | 14. c |
| 2. d | 15. d |
| 3. a | |
| 4 c | |
| 5. d | |
| 6. b | |
| 7. a | |
| 8. b | |
| 9. d | |
| 10. a | |
| 11. d | |
| 12. a | |
| 13. c | |

### True/False

| | |
|---|---|
| 1. T | 14. T |
| 2. T | 15. F |
| 3. F | |
| 4. F | |
| 5. T | |
| 6. F | |
| 7. T | |
| 8. F | |
| 9. T | |
| 10. T | |
| 11. F | |
| 12. T | |
| 13. F | |

### Matching

| |
|---|
| 1. j |
| 2. h |
| 3. c |
| 4. b |
| 5. g |
| 6. l |
| 7. k |
| 8. i |
| 9. f |
| 10. e |
| 11. a |
| 12. d |

### Essay
1. pp. 593-594
2. pp. 595-597
3. pp. 601-602

# Ma petit étoile

# À Joanna

Catalogage avant publication de Bibliothèque et Archives Canada

Bland, Nick, 1973-
[Twinkle. Français]
Ma petite étoile / Nick Bland, auteur et illustrateur ;
texte français
d'Isabelle Montagnier.

Traduction de : Twinkle.
ISBN 978-1-4431-0200-1 (couverture souple)

I. Titre. II. Titre : Twinkle. Français

PZ23.B5647Ma 2017          823'.92          C2017-900140-X

Version anglaise publiée initialement en
2010 par Scholastic Australia.

Édition publiée par les Éditions
Scholastic, 604, rue King Ouest,
Toronto (Ontario)  M5V 1E1, avec la
permission de Scholastic Australia.

5  4  3  2  1       LFA
Imprimé en Chine
17  18  19  20  21

Les illustrations de ce livre
ont été réalisées avec de la
peinture acrylique sur
du papier.

Le texte a été
composé avec la
police de caractères
Opti Announcement.

# Ma petite étoile

Nick Bland

Texte français d'Isabelle Montagnier

SCHOLASTIC

Un beau soir, Pauline Pasketti contemple le ciel et imagine qu'elle est amie avec les étoiles. Chaque scintillement est un clin d'œil, un secret ou une autre merveille.

Soudain, quelque chose d'étrange se produit.

Impatiente de vivre une aventure, Pauline descend en courant et trouve...

une amie.

Ensemble, elles chassent la tranquillité de la nuit
qui s'emplit alors de rires joyeux.

Pauline et sa petite étoile partagent
même un ou deux secrets.

Mais bientôt, la petite
étoile doit retourner
chez elle.

Pauline Pasketti a
promis de l'aider.

Toutes les deux, elles imaginent différentes
façons d'envoyer un objet dans le ciel.
Mais la petite étoile est trop lourde
et le ciel trop loin.

le ciel

Chaque fois que Pauline
trouve une façon de
faire *monter* l'étoile,

elle *redescend*
aussitôt.

La petite étoile se dit qu'elle ne réussira jamais à rentrer chez elle.

Mais Pauline Pasketti a une autre idée.

Dans la grande ville, les immeubles touchent le ciel.

Il est enfin temps de *monter...*
*monter... monter...*

jusqu'aux étoiles.

Pauline Pasketti fait ses adieux, les larmes aux yeux.

Puis, en un clin d'œil,
la petite étoile disparaît.

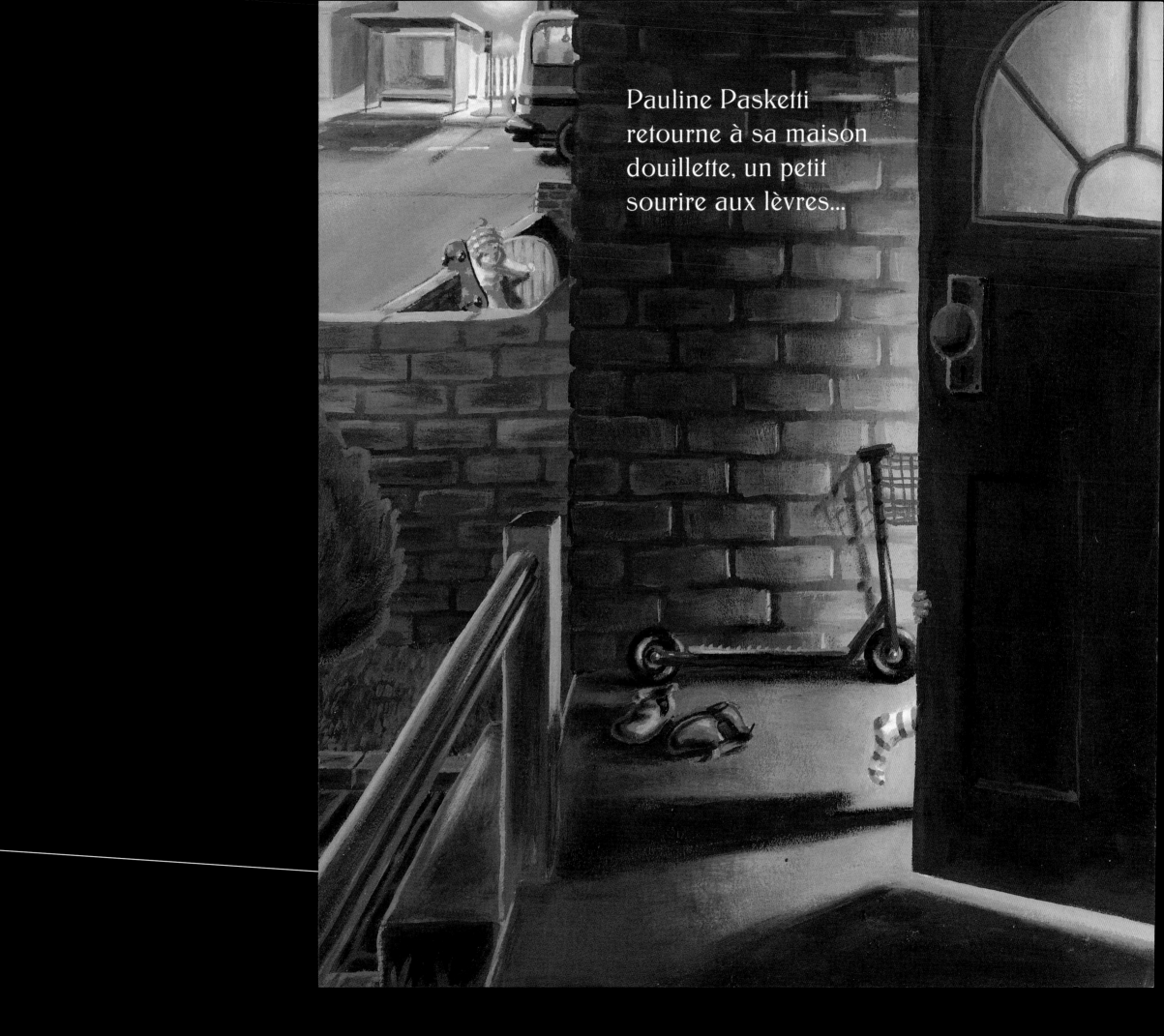

Pauline Pasketti
retourne à sa maison
douillette, un petit
sourire aux lèvres...

et un grand secret dans le cœur.

Puis elle s'endort en se demandant qui elle rencontrera le lendemain.